PRAISE FOR CATHY GLASS

'Poignant and revealing … real-life stories such as these have helped to move and inspire a generation' *Sunday Mirror*

'A true tale of hope' *OK!* Magazine

'Heartbreaking' *Mirror*

'A life-affirming read … that proves sometimes a little hope is all you need' *Heat* Magazine

'A hugely touching and emotional true tale' *Star* Magazine

'Foster carers rarely get the praise they deserve, but Cathy Glass's book should change all that' *First* Magazine

'Cannot fail to move those who read it' Adoption-net

'Once again, Cathy Glass has blown me away with a poignant story' The Writing Garnet, book blogger

'Brilliant book. I'd expect nothing less from Cathy … I cried, of course' Goodreads review

'… gripping page-turner from start to finish … emotive and heart-wrenching …' Kate Hall, book blogger

D0488776

'... another great read ... no complex narrative, just pure storytelling ...' 5* Kindle review

'Filled with compassion and love' Victoria Goldman, Lovereading

'Never disappoints and brings a tear to my eye' Hannah, book blogger

'Simply yet eloquently told ... Cathy's years of fostering experience shine a beam of light across the pages' Liz Robinson, Lovereading

'Amazing writing from an incredible lady' 5* Amazon review

'Wonderfully written book' 5* Kindle review

'A captivating insight into the life of a foster carer' Victoria Goldman, Lovereading

'I have read all Cathy Glass's books and none disappoint' 5* Amazon review

'Great job, Cathy Glass. Keep doing what you do and I'll keep reading' Goodreads review

A Family
Torn Apart

ALSO BY CATHY GLASS

THE MILLION COPY BESTSELLING AUTHOR

CATHY GLASS

A Family Torn Apart

**Three sisters and a dark secret
that threatens to separate
them for ever**

Certain details in this story, including names, places and dates,
have been changed to protect the family's privacy.

HarperElement
An imprint of HarperCollins*Publishers*
1 London Bridge Street
London SE1 9GF

www.harpercollins.co.uk

HarperCollins*Publishers*
1st Floor, Watermarque Building, Ringsend Road
Dublin 4, Ireland

First published by HarperElement 2022

3 5 7 9 10 8 6 4

© Cathy Glass 2022

Cathy Glass asserts the moral right to
be identified as the author of this work

A catalogue record of this book is
available from the British Library

ISBN 978-0-00-854084-5

Printed and bound in the UK using 100%
renewable electricity at CPI Group (UK) Ltd

MIX
Paper from
responsible sources
FSC™ C007454

This book is produced from independently certified FSC™ paper
to ensure responsible forest management.

For more information visit: www.harpercollins.co.uk/green

ACKNOWLEDGEMENTS

A big thank you to my family; my editors, Ajda and Holly; my literary agent, Andrew; my UK publisher HarperCollins, and my overseas publishers, who are now too numerous to list by name. Last, but definitely not least, a big thank you to my readers for your unfailing support and kind words. They are much appreciated.

CHAPTER ONE

IT TAKES COURAGE

The pandemic changed our lives. Although lockdown had been lifted, restrictions still applied so there were no large indoor gatherings; we had to wear face masks in public places, socially distance in queues and use antibacterial soap and hand gel at every opportunity. I wasn't the only one experiencing dry, chapped hands from all the hand washing!

Fostering practices had also changed with the pandemic, so most meetings, home visits and contact were now taking place online. Foster carers, like many parents, had become adept at keeping children amused and home educating those of school age. Some motivational speakers and life coaches were suggesting families could use the additional time to reunite and strengthen their bonds. In reality, the opposite was true, and many families isolated in their homes faced unprecedented challenges as jobs were lost, earnings fell and tempers became frayed. Some families who were already struggling fell into the abyss and referrals to the social services rocketed.

At the start of August I had just said goodbye to Jamey, whom I'd fostered since before Christmas. I knew it wouldn't be long before I was asked to take another child or children and I steeled myself, wondering what their sorrowful story would be. In over 25 years of fostering, I'd looked after many children who had suffered abuse and neglect, but no two children's stories are ever the same, and that was certainly true of the girls who arrived next.

In hindsight I wonder if the truth would ever have come out if Angie and Polly hadn't lived with me. I'm not saying I'm a better foster carer than others, but splitting up the girls from their older sister allowed them to disclose what was really going on. However, I'm jumping ahead of myself. It was Tuesday afternoon when Joy Philips, my supervising social worker (SSW), telephoned and their story began.

All foster carers in the UK have an SSW whose role it is to support and monitor the foster carer and their family in all aspects of fostering. Most referrals for children who come into care come to the foster carer through the SSW. Joy was in her early fifties, of average height and build, and had a wealth of experience. I found her caring, efficient and level-headed, although like everyone in children's services at present she was working flat out and was slightly stressed as a result of the pandemic.

'Did Emma have a nice birthday?' she began by asking.

'Yes, thank you. Very nice.' Emma was my granddaughter (Lucy and Darren's child) who had just had her second birthday. In line with current restrictions, we'd held her party outside – in my garden, with only immediate family present.

'Excellent. And you are all well?' Joy asked. It wasn't simply a polite question but had gained real significance since the start of the pandemic.

'Yes, we are,' I confirmed.

'No one in your household is having to self-isolate or awaiting a Covid test result?'

'No,' I confirmed. 'Paula and I are fine.' There was just my daughter Paula still living at home with me. I had divorced many years ago and my son, Adrian, lived with his wife, Kirsty, and my other daughter Lucy lived with her partner, Darren. We saw them as much as we were allowed, in line with the present restrictions.

'Good. I've had a referral for a sibling group of three girls,' Joy continued, getting to the real reason for her call. 'We'd obviously like to keep them together if possible, and it's preferable if they are placed in an all-female household.'

'Why?'

'The eldest, who's fourteen and has a different father to the other two girls, has made allegations of sexual abuse against her stepfather and would feel more comfortable in an all-female environment.'

It wasn't unusual to try to place victims of sexual abuse in female households where possible.

'I see. I'm sorry, Joy, but I can't take all three of them,' I said, with a stab of guilt.

'The younger two are used to sharing a bedroom.'

'It's not that, it's the work involved. I'd be spread too thinly and couldn't meet their needs.' I'd said this in the past to Joy, but I understood why she was asking. With so many children coming into care, and with some foster carers having to shield because of health concerns, and children's homes full or in quarantine, those carers that were able to take extra children were being asked to.

'Even with Paula there to help you?' Joy asked.

'Yes. She's furloughed for now, but she could go back to work soon,' I pointed out. 'Then there would just be me. Sorry, Joy. I know my limitations. I can't take all three.' The government had introduced a scheme so that businesses could furlough their workers rather than make them redundant. It meant that employees had a job to return to once the work picked up again.

'I thought you might say that,' Joy admitted. 'But I wanted to ask. So can you take the younger two? Angie and Polly are six and four years old.'

'Yes, but what about the older girl?'

'There is someone who can take Ashleigh if we can't keep them together. She's a single carer who has just returned to fostering after a long break so doesn't feel up to taking all three girls as her first placement.'

'OK, fine. I can take Angie and Polly,' I said. 'When are they coming?'

'Soon. This afternoon. Their father is still with the police but he will be bailed later and is returning to the family home to live. The children need to move before then. The girls' mother is standing by him.'

'Even though it means she's losing her children into care?' I asked, amazed.

'Yes. Their social worker, Fatima Hadden, will tell you more, but the girls' mother doesn't believe her daughter's claims and is siding with her husband.'

'Oh dear. That poor child,' I said.

'Yes,' Joy agreed.

It takes a lot of courage to disclose sexual abuse, and not to be believed is devastating for the victim and compounds the harm already done to them, often scarring them forever.

CHAPTER TWO

I WANT TO GO HOME

Half an hour later, Fatima Hadden, the children's social worker, telephoned. Our conversation didn't get off to the best start. Having introduced herself, she said quite brusquely, 'So you *really* can't take all three girls?'

'No, I'm sorry. I did explain to Joy.'

'Who's Joy?'

'My supervising social worker.'

'Oh, yes. Too many new names to remember. I haven't been in the post for long. Remind me why you can't take three children. I promised their mother I'd try to keep them together.'

'I'm a single-parent foster carer. It would be unfair to the girls, as I couldn't give them all the attention they'd need.'

'They may not need much attention,' Fatima replied, which I found an odd thing to say. 'They seem well behaved and the family hasn't come to the attention of the social services before.'

'What I mean is that I couldn't foster all three children to a good standard,' I said. 'And if I'm honest it would be too much for me. Joy understands.'

I heard her sigh. I felt slightly annoyed. I knew the social services were stretched and under pressure, but I was doing my best to help.

'I'll have to tell their mother they will need to be split,' Fatima said, as though thinking aloud. 'And set up regular contact as a peace offering. I take it you know why the girls are coming into care?'

'Only a little. Joy said the eldest, Ashleigh, has accused her stepfather of sexual abuse and their mother is standing by him.'

'That's it in a nutshell. Had she kicked him out and denied him access to the girls pending the police investigation there would have been a good chance they could have stayed at home. But as she refuses to believe he has done anything wrong – despite the evidence – she has given me no choice.'

'What is the evidence?' I asked.

'Apart from what Ashleigh is saying, you mean?'

'Yes.'

'She took herself to A&E and told the doctor her stepfather had raped her. She was examined and she'd definitely had sex. That's when we got involved. The full medical report will follow.'

'Oh, I see. How awful. Is there any suggestion that Angie and Polly have been abused too?' I asked. It was important I knew.

'They're not saying at present, but they're not saying much at all. I guess they are traumatized by what has happened. The police will interview them separately. Obviously if Angie or Polly disclose anything to you about their father touching them inappropriately, tell me straight away.'

'Yes, of course. He is Polly and Angie's natural father and Ashleigh's stepfather?' I checked.

'That's correct.'

'Do either of the girls have any special needs, allergies or dietary requirements?' I asked while I had the chance.

'Not as far as I know. I'll bring the placement information forms with me. I'm just waiting for my colleague and then we'll set off.'

We said goodbye and I replaced the handset in its stand with a very heavy heart. I'd taken the call in the living room, which is at the rear of my house. I stayed where I was, gazing towards the open patio doors and the garden beyond. It had been a hot, sunny morning, but now the sky had darkened and storm clouds were gathering.

As a foster carer I'd looked after children before who'd been sexually abused, and the perpetrator was often someone known to them. Stranger danger is quite rare and the majority of abusers are either a family member or friend, which makes it all the more difficult for the victim to tell and deal with the truth. To some extent I could understand why the girls' mother was struggling to believe her partner would do such a dreadful thing. We have to trust in order to love and have relationships, and then something like this happens. She would be in shock right now. Would she feel differently when she'd had time to think about it? From what Fatima had said they were just an average family, so this had come like a bolt from hell.

Deep in thought, I went over and closed the patio doors. As I did a large raindrop splattered onto the patio, followed by another and another, turning the light-grey patio stones darker.

7

'Is Sammy in?' my daughter Paula asked, coming into the living room and breaking into my thoughts.

'I'm not sure, love.' I glanced around but couldn't see our cat.

Sammy hated the rain so I opened the patio door again and called, 'Sammy!'

He shot out from under a bush and ran in, shaking his wet fur as he landed.

'I've just had a phone call from a social worker,' I told Paula. 'I've agreed to foster two little girls – Angie is six and her sister Polly four. They have an older half-sister, and I was asked to take her too, but I've said no, that it would be too much. I did right, didn't I?' Paula, now twenty-six, had grown up with fostering and knew what was involved.

'Yes, you did right, Mum. I can help now but I'm hoping I will be able to start work again soon.'

'That's what I said.'

'Why are they in care?' she asked, stroking Sammy.

'Their elder sister has accused their father of rape.'

'That's awful.'

'I know. So if the little girls say anything relevant about their father let me know and I'll pass it on to their social worker.'

'Yes, of course. Do you want some help making up the beds?'

'Thanks, love. Hopefully they're not bringing coronavirus with them.'

Since the start of the pandemic this was a real worry for foster carers. Children coming into care were not being tested for Covid and neither were those they had been living with. Once the children had arrived I could protect us all and follow government guidelines, but I had no idea if they were already carrying the virus. It was a risk we had to take and for this reason some carers had stopped fostering.

Half an hour later Paula and I had raided the airing cupboard for fresh linen, and the bedrooms were ready with bright, decorative duvet covers, matching pillow-cases and some cuddly toys from my spares propped up on the pillows. Hopefully the girls would arrive with some of their belongings, but it couldn't be guaranteed. It's prefer-able if the child has some of their own clothes and favourite toys, which are familiar to them – it helps them settle into a strange house – but if they don't, we make do from my spares until I can buy new. I'd left the beds where they were in separate rooms, but if their social worker wanted them to share a bedroom as they had been doing at home then Paula and I could move one of the beds.

The storm had ended and the sun was now trying to come out as the front doorbell rang. Paula picked up the face mask she had ready and stayed in the living room while I went to answer the door. Sammy, always wary when the bell rang, ran upstairs and watched from the landing. I took a disposable face mask from the hall stand where I kept a few and slipped it on before I opened the door.

'Hello, I'm Cathy,' I said. Two small, petrified girls looked back at me. I hoped they could see that my eyes were smiling and welcoming above the mask.

'This is Angie and Polly, and I'm Fatima,' their social worker said, easing the girls over the threshold. 'This is my colleague, Liz.'

'Hi, we're in the living room,' I said. 'At the end of the hall.'

'We?' Fatima queried as she led the way down the hall. She and her colleague were wearing masks.

'Yes, my daughter Paula is in there,' I replied unnecessarily; Paula was already introducing herself as I followed them in.

Fatima was a solidly built woman with a loud voice and strong presence. Very good for decision making and dealing with unruly parents, I thought, but the girls seemed worried and were keeping well away from her.

'Let's get some air in here,' she said, and opened the patio doors. Keeping a room well ventilated was thought to reduce coronavirus transmission.

'Would anyone like a drink?' I offered.

'Black coffee, no sugar,' Fatima said.

'Nothing for me,' Liz replied.

'What about you?' I gently asked the girls. They were standing by Liz.

Angie shook her head while Polly sucked her thumb.

'Maybe later then.'

'I'll get the coffee,' Paula said, and left the room.

'You've got her well trained,' Fatima quipped.

I smiled politely and looked at the girls. 'Would you like to play with some of these toys?' I asked. Paula and I had put some toy boxes in the living room.

Angie shook her head and little Polly said a quiet, 'No.'

'I've got some of their belongings in my car,' Fatima said. 'We'll unload later.' Then to the girls, 'So this is your new home for the time being. Isn't it nice?'

I thought that two little girls who'd just been taken from home were unlikely to think my house was nice.

They appeared well cared for and although there was a two-year age gap between them they looked very similar, with brown hair cut in the same style and wearing similar floral-patterned dresses. They both had bright red sandals with white lacy ankle socks. They were clean and their clothes looked new, unlike some of the children I'd fostered who'd arrived grubby and with holes in their clothes and shoes.

Fatima had slipped her face mask under her chin so she could talk more easily. I did the same. We were sitting on opposite sides of the room with the patio doors wide open, so I thought it was reasonably safe to do so.

'Placement forms,' Fatima said, taking paperwork from her bag. 'Sign the last page, please.' She placed a biro and the forms on the coffee table. I checked our details and signed. It was the agreement for me to foster the girls and also gave permission for me to seek emergency medical treatment for them if necessary. I handed back the signed page. 'You can read the rest later,' Fatima said. 'We'll keep our visit short.'

I knew this was current practice. If a meeting was necessary and couldn't be done virtually – for example, when placing children – then it was kept to a minimum to reduce the risk of transmitting the virus.

'Their mother said they didn't have much lunch,' Liz said. 'So can you make sure they have plenty to eat.'

'Yes. Although it might take a while before they regain their appetites after all the upheaval. Do we know what they like and dislike?'

'No, only that they haven't got any food allergies,' Fatima said. 'You can ask their mother what they like when you call her later.'

Paula returned with Fatima's coffee and a plate of biscuits, which she placed on the coffee table within reach, then she sat next to me.

'You're tempting me,' Fatima said as she helped herself to a biscuit. 'I'm supposed to be on a diet.'

'Aren't we all,' Liz said.

I glanced at the girls. 'Would you like a biscuit?'

They both shook their heads shyly. They looked so lost and alone.

'Would you like Paula to read you a story?' I suggested. 'She's good at reading stories.'

Angie nodded. Paula took a picture book from the shelf and sat on the sofa with the girls beside her.

'There! They're settling in already,' Fatima said, pleased. She drank some of her coffee and took another biscuit. 'Contact,' she announced. 'I want you to monitor it. I've told their mother you will phone every day. Make sure you call her today after we've gone. You know how to make a Zoom call?'

'Yes.'

'The Family Centre will be sending the login details by email.'

'What time shall we call today?'

'As soon as possible after we've gone.'

'And the other days?'

'Arrange it with their mother. The children are in care under a Section 20, so she has some say.'

Section 20 (of the Children Act) is also known as accommodated and is when a parent(s) agrees to place their child in care voluntarily. There is no court order and the parents retain legal rights over their child.

Fatima's phone rang and, taking it from her bag, she stood. 'I need to take this,' she said, and left the room. She went into the hall but spoke so loudly we could hear every word. It sounded as though there was a problem at her home, but she despatched them quickly with, 'I can't discuss it now. I'm placing children. I'll call you later.'

She returned to the living room and, dropping her phone into her bag, sighed. 'Families! Love 'em or hate 'em, we can't be without 'em.'

I smiled.

'Now, where were we,' she said. 'Speak to the girls' mother about what they like to eat and make sure you call her. Oh, and by the way their father isn't allowed to talk to them.'

'No, all right. What about contact with their sister, Ashleigh?' I asked.

'Yes, you need to phone her too. It's all in the email I've sent you. I'll have a quick look around the house now and then we'll be off. Liz,' she said, turning to her colleague, 'can you unload the car while I see where the girls will be sleeping. Angie, Polly, do you want to come with us to see your new bedrooms?'

Angie shook her head while Polly snuggled closer to Paula, who'd also lowered her face mask.

Fatima finished her coffee, then repositioned her face mask for the tour, as I did. Liz let herself out of the front door and I showed Fatima into the kitchen-diner and then the front room. She nodded and said, 'Fine.'

Upstairs I showed her the girls' bedrooms, explaining that I could move a bed if she wanted them to share.

'No. Lucky girls, having their own rooms,' she said. 'I had to share with four others when I was growing up. It's

13

not funny when you're a teenager.' Which wasn't really the point. It was about what the girls were used to and felt comfortable with, but I didn't comment. I'd see how the sleeping arrangements went and change them if necessary.

'I'll ask their mother about their bedtime routines,' I added, as I continued the tour by showing Fatima the bathroom and the other bedrooms.

'Nice house,' she said as we returned downstairs.

Liz had brought the girls' bags in from the car and was now waiting in the hall, mask on, ready to go.

'Looks like you've got some unpacking to do,' Fatima remarked, referring to the bags. 'But don't forget to call their mother or I'll be in for it.'

'I won't forget,' I reassured her.

I waited in the hall with Liz while Fatima went into the living room to say goodbye to the girls.

'Have a good evening,' she said to me, and I saw her and Liz out.

I closed the door, hung my mask on the hall stand and returned to the living room. The girls were still sitting next to Paula, who had taken off her mask. We only needed masks on in the house if someone came inside, which, in line with current restrictions, wasn't often.

'Would you like a drink now and something to eat?' I gently asked the girls. 'Then we will phone your mummy.'

'I want to go home,' Angie said, her bottom lip trembling. 'I want my mummy.'

'I want Mummy,' Polly said.

They both began to cry. Floods of tears that broke my heart.

'Come on, love,' I said to Polly. I took her onto my lap as Paula tried to comfort Angie.

Both girls continued to cry pitifully, probably like they'd never cried before. Heart-breaking sobs that racked their little bodies and tore at their souls. It was agony to witness, and there was little Paula or I could do to ease their pain. They wanted to go home, but that wasn't likely to happen for a very long time, if ever. It wasn't safe. Their half-sister had accused their father of rape, a heinous crime that, if convicted, carried a maximum sentence of life imprisonment.

CHAPTER THREE

A SORT OF HOLIDAY

Angie and Polly were inconsolable and quickly became hysterical. Then Polly jumped from my lap and, crying, ran to the front door. I went after her.

'I want Mummy. Daddy! I'm here,' she wept, banging on the front door with her little fists, hoping they would rescue her. 'Mummeeeee! Daddeeee!'

'Come on, love. Calm down,' I said, trying to hold her. 'Once you've stopped crying we can video call your mummy. We can't have her seeing you like this.' I thought the poor woman would be upset enough, having had her children taken away, and didn't need to see her daughters so distraught.

I picked up Polly, soothing her as I carried her back to the living room where Paula was still trying to comfort Angie. I sat her on the sofa next to her sister.

'Girls, listen to me,' I said, kneeling down in front of them so I was at their eye-level. 'We're going to dry your tears now and Paula will get you a drink while I go into the front room and get my computer ready so we can video call your mummy. Have you ever used a video call before?' I was hoping to pique their interest and distract them from their grief. 'Maybe on a phone?' I suggested. 'It's when you can see the person as well as talk to them.' It can be a difficult concept for young children.

Angie nodded. 'We call Nana when we aren't allowed to see her because of the virus,' she said.

'Good girl. Well done. That sounds right.'

'Do you remember using it?' I asked Polly.

She gave a small nod.

'Excellent.' I smiled. 'Now, let's dry your tears and get your drinks.'

I wiped their eyes and then Paula held Angie's hand and I held Polly's as we took them into the kitchen-diner. Paula opened the fridge and a cupboard to show the girls what drinks we had.

'Blackcurrant,' Angie said, in a tiny, quaking voice.

'I want blackcurrant too,' Polly said, standing close to her sister.

'Great.' I smiled at them. They were lovely girls and it was awful seeing them so distraught. 'And what about something to eat?' I asked. 'We'll have dinner soon, but you could have a sandwich now.'

'I want a chocolate biscuit,' Polly said.

'Mummy doesn't let us have a lot of sweet things,' Angie said. Bless her.

'I don't think she'll mind this once,' I said. 'Paula will get you what you want while I'm in the front room seeing to the computer.' Indeed, Paula was already taking down the biscuit tin and opening it. I left them to it.

I was using the desktop computer in the front room as the larger screen on the monitor gave a better experience for video calls. Also, I'd learnt from using video calls for contact that sometimes the parent wasn't ready or didn't answer. I usually made sure they were there and could talk before I brought in the child. Prior to the pandemic, children usually saw their family in person at the local Family Centre.

I opened the email with the contact arrangements. It wasn't a Zoom call as Fatima had said, but Skype, which was fine as I already had the software on my computer as well as other video and conference-call platforms. Foster carers, like many others, had had to get used to this software, and 'virtual' was fast becoming the new norm. The girls' mother was called Selina, and I noted her Skype contact details. The email said to call this afternoon and then at 4 p.m. on all the other days. I assumed this was in preparation for when the schools returned the following month, as contact for school-age children was generally held after school.

I launched Skype, added Selina as a contact and clicked the icon for a video call. It rang for a while and then a woman appeared, and I knew straight away it was the girls' mother. Her daughters had the same petite features and similar hair and eye colouring. She had clearly been crying. Her face was red and puffy and lined in anguish.

'Selina, I'm Cathy, your daughters' foster carer,' I said gently. 'Can you hear me OK?'

She nodded, her face crumpled and, holding her head in her hands, she wept. She clearly wasn't coping at all and witnessing her distress was as bad as it had been with Angie and Polly. I felt helpless and also guilty, as I had her children.

'Shall I call you back later?' I asked after a while.

'No. Stay, please.' She lifted her head. 'Where are they?'

'In another room, having a drink and a biscuit. My adult daughter is with them.'

She reached for a tissue and wiped her eyes. 'I can't believe this is happening to me,' she said, fighting back more tears. 'My poor girls. How are they?'

'They're missing you, obviously, but they're calm now. I'm hoping you can tell me about their routine and what they like to eat. It will make it easier for them to adapt to being here.'

'He didn't do it,' she said imploringly. 'I don't know why but Ashleigh has made this up. I told the social worker and the police Tim would never hurt any of them, but they didn't believe me. Tim is a good man. He loves Ashleigh as his own daughter, although she can be very difficult at times. He tells her off, but she deserves it. I can't believe this, I just can't.' She began crying again.

I closed the door to the front room so the girls couldn't hear. There was little I could do but wait for Selina to recover. Contact at the Family Centre is monitored by a contact supervisor who is present the whole time. The foster carer usually only meets the parents for brief periods at the start and end of contact when they drop off and collect the child. Now, with virtual contact, the boundaries had disappeared and foster carers were supervising contact as well as finding themselves in the role of confidant and counsellor.

'I can appreciate how difficult and upsetting all of this is for you,' I said. 'But please be reassured, I will look after your daughters very well.'

'The police and social services just turned up at our door without any warning,' Selina said, reliving her nightmare. 'We all had to stay in one room while they searched the house. They took away Ashleigh's bedlinen and some of her clothes. Tim was taken to the police station for questioning. They've also taken our phones and laptops. Tim had to buy another one after they released him. He needs it for work. He said I shouldn't have agreed to the children going into care, but I didn't have a choice. That social worker said if I didn't sign then they would apply for a court order. I thought I'd be able to see them. I don't know why I can't see them. It's not as though we're in lockdown.'

'You'll need to ask Fatima that and to talk to a solicitor. Have you got one yet?'

She shook her head and wiped her eyes again. 'I've got to phone one tomorrow. But we've done nothing wrong. I'm not even allowed to know where Ashleigh is.'

'I think that's normal given the allegations she's made, but ask Fatima and your solicitor,' I said again. It was the only advice I could give her.

'I've been trying to think why Ashleigh would say such wicked things and I think it could be jealousy. She's always been a bit jealous of Angie and Polly and says they get all the attention and Tim loves them more than her. But that's not true. Of course they need more attention, they're younger and there's only two years between them. But I make it up to Ashleigh, I'm sure I do.'

I nodded.

'So why is she behaving like this?' Selina asked, tears running down her cheeks. 'They told Tim he should move out. But this is his home and he has nowhere else to go. He's done nothing wrong.'

'Have you got someone there to support you?' I asked, very concerned.

'Just Tim, and he's in pieces. I can't tell my mother; it would kill her. I don't know what I'm going to do.'

'I'm so sorry, but I think it might be better if we called back a bit later for you to speak to Polly and Angie, don't you?'

'No, I need to see them now. I promise I won't cry.'

Selina was inconsolable and I knew she wouldn't be able to hold it together to speak to the girls, but she had the right to talk to them. I waited while she dried her eyes and composed herself as best she could, then I went to fetch the girls. They had finished their drinks and were sitting at the table with Paula, who was talking to them in a quiet, reassuring manner.

'You can come and speak to Mummy now,' I said with a smile.

They clambered off their chairs and came with me as Paula cleared the table. 'Thanks for your help, love,' I said.

I showed Polly and Angie into the front room, but as soon as they saw their mother on screen they both began to cry, as did Selina. I sat them on chairs in front of the monitor so they could both see her and I stood to one side. The girls wept, rubbed their eyes and pleaded with their mother to be allowed home.

'Can we come home? We promise to be good.'

Selina was in no fit state to give them the reassurances they needed and just cried bitterly.

'You've done nothing wrong,' I told the girls. Like many children who come into care, they seemed to think it could be their fault. 'Don't be upset. Mummy is going to be all right. She's just missing you.'

'I love you,' Selina said, trying to stem her tears.

'We want to come home,' Angie said. 'We love you, Mummy.'

'I love you both very much,' Selina replied, tears flowing.

'When can we come home?' Angie asked.

'Not just yet, love,' Selina managed to say. 'You have to stay at Cathy's for a few days while Daddy and I get this mess sorted out.'

'What mess?' Angie asked, her voice breaking.

'Where's Daddy?' Polly asked.

'He's here with me, love.'

'Can we see him?'

'Not today.'

'Can you tell him we want to come home?' Angie asked.

'Yes, he knows.'

'Can he come in the car and fetch us?'

'No, love.'

'Why not?' Angie asked.

'Because of something Ashleigh said,' Selina replied.

'What?'

I was ready to intervene. The girls didn't need to know the details and given that they were going to be interviewed by the police it was better they didn't talk about it, as it could influence what they said. Thankfully Selina didn't go into details. 'It's a misunderstanding,' she said. 'We'll sort it out.'

'Is Daddy upset too?' Angie asked.

'Yes, love.'

It was now obvious to me that the girls loved their father, and I was struggling to believe he could have harmed them, but I knew enough of paedophile activity to understand that appearances can be deceptive, and if one child in a family had been abused then the others are in danger.

Selina was crying openly, and Angie and Polly were quickly becoming hysterical. They begged their mother to come and get them. Angie was barely able to get her words out through her sobs and Polly was now saying she felt sick. I thought it was time to wind up. They'd seen each other and hopefully when we called tomorrow they would be calmer and starting to adjust.

'Do you all want to say goodbye and we'll phone again tomorrow?' I suggested to Selina.

She nodded, as wretched as the girls. I think she'd come to the end of her reserves and seemed ready to collapse. 'Bye, my darlings,' she said. 'Daddy and I love you both so much. Don't ever forget that.'

'We love you,' Angie wept. Polly was crying so much she couldn't speak and clung to her sister.

'We'll call again tomorrow at four o'clock,' I said. 'Take care.'

Selina nodded and ended the call.

That poor woman, I thought, but in all honesty the contact had done more harm than good. It hadn't reassured any of them and again I hoped it would improve tomorrow. Now I'd spent some time with the girls and seen how close they were and how they supported each other – Angie was still cuddling Polly – I wondered if they might be better off sharing a bedroom, but I'd let them decide.

I dried their tears and, explaining I was going to show them their bedrooms, I took them upstairs. Paula came out of her room.

'Oh dear,' she said, seeing their grief-stricken faces.

'I know. I'm trying to distract them. I think they might be better sharing a bedroom.'

'OK.'

'This way, ladies,' I said brightly to Angie and Polly, trying to divert their attention from their misery. 'You have a choice. While you are staying with me you can have your own bedrooms or share.' I showed them the rooms.

'Do we have to sleep here?' Angie asked forlornly.

'Yes, love, for now.'

'I want to go home,' Polly said.

'I know. But that's not possible at present. Did Fatima, your social worker, explain about me being a foster carer?'

Angie nodded.

'Good. So you know I sometimes help parents look after their children like I am going to look after you. The first thing we have to decide is where you will be happiest sleeping. Together or in your own rooms?'

'I want Polly with me,' Angie said.

Polly was nodding, so the decision was made.

'Let's do it,' Paula said.

Only one of the rooms was big enough to take two single beds, and we could really have done with my son Adrian's help. Over six feet tall and muscular, he would have made short work of moving the bed; as it was, it took Paula and me a lot of effort and some time. Enlisting Angie and Polly's help, we took off the bed linen, then Paula and I removed the headboard and upended the bed. Making sure the girls were safely clear of our route, Paula and I manoeuvred the bed out of the room, along the landing and into the next bedroom, where we lowered it into position and fixed the headboard back in place. We then encouraged Angie and Polly to help us make it up with the linen and pillows. There were brief moments as they helped when their little faces lost some of their sorrow, which was lovely to see, although they remained quiet, withdrawn and close to tears.

The beds were right up close to each other, touching, as it was the only way they would fit in. Satisfied we'd done our best, Paula took the girls downstairs to start making dinner – it was after five o'clock – while I fetched and then unpacked their bags. As well as day- and night-clothes, underwear and so forth, there were two soft toys, which I assumed were favourites and should help the girls settle tonight.

I returned downstairs where Paula was putting the finishing touches to pasta in a cheese and tomato sauce – a favourite of most children. Selina had been in no fit state to talk to me about the girls' likes and dislikes or their routine, so I'd ask her again tomorrow. Sammy had appeared and was watching Paula as the girls sat quietly at the table with their drinks. I smiled at them reassuringly, fed Sammy, then sat at the table to eat. Angie and Polly were very subdued and said they weren't hungry, but with a lot of encouragement they ate a little, followed by a scoop of ice cream each. They looked shattered, so once we'd finished I took them upstairs for their baths as Paula cleared up the dinner things. They didn't say a word as I ran the water and then helped them in. It was only a quick bath, but it gave me the chance to see that there weren't any suspicious cuts, burns or bruises on their bodies as I have seen on some children I'd fostered.

I helped them out of the bath, wrapped them in fresh towels and encouraged them to dry themselves. Paula came to help and we dressed them in their pyjamas, which had been sent from home. They had a child's toiletry bag each containing a toothbrush, flannel and toothpaste. Angie said they used these when they went on holiday.

'Are we on holiday now?' little Polly asked.

'A sort of holiday,' I said.

'Can Mummy and Daddy come?' she asked.

My heart went out to her. 'Not this time, love.'

Paula and I waited as they brushed their teeth. Although they weren't crying, they weren't far from it. Once they'd finished in the bathroom, I showed them where my bedroom was and said if they needed me in the night they should call out and I'd come straight away. Paula also showed them her bedroom, then we took them into their bedroom. Polly seemed surprised to see their favourite cuddlies on the beds and she picked up hers and held it to her face. It would smell of home and hopefully offer some comfort. They both had a soft-toy rabbit: Polly's was pink and Angie's was pale blue. Paula asked them if they had names and Angie nodded, although neither of them felt like telling us right now. They were exhausted and also probably traumatized by all that had happened.

As they climbed into their beds I drew the curtains, leaving a gap in the middle so the room wasn't completely dark. It was still light outside, the sun having not yet set. Polly reached out for her sister and they held hands. Paula asked them if they'd like a bed-time story, but they didn't.

'Where's Mummy and Daddy?' Angie asked in a small fragile voice.

'At home, love,' I replied.

'Can I see them?' Polly asked.

'We'll phone Mummy again tomorrow.' It was all I could offer.

'I want to go home,' Polly said.

'I know.'

They shed a few more tears and Paula and I sat on their beds and soothed them, but they were so tired it was only a matter of minutes before their eyes closed and they were both asleep. We crept from the room, leaving the door open so we could hear them if they woke. I find the first twenty-four hours are usually the most distressing for children coming into care and then, little by little, they adjust and start to settle.

CHAPTER FOUR

A DISTURBED NIGHT

Once Polly and Angie were asleep, Paula went to her bedroom to have some time to herself and I went downstairs to write up my log notes. All foster carers in the UK are required to keep a record of the child or children they are looking after. This includes appointments, details of the child's health and wellbeing, and any disclosures they may make. As well as charting their progress, it can act as an aide-mémoire if necessary. The record needs to be objective and accurate and can be requested by a judge in childcare proceedings, and indeed by a criminal court. Aware that very serious allegations had been made against the girls' father, I was meticulous in recording what they'd said about him. They clearly loved and missed him and seemed very close, but that wasn't for me to comment on. I simply recorded how they'd been since arriving.

Once I'd finished the log for both girls, I began reading the placement information forms that Fatima had left. It gave the children's full names, dates of birth, home address, ethnicity, religion, first language, reasons for being in care and any relevant history. They appeared to be a typical family and had no previous involvement with the social services. Their father sold cars for a living but was furloughed at present, while Selina was a full-time mother. Ashleigh was the child of her first marriage, and she still saw her birth father. Other significant adults listed only their maternal grandmother; their maternal grandfather was dead, and the paternal grandparents lived abroad. In the section for schools, I noticed that Polly was due to start school in September – the same school her sister attended and where Polly already went to nursery. My heart clenched. It's a big step for any child, starting school, and Polly would be doing it with the added anxiety of being in care. Also, it was highly unlikely Selina would be taking Polly to school on her first day – a milestone for all parents – as it was only four weeks away. I would take plenty of photos for Selina, but it wouldn't be the same as her actually being there.

I made a note of the school so I could check their website for details of term dates, school uniform suppliers and so forth, then read on. There was a place on the form where the referring social worker, Fatima Hadden, could record if the child had been sexually abused or was presenting with sexualized behaviour. I took a deep breath as I read: *There is a strong possibility Polly and Angie have been sexually abused as their older sibling has accused their father of rape. The foster carer needs to be aware and report any inappropriate sexual behaviour.* Sexualized behaviour or age-inappropriate sexual behaviour can be an indication of sexual abuse. While some sexual behaviour in young children is normal as they start to explore their bodies, others give cause for concern; for example, a child touching their own genitals is normal, but rubbing themselves against an adult or mimicking sexual acts is worrying. It's a subject most parents don't have to deal with, but sadly in fostering we do, too often, and we can't afford to be squeamish about it.

Nowhere on the form or in the email were the contact details for Ashleigh's carer, but Fatima had told me that Polly, Angie and Ashleigh would be having regular contact. I emailed both the Family Centre and Fatima asking for details of sibling contact, copying in my supervising social worker, Joy. It wasn't the first time something had been overlooked or missed with so many still working from home.

I checked some other emails and then shut down the computer. I texted my daughter, Lucy, and son, Adrian, saying we were fostering two little girls and we'd speak soon. Although they'd both left home, they lived locally and we saw each other as much as the current pandemic restrictions allowed, which at present was outside.

Aware that I was likely to have a broken night's sleep, I went to bed just before ten o'clock. Paula was in her bedroom listening to music but was also going to get ready for bed soon, so we said goodnight. I never sleep well when there is a new child or children in the house as I'm half listening out in case they wake, frightened – and Angie and Polly were more upset than most. I was exhausted. It's emotionally draining trying to help young children in distress.

The girls were asleep when I checked on them before I went to bed, but around midnight they woke crying out for Mummy and Daddy. I didn't know which one of them had woken first, but in the few seconds it took for me to throw on my dressing gown and go round the landing to their bedroom they were both sitting up in bed, crying hysterically. I went in, turned up the dimmer light a little and closed their bedroom door in the hope that they hadn't woken Paula. I tried to calm them.

'I want Mummy!' Angie sobbed.

'Daddy!' Polly screamed through her tears.

'We'll phone Mummy tomorrow,' I said.

'I want to go home!' Angie yelled. 'I want to go home now!'

It was pitiful to see, and they took little comfort in me being there; their bond was firmly with their parents. Of course their cries woke Paula and she knocked on their door and came in. For a moment they looked at her, startled.

'It's my daughter Paula,' I reminded them.

She joined me, sitting on the edge of a bed and trying to calm them. It was easier with two of us as we could look after a child each.

'What does Mummy do if you wake in the night or are upset?' I asked them, wondering if she sang a song as I used to do with my children.

'She comes into my bed,' Polly said, between sobs.

'Or Daddy does,' Angie added. 'Sometimes we go in their bed.'

None of these were really appropriate for a foster carer, so I said, 'We'll sit with you until you are asleep.'

Paula and I persuaded them to lie down, tucked them in, gave them their soft toys and then sat with them, stroking their foreheads and reassuring them that everything was going to be all right. Slowly their eyes began to close and eventually they returned to sleep. We quietly stood and crept from the room. I dimmed the light again but left their door open.

'Thank you for your help, love,' I whispered to Paula on the landing. 'But if they wake again you stay in bed and I'll go.'

'It's OK. I can help as I don't have to be up early for work.'

'Thanks, love.'

I kissed her goodnight and we returned to our beds. All my children were very supportive of fostering and I couldn't have managed without them.

It was just after 3 a.m. when I heard the girls sobbing again, but this time they didn't wake Paula. I went to them and Polly was out of bed saying she wanted to go to the toilet, so they both went. I then took them back to bed and sat with them until they fell asleep again. It was near four o'clock before I returned to my bed and two hours later they were awake again, calling out for Mummy and Daddy. I went into their room. They were sitting up in their beds, not sobbing hysterically but looking very miserable. I guessed they wouldn't go back to sleep again, and it was now light outside.

'It's a bit early to get up yet,' I said. 'So I'd like you to stay here while I get dressed. Mummy has sent some of your toys. What would you like to do?'

I showed them what had been packed and they both wanted the tablet. 'You can share it,' I said.

'We do,' Angie said, and Polly climbed into her bed.

'When can we see Mummy?' Angie asked, her voice slight.

'We're going to video-call her later today at four o'clock. It's a nice day so we can play in the garden later. I've got a paddling pool you can go in.'

'When's four o'clock?' Polly asked.

'I know,' Angie said. 'It's when the big hand is straight up and the little hand is on four.'

'Yes, well done, that's right, good girl,' I said.

'Mummy taught me to tell the time.'

'Excellent.'

I checked what they were going to play on the tablet and then, telling them I would be in the bathroom, I left to have a shower. As I dressed I could hear a faint tune coming from the game they were playing on the tablet. Once ready, I returned to their bedroom to find them both asleep in one bed. I switched off the tablet, crept from their room and, resisting the temptation to return to my bed, I went downstairs. I made coffee, fed Sammy and let him out for a run. As I opened the back door the sweet smell of jasmine floated in. It was going to be another warm day and my spirits lifted. There would be plenty I could occupy them with outside and hopefully the video call this afternoon would make them all feel a bit better.

Angie and Polly slept for another hour and then I heard Angie cry, 'Cathy!'

I hurried upstairs. Both girls were out of bed, Polly close to tears.

'What's the matter?' I asked. They were both looking worried.

'She wet the bed and I'm wet too,' Angie said, pointing at her sister.

'Don't worry. We'll soon have you both dry. It can't be helped.'

'Is she in trouble?' Angie asked.

'No, of course not. It was an accident. Do you get into trouble at home for wetting the bed?'

Polly shook her head while Angie replied, 'I never wet the bed. I'm a big girl.'

'I know, love. Now, let's find some clothes for you both and then you can have a quick bath and dress.'

I let them choose what they wanted to wear from the clothes their mother had sent. They both used the toilet and then, as I ran a bath for them, I heard Paula's door open and she appeared.

'Hi,' she said, smiling. 'How are you today?'

'OK,' Angie said quietly. Polly was playing with a bath toy.

I asked Paula to stay with them while I stripped the wet bed and put the linen and their pyjamas into the washing machine. It would soon dry on the line. When I was finished I returned upstairs.

'Is it four o'clock yet?' Polly asked as soon as she saw me.

'Not yet, love.'

Indeed, it wasn't yet 8 a.m., so I thought it was going to be a very long day!

Once the girls were out of the bath and dressed, Paula showered and dressed. By nine o'clock we were all having breakfast together and I'd lost count of the number of times Polly had asked if it was time to call Mummy, and Angie had told me she wanted to go home. But at least they weren't sobbing hysterically and were eating. They remained subdued, though. As we ate I asked them what sort of things they liked and Angie said fish fingers – a favourite of many children.

'I like fish fingers with baked beans,' little Polly added.

'Excellent. We'll have those for lunch and perhaps Mummy can suggest some other things when we phone her later.' I should have known it was the wrong thing to say.

'When can we phone Mummy?' Polly immediately asked, looking very sad.

'I miss Mummy and Daddy,' Angie said, rubbing her eyes.

'I know you do, love. Now finish your drinks and we can go into the garden. It's going to be a lovely day.'

At nine-thirty we went outside, and we weren't the only ones. Children's voices could be heard coming from neighbouring gardens as they, too, made the most of the fine weather. I unlocked the shed where the garden toys were kept and let the girls choose what they wanted to play with. Over the years we had accumulated plenty of outdoor play equipment, including bikes and scooters for many ages, bats and balls, hoops, dolls' prams and skate-boards. My mobile rang. It was Joy, so I went inside to take the call, leaving Paula in charge of the girls. As my supervising social worker, Joy was calling to discuss the girls and see how they were doing.

'I've just spoken to Fatima,' she said. 'And she tells me the girls have already settled in.'

'I wouldn't say that,' I replied, taken aback. 'They were very upset yesterday – hysterical. They're a bit better today but they desperately miss their parents. I've recorded it in my log.'

'Yes, I saw that, and your email. Fatima will send you the details of Ashleigh's contact.'

'Thank you.'

'What are Angie and Polly doing now?' Joy asked.

'They're in the garden with Paula.'

'I'll need to set up a virtual home visit so I can see them. I'll email you the details.'

'All right.'

The carer's supervising social worker and the child's social worker are expected to visit the carer and see the child in placement during the first week. Now, these visits were virtual, online. 'And you've got everything you need to foster Angie and Polly?' Joy asked.

'Yes. Some of their clothes and toys have been sent from home.'

'Hopefully more will follow. And they have contact every day with their mother?'

'Yes, but it's only a video call. They really struggled yesterday. I know some face-to-face contact is going ahead at the Family Centre. Why aren't Polly and Angie having some, do you know?'

'Fatima doesn't trust their mother not to scare the girls into silence,' Joy said. 'There is a strong possibility that they too have been sexually abused by their father or have some knowledge about what has been going on. Fatima said when Ashleigh told their mother of the abuse she called her a liar and said if she ever repeated it she would never speak to her again. The police will interview the girls as soon as possible. In the meantime, Fatima doesn't want their mother getting at them, so you will need to be vigilant during the video contact.'

'Yes, of course.' I knew that sometimes it only took a look from an abusive parent to threaten a child into silence. Yet … 'The girls seem very close to their parents and not frightened of their mother,' I said. 'They haven't stopped asking for her and their daddy.'

'But we know that some families are so dysfunctional that abuse becomes the norm.' Which was true. 'As Angie and Polly settle in and trust you they could begin to disclose, so be alert.'

'I will.' I'd been in a similar position before.

Joy finished by saying she'd email me the details of her virtual visit, and we said goodbye. I took my phone with me and returned to the garden. Paula had uncovered the sandpit and Angie and Polly were playing with the sand toys. I paused for a moment and watched them. I'd fostered sexually abused children before and those from highly dysfunctional families, and usually there were indicators, tell-tale signs, from very early on. I hadn't seen that yet in Angie and Polly and my gut feeling (from all my years of fostering) was that they hadn't been abused by their father and weren't scared of him or their mother. Their family didn't seem highly dysfunctional. The girls appeared to have been well brought up and were unlikely to have kept talking about and asking for their parents if they'd been abused. Which left me with the other option that their father had differentiated between his own children and his stepdaughter, and had only abused Ashleigh; perhaps seeing her as a sexual being rather than his child. He was still a paedophile, but it would explain Angie's and Polly's bond with him. Time would tell if I was right.

CHAPTER FIVE

IS IT DADDY'S FAULT?

Despite all Paula and I did to keep Angie and Polly occupied, they fretted for their parents all day, continually talking about their mummy and daddy, and yearning for four o'clock when we could video-call their mother. From what they said their mother organized many activities during the school holidays, including family outings – when pandemic restrictions allowed – and had helped them with the online learning Angie's school and Polly's nursery had set during lockdown. She sounded like the model parent. But by the afternoon I noticed that although they'd talked a lot about their parents and their home life, neither of them had mentioned Ashleigh. I wondered if Fatima was correct and the girls knew something about the abuse and had been warned into silence.

'Does Ashleigh go with you on family outings?' I asked. We'd returned to the garden after lunch. They'd been in the paddling pool and I'd just dried them off.

'Sometimes,' Angie replied.

'She is naughty,' Polly said.

'In what way, love?'

Both girls stopped what they were doing and looked at each other. Neither of them spoke. I felt a stab of unease.

'How is Ashleigh naughty?' I asked, again keeping my voice light.

'She argues,' Angie said. 'She doesn't do as she's told.'

'She argues with Daddy,' Polly added.

'I see. Do they argue a lot?'

Polly nodded while Angie said, 'Sometimes they shout at each other and Ashleigh runs out of the house, angry. She doesn't come back until very late.'

'After we're in bed,' Polly said.

'Oh dear, that must be worrying.'

'I don't like it when they argue,' Polly said, pulling a sad face.

'Ashleigh wants to live with Nana. I think she should,' Angie said. 'But Daddy says she can't.'

'Why?'

Angie shrugged. 'Don't know.'

'What sort of things do they argue about?' I asked. 'Do you know?'

Polly, bored with my questions, went to ride the tricycle while Angie replied, 'They argue about lots of things. Sometimes about her going out, and make-up, and her boyfriend.'

'So she has a boyfriend?'

'We think so, but no one has seen him.'

'Why do you think she has a boyfriend then?' I asked.

'She keeps wanting to go out to see him and I hear her talking on the phone. Daddy gets angry and says she's too young to have a boyfriend.'

'Does she spend time alone with Daddy?'

Angie nodded. 'He takes her out in the car sometimes. She doesn't want to go but Mummy says she has to.'

'Why?'

'To make it up, I guess.'

'Are they away for long?'

'Sometimes.'

'Is she better when she returns?' I asked.

'Not really. She doesn't like our daddy.'

'How do you know that?'

'Just do. She has another daddy she likes better. Is it time to phone Mummy yet?' Angie asked, changing the subject.

I checked the time on my phone. 'Not yet, love. Don't worry, I won't forget. I've set the alarm on my phone.'

Angie picked up a ball and wandered listlessly to the bottom of the garden where Polly was watching a bug on the grass. Paula had gone indoors a short while before. I pondered what the girls had just told me. It seemed their father had a very different relationship with Ashleigh to the one he had with Angie and Polly – far more fiery and confrontational, by the sound of it – but how much of that was due to normal teenage angst causing Ashleigh to test the boundaries? Abused children can be very angry, but then so can some teenagers. It's a difficult stage in life as they leave childhood and approach adulthood, often with the pressure of doing well at school. I would write up what Angie and Polly had said later in my log. It could be something or nothing.

Paula returned to the garden with a tray of cold drinks and a snack for the girls, then shortly before four o'clock I left her with them while I went indoors to set up the video call to Selina on my computer. There was an email waiting for me from Fatima saying that Polly and Angie should have virtual contact with Ashleigh once a week and she'd leave it to me and Ashleigh's carer to arrange.

But there were no contact details for the carer and they hadn't been included in the placement information forms, so I replied to Fatima's email asking for them.

At exactly four o'clock I video-called Selina, hoping she'd be feeling a bit better, or could at least hold it together to speak to the girls. I knew I was asking a lot, but if children in care see their parents distraught it compounds their separation anxiety and feelings of guilt.

Selina was waiting for my call. She looked pale and sad, but at least she wasn't crying as she had been yesterday. I guess there is only so much crying you can do.

'How are you?' I asked gently.

She shrugged dejectedly and took a deep breath. 'I'll try not to be upset while I talk to Angie and Polly,' she said. 'We spoke to a solicitor this morning – a different one to the one Tim has for the allegations.'

I nodded.

'The solicitor said I should be seeing my children properly, not just online. He's going to speak to the social worker and, if necessary, apply to the court. Some parents are seeing their children if they are going home, as it's detrimental to their relationship if they don't. I said we were thinking of simply bringing Angie and Polly home as they are in care voluntarily. I felt bullied into signing that Section 20.'

'What did the solicitor say?' I asked. Selina seemed to want to talk.

'He advised us against it. He said if we did and the social services believed the girls were in danger then they would apply to the court for a care order. The girls would still be in care and we'd have fewer rights than ever. He seemed to know what he was talking about.'

I nodded again.

'He also said that it would help me to regain custody if Tim moved out as the social services would not consider returning my children while he was here, with such a serious allegation hanging over him. But Tim says it would be like an admission of guilt. He's done nothing wrong so why should he move out?'

'I understand, but it's usually best to follow the solicitor's advice.'

'I don't know what to do,' Selina said with another heartfelt sigh. 'It's a nightmare. It really is. I didn't sleep at all last night. The house is so empty without my children. I still haven't heard from Ashleigh. I know Tim can't talk to her, but there is no reason why she can't speak to me. Have you heard from her? Fatima said the girls would be able to stay in touch.'

'Not yet. I'm waiting for her carer's contact details,' I said. 'Polly and Angie are looking forward to talking to you. Shall I fetch them now? They've been playing in the garden.'

'Yes, please.'

I went into the garden and called the girls. 'It's time to talk to Mummy.'

They immediately stopped what they were doing and ran towards the house, their expressions a mixture of relief, delight and concern.

'Mummy! Mummy!' Polly cried at the top of her voice, while Angie looked serious. I'd already noticed that Angie tended to internalize her feelings more than her sister and went quiet or looked grumpy rather than saying what she was feeling.

Both girls perched on the chair in front of the monitor

and I stood to one side. As soon as Selina saw them her eyes glistened with tears, but she managed to hold them back.

'Mummy, I'm so pleased to see you,' little Polly said.

'When can we come home?' Angie asked, her voice flat.

'Soon, I hope, love. We have a solicitor helping us now.'

'I want to come home,' Polly said in a small, plaintive voice.

'I know, love. I want you here, but it's not my decision.' I could see more tears welling.

'Tell Mummy what you've been doing,' I prompted.

'We've been in the paddling pool,' Polly said. Angie stayed quiet.

'I'm taking lots of photos,' I said. 'I can email them to you.'

'Thanks. But they don't have their swimming costumes.'

'I gave them some from my spares, and a sun hat each. I put sun lotion on them too.'

'What about you, Angie? Did you go in the pool?' Selina asked.

'A bit,' she said quietly. 'But I want to come home.'

'I know, and we're doing all we can to make that happen,' Selina replied, her voice catching.

'Why can't we come home?' Polly asked.

'Because of a misunderstanding,' their mother said. 'Try not to worry. Daddy and I will sort it out. I had an email today about school in September,' she said, changing the subject. 'It's going to be a bit different when you go back because of the coronavirus. Classes will have different start and end times and there will be spaces between the tables.'

Which reminded me that I needed to give the school my contact details.

'I'll have to buy you both a new school uniform and shoes,' Selina continued, apparently assuming the girls would be home by then. I thought it was highly unlikely, but then again if their father moved out and the social services were satisfied the girls were no longer in danger they could be returned quite quickly.

Selina continued to talk about their school and then asked what their bedroom was like. Polly tried to describe it, while Angie said grumpily, 'It's not like my bedroom at home.'

'I can send you some photos of my house,' I said to Selina.

'Then I'll be able to see where you are living,' she said to the girls.

I thought Selina was doing all right, not breaking down. It must have been so difficult for her, but then Angie said, 'Don't you want us any more?'

That was it. Selina's face crumpled. 'Yes, of course I want you. I love you both so much. This is all about something Ashleigh said.'

'Don't cry, Mummy,' Polly said, close to tears herself.

'So make Ashleigh go away,' Angie said. 'Then we can come home.'

'It's not that easy,' Selina said, wiping her eyes. 'And Ashleigh isn't here either. I don't know where they've put her.'

'She could be with her other daddy,' Angie suggested.

'Why would you say that?' Selina asked.

Angie looked worried, as though she'd said something wrong, and Selina was clearly struggling. I was there to supervise contact and make sure it was a positive experience. 'Perhaps change the subject,' I suggested to Selina. 'They've been telling me of the types of things they like to eat.'

'Have you had dinner?' Selina asked.

'No. It's not dinner time yet,' Angie said, bluntly. Her mother looked even more hurt.

'Online contact is difficult for young children,' I said. 'The onus is on sitting and talking. Perhaps next time you may like to read them a story from a favourite book? It helped with the last child I looked after.'

'All right,' Selina agreed, without much enthusiasm.

'What is your favourite book?' I asked the girls, trying to encourage conversation.

'I like *The Very Hungry Caterpillar*,' Polly said. 'I know it off by heart.'

'Wonderful,' I enthused. 'Would you like to say it to Mummy?'

'In the light of the moon a little egg lay on a leaf …' Polly began cutely. And then continued reciting what she remembered of the children's classic. I prompted where necessary, for like many parents and carers I knew the words off by heart. She did well and was even smiling by the end. Angie was still looking grumpy.

'Do you want to say a rhyme for Mummy or tell her about your favourite story?' I asked her.

She shook her head.

'I think Angie blames me for what is happening,' Selina said. Angie was looking away.

'I'll explain to her again later,' I reassured her.

Polly then said she wanted to use the toilet. I couldn't leave Angie with her mother unattended, so I suggested we wound up. The video call had lasted twenty minutes, which is as long as you can expect young children to sit in front of a computer trying to make conversation. It was different with face-to-face contact when time could be spent playing.

Selina agreed and they said a very sad goodbye, kept short by Polly urgently needing the toilet. I took the girls straight upstairs and they both used the bathroom. They were quiet but not as distraught as they had been the day before after talking to their mother. I asked if they wanted to go into the garden again, but they didn't. Angie said they watched television at this time, so I settled them in the living room with a children's programme, while I took the opportunity to send some photographs to their mother. I already had some of the house that I'd used before with other parents. I sent those and some of the photos I'd taken today in the garden. Hopefully it would help Selina. I checked on the girls in the living room and then began preparing dinner for later.

After we'd eaten Paula and I read the girls bedtime stories and then at seven o'clock I began their bath and bedtime routine. Polly asked when they could next see Mummy and I said we'd video call her tomorrow and every day at four o'clock. I said again that the reason they were in care was to help Mummy and it wasn't their fault.

'Is it Daddy's fault?' Angie asked.

'Some things have been said that need sorting out,' I replied. 'To make sure you are all safe.' That was all they needed to know for the time being at their age.

'I think it is his fault,' Angie said.

'Why?'

'Because he tells off Ashleigh and they argue.'

I changed the subject.

I was hoping for a less disturbed night. Both girls were tired from the broken night before and being out in the fresh air all day. I settled them in their beds and Paula came to say goodnight, then, leaving the door open, we came out. The girls knew to call me if they needed anything, but I wanted them to get into the habit of going off to sleep by themselves as children of their age normally do. I was assuming they would be with us for some time, so it was important I established a routine.

Paula returned to her room while I went downstairs. Lucy video-called and we had a chat. She'd spoken to Paula earlier when I'd been busy. She said she'd taken Emma to their local park that afternoon and suggested we meet there again soon, as current pandemic restrictions allowed. We'd just finished when my phone rang from a number I didn't recognize.

'Hello?' I answered tentatively.

'Is that Cathy Glass?' a female voice asked.

'Speaking.'

'It's Janet here.'

'Janet?' I asked, puzzled. I knew a Janet, but this wasn't her voice.

'Ashleigh's carer,' she clarified. 'You're fostering her sisters, aren't you?'

'Oh, yes, sorry. I wasn't expecting your call. I didn't even know your name.' I continued into the living room.

'I thought I'd grab the chance to phone while I could. It's been non-stop here since Ashleigh arrived. What with the social workers and the police, I haven't had a minute to myself! Ashleigh's out so I decided to put the time to good use and phone you.'

'Great. We can arrange video-call contact for the girls. Where has Ashleigh gone?' I asked.

'Goodness knows!' Janet said with a sigh. 'She wouldn't tell me. You know what teenagers are like. They're either on their phones or out.'

Immediately I had concerns.

CHAPTER SIX

DO YOU FEEL SAFE?

'And you don't know where Ashleigh has gone?' I asked her carer.

'No. She's a closed one. I've tried talking to her but apart from "don't know" and some shrugs, I'm not getting anywhere.'

'It's early days yet,' I said. 'It will take time for her to trust you and open up, especially after what's happened.'

'Can you believe what her stepfather did!' Janet exclaimed, shocked.

'I know, it's dreadful, but we see so many bad things as foster carers, don't we?'

'It's a long time since I fostered,' Janet admitted. 'Fifteen years. And back then we used to foster babies and infants. I stopped fostering when my husband died.'

'I am sorry for your loss,' I said.

'Thank you. He was only forty-five. I hadn't thought about returning to fostering until they said on the news that there was a big shortage of foster carers. I was fast-tracked. The assessment and training were all done online – I'm still doing some of the training. I was police-checked, but I only had one visit from the assessing social worker, towards the end. If I was hoping for some company, I was disappointed.' She gave a small laugh.

'Yes, most meetings, training and visits are online at present because of Covid.'

'They wanted me to take all three girls because I have the room,' Janet continued, clearly appreciating the opportunity to chat. 'My own two children are adults now and no longer live with me. I was surprised when they asked me to take all three; I didn't feel up to that, so I said I'd just have the eldest. I couldn't be running around after little ones again. I'm not as young as I used to be.'

Janet wanted to talk, so I listened as she told me about how well her own children were doing, although she didn't see them very often as they were busy with their careers and lived in another part of the country. She said her best friend had moved away and others had stopped going out because they were worried about catching coronavirus. She sounded lonely, saying she felt that fostering would give her something to do and also the allowance would come in handy. Foster carers receive an allowance towards the cost of looking after the children they foster. But as she talked my thoughts kept returning to Ashleigh.

'What time does Ashleigh have to be back?' I asked.

'She didn't say, but it's still light outside.'

'And you don't know where she might have gone?'

'No. I didn't like to pry. Why? You seem worried.'

'I am a little. She must be in a highly emotional state and vulnerable after what she's been through.'

'She'll be with her friends,' Janet said. 'That's what they do at that age. I remember my two being out with friends on a nice summer evening during the school holidays. Obviously once the new term starts she'll need to be in more doing her schoolwork.' Which rather missed my point.

'Does Ashleigh have her phone with her?' I asked.

'Yes, why?'

'Maybe you could text? Make sure she's all right, and tell her what time you'd like her back,' I suggested as tactfully as I knew how.

'She won't like that, I can tell. She's got a bit of an attitude.'

'She's fourteen. I think many young people have an attitude at that age. I know I did.' Then I added: 'Didn't her social worker talk about coming-in times, pocket money and so forth?'

'No. She wasn't here long. She's doing a virtual visit in a few days.'

'OK. Perhaps bring it up then and put the ground rules in place. It should be easier with the social worker present, assuming she is on the same page as you. I hope you don't mind me suggesting all this, but I've fostered a lot of teenagers over the years and have learnt what usually works.' I trusted I wasn't undermining Janet's confidence, but it was a long time since she'd fostered and back then it had been infants. Also, she'd been fast-tracked and from the sound of it hadn't had much training.

'No, you talk away,' she replied. 'I'm grateful for the company. It's been a lonely year with lockdown and all the restrictions. Some days I felt like climbing up the walls.' Janet then told me of her experiences during the pandemic and people she'd heard of who'd been very ill, some being admitted to hospital. It was a topic on everyone's lips.

Eventually, with the evening passing, I drew the conversation back to the reason for her call – arranging video contact for the girls. 'Fatima said once a week, so bearing in mind they will be at school next month how about Saturday morning around ten o'clock?' I suggested.

'OK with me. And maybe once they're all back at school you and I can meet for a coffee?'

'Yes, sure. That'll be nice.'

We said goodbye and I added Janet to the contacts list in my phone, then I checked on the girls. They were sleeping soundly. I returned downstairs and about twenty minutes later I received a text from Janet.

Messaged Ashleigh like you said. She replied she was with a friend and would be back later.

OK. Maybe you could tell her the time you'd like her back? How is she getting home?

On the bus, I guess.

I didn't feel I could say any more. The chances were I was worrying unnecessarily, but given the trauma Ashleigh had been through, if I'd been her carer I'd have felt happier having her home for a few days, or at least knowing where she was, who she was with and how she was getting home.

I heard nothing more from Janet for the rest of the evening and I switched off my phone before getting into bed as I usually do, unless I'm on standby for an emergency placement, when I have to leave it on.

Angie and Polly woke once during the night – a huge improvement on the previous night. I resettled them without waking Paula. When I switched on my phone in the morning I had a text message from Janet, sent during the night, saying she'd had to wait up for Ashleigh, who hadn't returned until nearly midnight.

Perhaps I should give her a front door key?

I texted back: *Update Fatima and discuss the front door key with her. I only give out keys when the young person has shown they are responsible enough to have one.*

I suppose Janet thought that if Ashleigh had her own key, which many young people her age do, she wouldn't have to wait up for her. But Ashleigh had only just arrived, and in very distressing circumstances. Personally, I would have wanted her in at a reasonable time and with arrangements in place for her safe journey home. I would also have wanted to know exactly where she was going. Boundaries are a sign of caring, although young people don't always see it that way.

I helped Polly and Angie wash and dress. By the time we were downstairs having breakfast, I'd lost count of the number of times they'd asked when they would be seeing their mummy and how long it was till four o'clock. Angie could tell the time, but it didn't stop her from asking. Apart from talking about their mother, they remained subdued and disinterested in anything else. So great was the strength of their bond with their mother that they would take longer to adjust to being in care than a child who didn't have the same attachment.

Once Paula was up and dressed and had had eaten something, we went to a local park – about a fifteen-minute walk – as it was another fine day. I hoped it would give the girls some distraction from pining for home, but when they spoke it was about their parents and family life. The benches in the park were still taped off, as was some of the children's play equipment, to maintain social distancing. Although lockdown had been lifted we still had to keep two metres from others, and wash and sanitize our hands regularly. Like most others, I was carrying antibacterial wipes with me at all times.

Polly and Angie didn't want to play on the children's apparatus or play with the ball I'd brought from home, so we walked over to the duck pond, but they weren't interested in that either.

'Mummy takes us to a nicer park,' Angie said, clearly resenting me, which was only to be expected.

'Is it time to phone Mummy yet?' Polly asked.

'No yet, love. I'll tell you when it is.'

We spent about half an hour in the park, then we began the walk home. My phone bleeped with a text message. It was from Janet, saying Ashleigh had only just got up and was planning on going out again. Did I think that was all right?

Do you know where she is going? I texted back.

A few minutes later my phone rang, and it was Janet.

'No, I don't know where she's gone,' Janet said, clearly irritated. 'I tried talking to her, but she ignored me and let herself out the front door. Cheeky madam!'

'I think you need to speak to Fatima,' I said. 'Give her a ring now.'

'I hope I'm not in trouble, but I couldn't really stop her going. She's hard work. Perhaps I should have taken Polly and Angie instead.'

'All children present some challenges,' I said. 'They are missing their mother dreadfully. Speak to Fatima.'

'I will if she's there. She doesn't always answer.'

'Then leave a message.'

It was lunchtime when we arrived home and I said I'd make us a picnic to have in the garden. Only Paula and I showed any enthusiasm for this plan, and Polly asked how long it was from lunch to when we telephoned Mummy.

'About four hours,' I said.

Paula and I involved the girls in putting together a picnic lunch and then set it out on a rug under the tree in the garden. For a short while they were occupied, but their thoughts were never far from home.

'We have picnics with Mummy and Daddy,' Polly said mournfully.

'That's nice,' I replied.

'Mummy's picnics are nicer than yours,' Angie told me.

'Don't be rude,' Polly admonished.

I couldn't help but smile. 'It's OK,' I said. 'I understand Angie is a bit annoyed with me at present.'

'Why?' Polly asked innocently.

'Because she is blaming me for not being allowed home. But it's not my fault. Don't you worry. Eat up.'

With a lot of encouragement, the girls ate a reasonable amount and fed Sammy a few morsels when he came over to investigate. I fetched ice cream for dessert. Once we'd finished we enlisted the girls' help to clear away. They didn't want to stay in the garden to play so we all went inside. It was one o'clock: three hours until we video-called their mother. I was looking in the toy cupboard for something to occupy them for the afternoon

– maybe painting or clay modelling – when the doorbell rang.

'You stay with Paula and carry on looking in the cupboard for something you'd like to do while I see who that is,' I told them.

I opened the front door to two plain-clothes police officers. 'Cathy Glass?' the lead officer said as they showed me their IDs.

'Yes.'

'We're from the Child Abuse Investigation Team. I'm Mel Robinson and this is my colleague, Kierston Smith. You're fostering Polly and Angie Fletcher?'

'Yes.'

'We'd like to have a chat with them.'

'Now?'

'Yes, please. Didn't their social worker, Fatima Hadden, tell you we were coming?'

'No. She must have forgotten. Come in.'

The Child Abuse Investigation Team (CAIT) investigates allegations of abuse and neglect towards children and young people under eighteen involving family members, carers or people in a position of trust.

'The girls are in here,' I said, showing the officers into our kitchen-diner where Polly and Angie were still looking in the toy cupboard with Paula.

I guessed the officers were in their thirties. They would have additional specialist training in questioning children.

Polly and Angie stopped what they were doing as we entered and immediately looked concerned.

'Hi, I'm Mel and this is Kierston,' Mel said. 'There is nothing to be worried about. We are police officers. We'd like to talk to you both if that's all right? Your social worker knows we're here.'

'This is my daughter, Paula,' I said, introducing her.

'Hi,' Mel said as Kierston pulled out a chair from under the table and sat down.

'If you don't need me, I'll be upstairs,' Paula said.

'That's fine, you go,' Mel smiled.

Angie and Polly were still standing by the open doors of the toy cupboard looking very worried. Mel went over. 'That's a lot of toys,' she said, also drawing out a chair so she was sitting at the girls' eye level. 'What do you like to play with?'

Angie shrugged and then said, 'Nothing,' in a small voice. Polly shook her head.

'We've been talking to your sister, Ashleigh,' Mel said gently. 'And now we'd like to talk to you. Is that all right?'

Polly nodded, while Angie just stared at Mel. It would have helped if I'd known the officers were coming so I could have prepared the girls for their visit.

'You had an upset at home, do you remember?' Mel asked them.

Polly nodded.

'What do you remember?' Mel asked. Her voice was soft and non-threatening. I saw Kierston quietly take out a notepad and pen.

'Mummy and Daddy were upset,' Polly said.

'Do you know why?' Mel asked.

Polly shook her head, but Angie replied, 'Because of something Ashleigh said about Daddy.'

'Do you know what it was?' Mel asked. I stood to one side, watching.

'I don't know, but it must have been bad, because we had to leave Mummy and Daddy and come here,' Angie said.

'Do you know why you are staying here?' Mel asked in the same gentle tone.

'Cathy says it's to keep us safe,' Angie replied, and Polly nodded. So they have been listening, I thought.

'Do you feel safe here?' Mel asked.

Both girls nodded.

'Did you feel safe at home?'

'Yes,' Angie said, and Polly nodded again.

'Do you think Ashleigh felt safe at home?' Mel asked as Kierston noted what the girls had said.

Angie looked thoughtful and then said quietly, 'I don't think so.'

'Why don't you think Ashleigh feels safe at home?' Mel asked.

'Because she argues with Mummy and Daddy,' Angie said. 'Sometimes they shout.'

'What do they argue and shout about? Do you know?' Mel asked.

'Staying out late,' Polly said.

'Anything else?' Mel asked.

'Ashleigh thinks Daddy loves us more than her, but it's not true,' Angie said.

'Why should she think that?' Mel asked.

'I think it's because she has another daddy,' Angie said.

'The one who doesn't live with her,' Mel clarified.

'Yes.'

'Is she afraid of your daddy – the one she lives with?' Mel asked.

'I don't know,' Angie said, and took a toy from the cupboard.

'You're doing well,' Mel said. 'Who gives you a bath at home? Mummy or Daddy?' she asked.

'Both,' Angie replied.

'Are you ever frightened of Daddy?' Mel asked.

'Only when he shouts,' Angie said, as Kierston wrote.

'Does he shout much?'

'Sometimes. Can we go now?'

'Yes, of course,' Mel smiled. 'You've done very well. One last question. Has anyone ever touched you in a way that made you feel worried or hurt you?'

'No,' Angie said.

'No,' Polly agreed. 'I want to play.'

'Yes, of course. Thank you for your help.'

I wasn't sure how much use their chat had been.

Mel looked at me. 'Can we talk to you alone?'

'Yes, of course. I'll ask Paula to stay with the girls. Just a minute.'

I called upstairs to Paula and asked her to come down to look after Polly and Angie as the officers wanted to talk to me. She came straight away and stayed with the girls in the kitchen-diner where most of the toys were kept in cupboards, while I took the officers into the living room. Mel shut the door so we couldn't be over-heard. Kierston still had her notepad and pen at the ready as we sat down, me on the sofa and the officers in the armchairs.

'You're presumably aware of the serious nature of the allegations Ashleigh has made against her stepfather?' Mel asked.

'Yes,' I said.

'Have Polly and Angie –'

But before we got any further the landline rang. Apologizing, I reached out and answered it. It was Fatima.

'Just phoning to let you know a police officer from CAIT will be coming to see Polly and Angie today.'

'They're here now,' I said.

'Good. Hopefully the girls will be able to tell them what they're not telling us.'

CHAPTER SEVEN

HIGH DRAMA

'It was their social worker telling me you were coming,' I told the police officers as I replaced the handset.

Mel nodded. 'I know Polly and Angie haven't been with you for long, but have they said anything about their relationship with their father?' she asked.

'They seem to have a good relationship with him,' I began as Kierston took notes. 'I've seen nothing to suggest he has abused either of them. They are desperately missing both their parents and talk as much about their father as they do their mother. I write up a log each day, which their social worker sees.'

'Yes, she mentioned it.'

'From what Angie and Polly have said their relationship with their father is better than his relationship with Ashleigh,' I continued. 'There seems to have been a lot of arguments between Ashleigh and her parents, but nothing to suggest he was abusing her, although they did spend time together away from the house, after an argument. It's all in my notes.'

'Can we access your notes?' Kierston asked, glancing up.

'Yes, I think so. You'll have to ask Fatima how you go about it.'

Kierston made a note.

'Do you speak to their mother?' Mel asked.

'Yes, I have to supervise their video-call contacts.'

'How often are they?'

'An hour every day.'

'Are you present the whole time?' Kierston asked.

'Yes.'

'How do the girls seem with her?'

'Fine. They love and miss her, and she's been very upset at being parted from her children, as you'd expect.'

'No threatening undertones or warning looks that you're aware of?'

'No.'

'We'll be speaking to someone at their schools to see if they have had any concerns about the girls.' This was usual practice when investigating a suspected case of child abuse.

'Is Ashleigh saying Polly and Angie have been abused too?' I asked, aware that they might not tell me.

'No,' Mel said. 'But then she's not saying much at all at present. We are trying to get her to come into the police station to record a video statement, but she's saying she's too stressed and upset at present. I know it's an ordeal, but we make it as easy as we can.'

'I know, I've taken children before and it often helps in their recovery.'

'Does Selina talk to you about what happened?'

'Yes, a little. She is very distraught and needs someone to talk to. She doesn't believe Tim is capable of doing what Ashleigh is claiming. I listen and have advised her to be guided by her solicitor or to speak to the social worker where necessary.'

'Have Angie or Polly displayed any sexualized behaviour? You know what that term means?' Mel asked.

'I do. I've seen it in other children I've fostered, but nothing in Angie or Polly. To be honest, apart from being traumatized by having to leave home, they seem very well adjusted – from a normal, loving family. But, of course, they haven't been with me long so it could all come out later.'

'If they do start to disclose, you'll let us know,' Mel said. 'Then we'll try to interview them at the station, but it's not worthwhile at present. I'll leave my card with you.'

'All right.'

Mel gave me her business card. 'Thank you for your time,' she said, standing. 'We'll just say goodbye and leave you to it. It's still nice and sunny outside,' she added, glancing through the patio windows.

'Yes, it is.'

I went with them into the kitchen-diner where Paula was showing the girls how to play the board game Snakes and Ladders. The officers said goodbye. I saw them out and returned to the kitchen-diner.

'How long before we can phone Mummy?' Polly asked.

I glanced at the wall clock. 'Two hours.'

'Can we tell Mummy about the police ladies?' Angie asked, frowning.

'Yes, love, if you want.'

'It's not a secret?' Angie asked.

I looked at her carefully. 'No, why? Do you have secrets at home?'

'Yes,' Angie said, and my heart sank. I thought Angie was about to disclose abuse.

'What kind of secrets?' I asked, my throat tight.

She thought for a moment. 'When it's someone's birthday we're not allowed to tell them about their presents.'

I allowed myself to breathe again. 'Yes. Any other secrets?'

Polly was nodding as Angie said, 'On Mother's Day we go shopping with Daddy. We buy Mummy a card and present, and we're not allowed to tell her until Mother's Day.'

'So that's a nice surprise for her,' I said. 'Lovely.'

In fostering we tend to differentiate between secrets, which can have dark connotations, and surprises, which are generally positive and welcome, although I know many families don't make that distinction.

Angie had fallen silent and said she didn't want to talk about home any more as it made her sad. Neither of the girls seemed very interested in the game of Snakes and Ladders so we packed it away. They didn't want to go into the garden either. In fact, they didn't want to do anything apart from phone their mother. Paula suggested they baked some cakes together. They weren't overly enthusiastic to begin with but gradually warmed to the idea. I left Paula with them while I went to my computer in the front room. As I worked I could hear them in the kitchen, making the cupcakes, and then putting them in the oven to bake. Paula even had the girls helping with the clearing up. When the cakes were ready we all had one. They were delicious straight from the oven and still warm. Angie and Polly forgot their upset for a short while and, once the cakes were cool, helped Paula ice them, and we all had another one.

Eventually it was time to video-call their mother and as usual I set up the call on the computer in the front room first. Selina was waiting and, while not crying, looked utterly wretched.

'Are you all right?' I asked. Obviously she wasn't.

'I've just had my ex, Ashleigh's father, shouting at me down the phone,' Selina said, clearly at the end of her tether. 'The social services told him Ashleigh was in care and the allegations she's made against Tim. He's furious. He's never liked Tim, and now he's saying he knew something like this would happen, which is ridiculous. The police are going to see him, and he said he can't wait to tell them what he thinks of Tim, then he will apply for custody of Ashleigh. I need this like a hole in the head.'

I felt sorry for Selina, but Ashleigh's birth father had a right to know his daughter was in care, and if he had information to add to the police investigation then of course he should tell them.

'I understand the social services have a duty to notify the natural parent if their child is taken into care, especially if they see the child regularly,' I said.

'He's out to make trouble. He left me for someone else and then regretted it. He's jealous of Tim, or was. Anyway, let me see the girls.'

I brought Angie and Polly into the front room. As soon as Selina saw them her eyes filled with tears, which upset the girls. 'I miss you so much,' she said.

'We miss you,' Angie cried.

'I want to come home,' Polly said, rubbing her eyes.

'Daddy and I are doing all we can to bring you home,' Selina said. 'What have you been doing today?'

I was hoping they might tell her of the nice things they'd been doing, but Angie said, 'Police ladies came here and we had to talk to them.'

'Today?' Selina asked, concerned.

'Yes.'

'What did they want?'

'They asked us questions.'

'What did you tell them?'

Both girls were looking worried, as if they had said or done something wrong. 'Probably best not to question them about it,' I said to Selina.

'Why not? I have a right to know.'

'They just asked them some questions,' I said.

'About Tim?'

'Some of them were, but I really don't think it should be discussed now. Have you got a book you could read to the girls?'

'No, I was going to get one, then I got distracted when Trevor phoned.'

I assumed Trevor was her ex, and then Angie confirmed he was by asking worriedly, 'Have you seen Ashleigh's daddy?'

'No,' Selina said. 'And he's not her daddy. Tim is. He's the one who brought her up and pays for everything, not him!'

Both girls were looking even more anxious, and I could see how arguments and bad feeling had developed at home. Some stepfamilies manage to blend successfully while others struggle.

'Tell Mummy about the cupcakes you made,' I suggested.

'We made cakes,' Polly said in a small, flat voice, as if it had been something to endure.

'Tell Mummy how you iced them,' I encouraged, hoping to show Selina something positive. Whenever she saw the girls they looked miserable – seeing her was bittersweet.

Angie and Polly made a half-hearted attempt to describe how they made and iced the cakes. Selina sat there, saying nothing, her thoughts clearly a million miles away. Having wrung as much as I could out of the subject of cupcakes, I suggested some other topics the girls could talk to their mummy about. The video call struggled on for about another ten minutes. Then Selina, who'd been preoccupied throughout, suddenly said anxiously, 'I'd better phone our solicitor before they close.'

They all said a hurried and tearful goodbye before Selina ended the call. Reassuring the girls that their mother was all right, I took them into the kitchen-diner where I got out paints, paper and colouring books. After a while they asked to watch some television as they usually did around this time at home. Once they were settled in the living room, I began to prepare dinner. I felt we were starting to get into something of a routine.

Paula joined us for dinner and then we read to the girls until it was their bedtime, at which point I took them up while Paula had some well-deserved 'me' time. Angie and Polly were used to going to bed at the same time at home so I kept that going, otherwise I would have taken Polly, the younger, up first. They were bathed and in bed by 7.30 and Paula came to say goodnight. I asked them if they wanted a kiss, but they didn't, preferring to kiss and cuddle their soft toys. I told them to call out if they needed me, as I would be downstairs. Leaving their bedroom door open and their light on low, we came out. Paula returned to her room and I went downstairs to the front room. I wanted to write up my log while the day was still fresh in my mind.

No sooner had I begun than my mobile rang. It was Janet, Ashleigh's carer.

'You'll never guess what's been going on here today!' she exclaimed as soon as I answered. 'Talk about high drama!'

'Oh dear, what's happened?' I asked, and stopped what I was doing.

'Once Ashleigh finally got up, I started to talk to her about coming-home times and who she was with, but she burst into tears and declared she was pregnant!'

'Oh.'

'You could have knocked me down with a feather! I phoned Fatima and she came here this afternoon and spent some time talking to Ashleigh, just the two of them. It turned out she wasn't pregnant after all. It was a false alarm. Between telling me and Fatima arriving, Ashleigh started a period.'

'That was fortuitous,' I said. 'Why did she think she was pregnant?'

'I assume because of her stepfather raping her,' Janet replied. 'Ashleigh wanted to speak to Fatima alone, so I left them to it. I'm sure you know that foster children have a right to speak to their social worker in private if they want.'

'Yes, the poor girl. Ashleigh's been through so much. Is she being offered counselling?'

'Fatima is making a referral, but Ashleigh says she doesn't want to go.'

'She may change her mind when the appointment comes through. Where is she now?'

'Out with a friend. She's promised to be home at a reasonable time. Like you said, I told her that once she'd proved herself I would give her a front door key.'

'And how is she getting home?'

'On the bus, I guess.'

The arrangements still seemed vague, but I didn't feel I could offer any more advice. 'We'll speak again on Saturday for the girls' video-call contact,' I said. 'I'm just going to write up my log notes.'

'Yes, I need to do mine,' Janet said. 'I'll let you know if Ashleigh keeps her promise and comes in on time.'

'OK.'

We said goodbye and just for a moment I wondered if Ashleigh had been telling the truth when she'd said she'd thought she was pregnant. I didn't know her, and I was probably doing her a big disservice, but I could picture the scene: Janet starting to put boundaries in place and then being thwarted by Ashleigh declaring she was pregnant. I hoped I was wrong, but she wouldn't be the first troubled child who'd made up something to gain sympathy and attention.

At nine o'clock Janet texted to say Ashleigh had returned and gone straight to her bedroom. *I feel like a landlady rather than a foster carer!* she messaged.

It's early days yet, I replied. *Glad she's back safely.*

Paula and I watched the news as we often did. The pandemic and the effect it was having across the world still dominated, with global infection figures and fatalities climbing, although not as sharply. In the UK we were being given regular reminders on television to wash our hands, maintain social distancing and follow the rules on mixing with other households. August is traditionally the main holiday season, and some ventured abroad, but not many, as returning home was becoming problematic due to countries being added to our list of those where travellers had to quarantine on arrival. However, the weather was good and a vaccine was being developed very quickly. Schools and colleges would be returning next month and any warning about a possible second wave seemed pessimistic and far-fetched. We were beating this virus, weren't we?

CHAPTER EIGHT

ANOTHER DIFFICULT CONTACT

Polly and Angie woke once during the night. I went to them as soon as I heard Polly's call. She wanted the toilet; they both went, then returned to their beds. As I lay in my bed I could hear them talking for a while before they fell asleep. They didn't wake again until 7 a.m., by which time I was awake but not showered and dressed. I asked them to stay in their beds while I got ready and gave them some books to look at. I wouldn't have done this with all the children I fostered, as some I had to watch the whole time. But Angie and Polly were used to amusing themselves for short periods at home, so I felt comfortable doing this.

I had a quick shower, then once dressed I took the girls downstairs in their pyjamas and they sat at the table in the kitchen-diner while I made breakfast. They had cereal and fruit, which they were used to having at home with a drink of juice. After we'd eaten I took them to wash and dress. Paula was up now. She knew I needed her help this morning as Joy had booked a supervisory visit for ten o'clock. Although it was virtual, I still needed to prepare.

Aware that Joy would want to see the girls and also all the rooms in the house (as she would normally have done in person), I was using my tablet so I could move around. As my supervising social worker, Joy normally visited every four weeks (in addition to two unannounced visits a year) when we discussed the child's progress, routine, health, education, cultural needs, contact and any issues that had arisen.

I explained Joy's role to Angie and Polly – 'To make sure I'm looking after you very well,' I said.

'Mummy looks after us very well,' Angie said.

'I know, love, and I'm helping her.'

Just before ten o'clock I left the girls with Paula in the living room while I set up the conference call on my tablet in the front room. Once logged in Joy began by asking if we were all well and I confirmed we were. She then asked, as she had been doing since the start of the pandemic, if anyone in the house was having to self-isolate or had been in contact with someone who had tested positive for coronavirus. I confirmed no one had.

I'd been copying Joy into my emails to Fatima and she had access to my log online so was more or less up to date.

'A lot of younger children are struggling with the online contact,' Joy said, aware that Polly and Angie were. 'Are there any plans for face-to-face contact?'

'Selina raised it with her solicitor, but I haven't heard any more,' I replied.

'Have Polly and Angie had online contact with Ashleigh yet?' Joy asked. Joy wasn't Janet's supervising social worker.

'No, tomorrow,' I replied, as Joy typed, making notes as we went.

We talked about the girls' emotional needs and how upset they were at being parted from their parents. Joy felt that I was doing all I could do to reassure and comfort them, and asked how I was keeping them occupied. I described a typical day and some of the activities Paula and I arranged for them. She asked if they'd had any accidents or illnesses as she did at every supervisory meeting. I confirmed they hadn't.

'Any concerns about their behaviour?' she asked.

'Other than the fact that they're very upset at being away from home, no.'

'Children react differently to being in care,' Joy said, which I knew.

We then talked about the girls' education and that Polly would be starting school the following month. I said I would contact the school nearer the time. Joy wanted to know if I had everything I needed to foster the girls and I said I did. We continued with my training needs. All foster carers attend ongoing training, regardless of how experienced they are, and are expected to complete a set number of training modules per year. I was up to date. At present training was online, which was convenient as I was able to slot most of it in around looking after the girls and my other commitments. Joy said she'd signed off my log notes online and asked me to do the same with the minutes from her last visit, which I would do later when our meeting had ended. With no other business, she asked to see Angie and Polly. I took the tablet into the kitchen-diner where Paula had organized modelling dough at the table.

'This is Joy, my supervising social worker I told you about,' I said to Angie and Polly, holding the tablet so they could see Joy, and she them.

Angie immediately slid from her chair and stood out

of sight of the cam. 'I don't want to talk to her,' she said moodily.

'No, OK, but Joy needs to see you,' I said. I turned the tablet so she was in view again.

'Hi, Angie,' Joy said with a warm smile. 'How are you?'

Angie hung her head and pouted.

'What are you doing?' Joy asked.

'Modelling with dough,' Angie replied in a subdued voice.

'That sounds fun. What have you made?'

'A cat,' Angie mumbled.

'Fantastic. Can I see it?'

Angie made no attempt to show Joy the model, so I picked up the piece of dough that looked most like a cat and held it so Joy could see.

'That's very good,' Joy enthused. 'Cathy's got a cat. Is it a model of him?'

'Can I go now?' Angie asked.

'Yes, of course,' Joy said. 'Thank you for talking to me.'

Angie returned to the table but sat out of Joy's sight.

'This is Polly,' I said, angling the tablet so Joy could see her.

Polly smiled shyly.

'Hi, Polly, are you modelling too?'

'Yes,' she said, sweetly.

'Fantastic. Can I see what you've made?'

Polly didn't show the same reluctance as Angie and proudly held up a large lump of blue dough. 'It's a cat, like Angie's,' she announced.

'Marvellous.'

'Does the cat have a name?'

'Sammy,' Polly said, and I smiled.

'Cathy's cat is called Sammy. Your model is very good,' Joy said.

'My model is called Sammy too,' Angie said, not wanting to be left out.

'Great. What else have you both made?'

'This!' Polly declared, holding up another large lump of dough that appeared to have horns. 'It's a dog, but I want to go home to Mummy.'

'I know,' Joy said. 'But Cathy is looking after you well, isn't she?'

Neither of the girls answered.

'If you need anything or have any worries, who do you go to?' Joy asked them.

'Cathy,' Polly said.

'Or Paula,' Angie added.

'Good.'

'Hi, Joy,' Paula called. She'd been out of view, so I turned the tablet towards her. She was rolling dough between her palms.

'You look busy,' Joy said. 'Thanks for all you're doing. I understand you're still furloughed.'

'Yes, for at least another month.'

They talked for a few moments as they would normally have done if Joy had visited in person. The SSW likes to see others living in the house as much as is practical.

'I'll let you get on then,' Joy said, winding up her conversation with Paula. 'Cathy, if there's nothing else, we'll do the tour now,' she said to me. 'Include the garden, please, as I didn't see it last time. It was raining.'

Angie stayed at the table with Paula and Polly came with me. I held the tablet in front of me and walked through the kitchen, panning the cam as we went so Joy could see all around. We went out of the back door, down the garden to where the children's play apparatus was, then back up and indoors, going in through the patio doors. I showed her the living room, down the hall, into the front room and then upstairs, where I went in and out of all the bedrooms.

'That's my bed,' Polly said, pointing as we went into the room. 'Angie sleeps there.'

'Wonderful. Very snug,' Joy said. 'And who is that sitting on your pillow?' Joy was referring to the soft-toy rabbit.

'Pink Rabbit,' Polly said cutely. 'And my sister's is Blue Rabbit.'

'They're good names,' Joy said, pleased Polly was talking to her. Joy had done better than me with the soft toys. When I'd asked their names neither of the girls had wanted to tell me, but then Joy wasn't usurping the role of their mother as I was. 'Do you like sharing a bedroom with your sister?' Joy asked.

But Polly had had enough. 'I'm going,' she said, and headed out of the room.

'Yes, she does,' I replied, and followed Polly out.

We'd finished the tour, so I returned downstairs with Polly and went into the kitchen-diner for Joy to say goodbye.

As soon as I closed the tablet Polly asked, 'Is it time to phone Mummy?'

'No, love.' It wasn't yet eleven o'clock. 'Let's go out,' I suggested. 'We'll take a picnic lunch with us. Where shall we go?'

'How about the animal sanctuary?' Paula suggested.

'Yes, good idea.'

The sanctuary was in a park a short car journey away. It was popular with local residents and housed birds and small animals that had been rescued and were now recovering or couldn't live in the wild. I'd often taken my children there when they were little as well as children I'd fostered. It survived on the small entry fee, donations and voluntary help. I knew they'd been struggling to stay afloat during lockdown when they'd had to close to the public.

Paula and I involved the girls in putting together a picnic lunch and half an hour later we set off. As I drove Paula told the girls what they might expect to see.

'I've been to a zoo,' Angie said.

'It's much smaller than a zoo,' I said, not wanting them to be disappointed.

'We saw lions at the zoo,' Angie replied.

'There won't be any lions at the sanctuary,' Paula said.

'I saw monkeys,' Polly told us.

'No monkeys either, but there will be lots for you to see,' I reassured them.

Despite them not seeing lions or monkeys, they did have a nice time at the sanctuary – as much as they were able to without their parents. One of the aviaries housed budgerigars and other brightly coloured, chirping tropical birds, which they liked, as well as the ducks on the pond that quacked loudly as we passed. There was also a rescued swan in the enclosure. There were other visitors apart from us and large signs everywhere reminded us to keep two metres apart and to use the hand sanitizer at the wash stations. As we continued round the one-way system we saw three huge pigs in a pen, one so fat it could barely stand.

'He's ugly,' Angie said, pulling a face.

I guessed he was, but I felt sorry for him as he looked at us sadly. A three-legged sheep had arrived since my last visit and Angie asked why it didn't fall over.

'Good question. It's because it can balance on its other three legs,' Paula said.

It was coping very well and as we watched it ran to the fence when it thought a visitor had food. The next enclosure had goats that were four-legged and appeared to be well. There were various owls in another large enclosure, but we couldn't see the hedgehogs in their compound.

'I expect they're asleep under that pile of leaves,' I suggested.

We spent some time looking for them through the wire netting and then moved on. We were at the sanctuary for an hour and a half, and then, having seen all the animals, we left, washing and sanitizing our hands on the way out. We returned to the car for our picnic hamper and sat on the grass to eat. The girls had mentioned their mummy and daddy a few times but not as often as they did at home when they were constantly waiting for four o'clock. Once we'd finished lunch we went to the children's play area. I kept an eye on the time and we left the sanctuary at 3 p.m. in plenty of time to video-call their mother at 4 p.m. Contact had to take priority over everything else, even though it was virtual.

Just before 4 p.m. I went into the front room to set up the video call while Paula looked after Angie and Polly. I was hoping that Selina had started to adjust to her children being in care and wouldn't be so distraught. I was also hoping the girls might share the details of some of our outing with their mother. As Selina accepted the call she was talking to someone off screen. It was a man's voice and I wondered if it was Tim, her husband. 'You're wasting your time,' he said, annoyed.

'I'm still going to tell her,' Selina replied, then speaking to me: 'Our solicitor has just telephoned and said the social services won't allow me any face-to-face contact with my children, and even if Tim moves out it's highly unlikely the girls can return. The social worker thinks I'm covering up for him or could even be involved in abusing the girls! There isn't any abuse! It's ridiculous!' Tears filled her eyes.

'There! I told you you'd only upset yourself,' Tim said off-screen.

'I am sorry,' I said.

I waited for Selina to recover and thought thank goodness the girls were in another room. Disappointing and upsetting as this news was for Selina, the social services must have had their reasons for denying contact. I wasn't really surprised they'd taken this view. Protecting the children from harm was paramount and at present Selina was still behind Tim 100 per cent, supporting him, and even denying any abuse had taken place. Abusers don't come with a label and it's often a long and difficult process to get to the truth, during which time the children need protecting.

'We'll do what I wanted to do in the first place and take it to court,' I heard Tim say.

'And lose all our parental rights!' Selina retaliated, wiping her eyes. 'You know what our solicitor said. At least with a Section 20 we have some rights.'

'What rights? Where are they?' Tim demanded

off-screen. 'You're not allowed to see the children and I can't even talk to them online.'

'Shall I call you back?' I asked Selina.

'No need!' Tim shouted. 'I'm going out!'

Selina looked away, presumably tracking Tim's movement as he left. I heard a door slam.

'Are you sure you don't want me to call back?' I asked.

'No. I need to see the girls.'

I waited for her to recover and then fetched Angie and Polly.

'Hello,' Selina said, putting on a brave face. 'How are you both?'

'We saw some animals,' Polly said. I was pleased.

'It wasn't as good as the zoo we went to with you and Daddy,' Angie said loyally.

'I liked it,' Polly said.

'Good,' Selina said. 'Did you like it, Angie?'

She shrugged.

'What else have you been doing?' Selina asked, forcing herself to make conversation.

'Nothing,' Angie replied.

'You made dough models and then helped make the picnic,' I prompted.

'We saw another lady,' Polly said.

'Really?' Selina asked, puzzled and concerned.

'Do you mean Joy?' I asked, and Polly nodded.

'It was my supervising social worker,' I explained to Selina. 'She visits regularly, as does the children's social worker. Fatima will be paying us a visit on Monday, but nearly all the visits are online at present.'

Selina gave a small nod and then said half-heartedly, 'What else have you been doing?'

'When can we come home?' Angie asked.

'Soon,' Selina said.

'Where's Daddy?'

'He's gone out.'

'Doesn't he want to talk to us?'

I saw Selina take a deep breath. 'Yes, more than anything in the world, but he's not allowed to at present.'

'Why?' Angie asked.

Selina was struggling. 'Do you have a book you can read to the girls?' I suggested, as I had done before. 'Otherwise, I can find one that Angie could read.'

'I don't want to read,' Angie said.

'I'll get a book,' Selina said, and disappeared for a few moments.

She returned with a children's book, which she read to the girls. It was a short story about a lost teddy bear. As she finished she said, 'I'll speak to you again tomorrow. I need to find Daddy now.'

CHAPTER NINE

GOING TO LIVE WITH NANA

On Saturday morning I explained to Polly and Angie that we would be making a video call to Ashleigh so they could see and talk to her like they did with their mother. They seemed pleased but not wildly ecstatic. My impression so far of the siblings' relationship was that while Polly and Angie were very close, they weren't close to their older sister, which I attributed to the age gap. I was planning on setting up the video call to Janet on my computer beforehand, as I had been doing with their mother and other virtual contacts since we'd begun using them at the start of the pandemic. While I wasn't antici-pating any problems in the girls speaking to their older sister, I thought it was wise to make sure she was there and able to talk.

But just before ten o'clock, as I was leaving Paula with the girls in the living room to make the video call to Janet, my phone began ringing. To my astonishment I saw it was a WhatsApp video call from Ashleigh. Her name showed together with her image. I wasn't even aware she had my number. Thrown, I continued down the hall, swiping the screen to accept the call as I went.

'Hello, love, this is a surprise,' I said, going into the front room. She had shoulder-length brown hair, and similar petite features to her mother.

'Is it? Janet told me to call you so I could speak to Angie and Polly.'

'Yes, that's fine. I was about to call Janet. No problem. I'll put the girls on. I expect Janet explained I'll be staying while you talk to them.'

'No.'

'Is Janet there?' I asked.

'She's downstairs.'

'Where are you then?'

'In my bedroom.' I could see some shelves behind her but that was all.

'She knows you're calling me?' I checked.

'Yes.'

'OK.'

I had no idea if Janet had been told to supervise the video-call contact or not. Ashleigh was fourteen so it was possible it wasn't felt necessary. Even so, had I been her foster carer I would have been in the same room as her for at least the first contact to make sure it ran smoothly. Also, I wouldn't have given another carer's phone number out without asking first.

'How are you doing?' I asked Ashleigh as I returned down the hall to the living room.

'Good,' she replied.

'It's nice to meet you at last,' I said. Then to Polly and Angie: 'Here's Ashleigh to talk to you.'

'My sister,' Polly said, while Angie looked wary.

Paula stood to make room for me on the sofa and held my phone so both girls could see Ashleigh. It was more difficult on the small screen of my phone than on my tablet or computer.

'Hi,' Ashleigh said, upbeat. 'Are you having a nice time there?'

Angie shook her head while Polly said, 'I want to go home.'

'I don't,' Ashleigh replied.

I looked pointedly at Paula, who was now sitting in a chair on the other side of the room. Her eyes rounded in astonishment. It was a long time, if not forever, since we'd heard a child or young person say they'd rather be in care than at home. What did that say about her home life? I wondered. More was to follow.

'Why don't you like Daddy?' Angie asked bluntly.

'Because he's horrible,' Ashleigh replied.

'No, he's not, and it's your fault we're here,' Angie said.

'It's not my fault,' Ashleigh snapped.

'Yes, it is. You're always arguing,' Angie said. 'And because of you we had to leave home.'

I would have liked to see where this conversation went in terms of what it divulged, but Ashleigh and Angie were getting annoyed and Polly was looking anxious.

'Let's talk about something else,' I said. 'What have you been doing, Ashleigh? I'm sure Angie and Polly would like to hear your news and then they can tell you theirs.'

Ashleigh looked a bit disgruntled, but then began telling the girls how she filled her days. 'I listen to music and watch television. I have a TV in my bedroom here and Janet has given me her Netflix password so I can watch what I want and not what she does. I've got loads of credit on my phone and I can go out with my friends whenever I want, and I've got new clothes.' I wondered if these had been issues at home.

'Mummy sent our clothes,' Angie said.

'She sent some of mine too, but these are much better,' Ashleigh replied. 'I get a clothing allowance here so I can buy what I want.'

'Did Janet go shopping with you?' I asked, out of interest.

'No, I went with friends. She gave me the money and my weekly pocket money. It's more than Mum used to give me. She gave me extra for lunch too, so I had McDonald's with my friends.'

'Tell Ashleigh what you've been doing,' I encouraged the girls.

Polly began talking about the animals we'd seen at the sanctuary, calling it a 'little zoo'. I was impressed by how much she'd taken in and remembered. Angie was still looking warily at Ashleigh.

'Which animal did you like most?' I asked Angie, trying to draw her into the conversation.

'I like lions,' she said. 'But there weren't any.' Paula threw me a knowing smile.

'OK, love. Maybe another time,' I said.

'What are you planning for today?' I asked Ashleigh, trying to keep the conversation going.

'I'm going out soon,' she said.

'You are being careful about mixing?' I reminded her. 'And following the Covid rules?'

'Yes, I'm only seeing one friend today.'

'Your boyfriend?' Angie asked.

'Maybe,' Ashleigh said, meaning she wasn't going to tell. 'I have to go now to get ready.'

'Are you going now?' Polly asked.

'Yes.'

'All right, love,' I said. 'It's been nice talking to you. Say hi to Janet for me.' Then to Angie and Polly I said: 'Say goodbye to Ashleigh.'

'Bye,' they chorused together.

'Bye,' Ashleigh said, and straight away ended the call.

I'm not sure how I'd imagined Ashleigh to be or what I'd been expecting from the contact, but it hadn't been this. They'd only spoken for five minutes and it had been hard work, not like the conversations between some siblings I'd fostered who'd become separated in care, who talked warmly and at length. But what struck me was how well Ashleigh was doing compared to the rest of her family. Her parents were in pieces and Angie and Polly were pining for them and their home, while Ashleigh seemed to be flourishing. It was a little over a week since she'd suffered the horrendous trauma of being raped by her stepfather, but now she appeared to be relaxed, was going out with friends, buying new clothes and doing what most teenagers her age do. Perhaps it was the relief of being away from home after years of living in fear of her stepfather. Even so, I would have expected some sign of the horror she'd been through. When the police officers had visited us Mel had said Ashleigh was too stressed and upset to go to the police station to make a statement. I wondered if she'd gone now. My other thought was that she could have buried her past suffering in order to cope, as I'd seen other young people do. I hoped Ashleigh got the help she needed to come to terms with her past.

'When can we phone Mummy?' Polly predictably asked a few moments after the call to Ashleigh had ended.

'Four o'clock,' I replied. 'But first, you're going to meet my other daughter, Lucy, and her family in the park.'

'Not the park again,' Angie sighed.

'It's a different one,' Paula said, with an indulgent smile.

'I like parks,' Polly said, bless her, and allowed me to give her a little hug.

I would have given both girls lot of hugs had they wanted me to, but at present they didn't. Some children arrived wanting to be held and cuddled all the time, while others didn't want to be touched at all. Age, past experience of physical contact and personality played a part. With Angie and Polly I thought it was loyalty to their parents that stopped them from letting me get close. Hopefully in time they would see that it was all right for me to hug and care for them, as it didn't detract from the relationship they had with their parents. Like most foster carers, I took my cue from the child on what they felt comfortable doing.

We met Lucy and family in a park close to where they lived. As it was Saturday there were lots of families there and some large groups, which strictly speaking was against the restrictions. We found a quiet corner to lay out our groundsheets and picnic. It was the first time Lucy and Darren had met Angie and Polly, and they made a fuss of them. They were nursery assistants and had plenty of experience in putting children at ease and making them feel welcome. My granddaughter Emma wanted all of my and Paula's attention. Now two years old, like many her age she knew her own mind and liked her own way, but it was her parents who put boundaries in place when we were all together, leaving me free to simply enjoy her. That's the wonderful thing about being a grandparent – you get all the good bits. If Emma became over-excited and annoyed then it was Lucy or Darren who calmed her.

Polly liked Emma. Angie less so; she turned her back if she came close or moved away. She asked me regularly if it was time to go yet and phone Mummy. I reassured her we would be back in plenty of time, although I thought this was more about being with my family. She knew we were never late video-calling her mother. I appreciate how difficult it is for looked-after children when the carer sees their family. It reinforces that they've lost their family. But as a carer you can't not see your own loved ones. We all went out of our way to make sure the children we fostered were included and felt part of the family, just as my dear parents always had when they'd been alive.

We didn't take the children to the area where the play equipment was as it was crowded and we had concerns about the virus being spread with so many children close together. Instead, after we'd eaten, we organized ball and hoop games on the grass, and hide and seek around the trunks of the large oak trees. Angie joined in and for a while forgot her unhappiness.

It was lovely spending time with Lucy and family, but we had to leave at 3.30 to go home for the video contact. Lucy and Darren came with us to the park gates where we said goodbye. They only lived a short walk away so hadn't brought their car.

Once home, Paula took the girls to the bathroom to thoroughly wash their hands while I unpacked the picnic hamper and then set up the video call.

I knew the moment I saw Selina she was feeling brighter. I was relieved. When she spoke she sounded more positive too.

'Hi, Cathy, how are you? How are Angie and Polly?'

'They're doing well. We've been out. We met up with my daughter Lucy and her family. How are you?'

'Much better, thank you. Can you get the girls now, please? I've got some good news to share with them.'

I suppose I should have asked what the news was, but it would have been awkward, and to be honest I'm not sure it would have stopped Selina from telling them anyway.

Angie and Polly were downstairs now and I brought them into the front room. As they sat in front of the screen Selina smiled and said, 'Great news. You're going to stay with Nana until you can come home again.'

Their little faces lit up. I knew from the placement information forms and the comments the girls had made that they had a good relationship with Selina's mother. But that didn't mean they could live there.

'When are we going?' Angie asked excitedly.

'Early next week,' Selina replied. 'Hopefully Monday.'

'I love Nana,' Polly said, also smiling.

'Sorry, Selina,' I said, interrupting. 'I haven't heard anything about this. When was it decided?'

'I spoke to Mum this morning and finally told her what had happened. She was very upset, but immediately offered to have Angie and Polly until this mess is sorted out. I should have told her sooner, but we've been in such a state we haven't been thinking straight. She spoke to Tim too and said she would support him in any way she could. It was just what we needed. She's a rock in times of trouble. She said straight away Tim was incapable of harming any of his children.'

'I see. Have you discussed all this with Fatima?' I asked.

'Not yet. We only decided this morning and the social services are closed all weekend apart from emergencies. I left a message on Fatima's voicemail and will phone her again first thing on Monday, then move Angie and Polly in the afternoon. Mum can collect them. They'll be much happier there – no offence to you.'

While the girls would very likely be happier with their maternal grandmother, and staying with a suitable relative was usually considered the next best option for children who can't live with their parents, it would need the approval of the social services.

'You will need to speak to Fatima,' I said. 'Even though the children are in care under a Section 20.'

'Yes, I know. I will on Monday.'

'When are we going to Nana's?' Polly asked, delighted.

'Very soon,' Selina said, with a smile.

'Yippee! What about school?' Angie asked, aware that she was due to return to school the following month.

'If you're not home by the start of term, Nana will take you to school in her car,' Selina said. 'The journey will be longer, but it'll only be for a short while, until you're home again.' Clearly they'd planned it all out.

'I can't wait to see Nana!' Angie exclaimed.

'Me too,' Polly said, grinning.

The rest of the video contact was excited talk about the girls going to live with Nana until they returned home. From what Selina said it seemed she thought she'd be able to see the girls at her mother's house whenever she wanted. Angie asked if they would see Daddy there too and Selina replied, 'Not straight away, but very soon.' I had no idea what she was basing this on, for as far as I knew the police were still investigating Ashleigh's allegations and no decision had been made by the social services. I feared it was conjecture and hoped for all their sakes that what Selina was telling the girls was correct.

Angie and Polly were in very good spirits that evening and continued to be so the following day. I lost count of the number of times they told Paula, me or our cat, Sammy, they were going to live with Nana and then go home. I explained to Paula what their mother had said and, aware of how the social services worked, she shared my concerns it had been premature to tell the girls. As carers, we never promise a child anything until we know for certain it's going to happen, especially in respect of them returning home or seeing loved ones again. Under-promise and over-deliver is our maxim.

On Sunday afternoon Adrian and Kirsty came to visit us, and as the weather was good we sat outside, maintaining social distance as we were supposed to. We weren't allowed to hug yet so like many others we'd got into the habit of elbow-bumping instead, which I felt was a very poor substitute for a good hug. But we had a nice afternoon. We talked, and Kirsty and Adrian played with Angie and Polly. As I watched them with the children I thought, not for the first time, they'd make very good parents if they decided to have a family. They were kind, gentle and caring. Kirsty was a primary school teacher and Adrian an accountant, working from home since the start of the pandemic. Angie and Polly told Kirsty and Adrian they were going to live with their Nana.

'Only if your social worker agrees,' I said, sounding another word of caution. They were undeterred. At their age, of course, they believed what their mother had told them.

As four o'clock approached I slipped indoors to set up the video call to Selina. She was there ready, smiling, and still in a positive frame of mind. I called in Angie and Polly, leaving Adrian, Kirsty and Paula in the garden about to erect the badminton net.

'Lovely to see you,' Selina said brightly as they sat in front of the monitor. 'How are you?'

'When can we come home?' Angie asked.

'Remember, you're going to Nana's first,' Selina replied. 'I hope tomorrow. I'll tell the social worker first thing in the morning. Daddy sends his love.'

'When can we see Daddy?' Angie asked.

'Very soon.'

'The arrangements will need to be cleared with the social services,' I warned again. But it had no effect.

'When you leave remember to thank Cathy for looking after you,' Selina said. 'Nana knows what you like to eat and I'll take some more of your clothes there.' So she continued until she wound up by saying: 'When we speak tomorrow you'll be at Nana's.'

As we returned to the garden the girls were skipping with delight – the happiest I'd seen them since they'd first arrived.

CHAPTER TEN

DRAWN INTO THE FAMILY'S CRISIS

I knew it was possible Fatima would approve the girls going to live with their maternal grandmother, and when she failed to log in for her virtual visit, which she'd booked for 10.30, I half assumed it was because the girls were leaving and she'd phone later with the details. The child's social worker, like the carer's supervising social worker, has a duty to visit regularly, although it was virtual at present. Polly and Angie were convinced they were going that afternoon and Angie kept telling me to pack, while Polly brought down their soft-toy rabbits and placed them by the front door, ready.

'I'll pack all your belongings as soon as I hear from Fatima you're definitely going today,' I told them. 'Don't worry. It won't take me long.'

'Mummy says we are going,' Angie said defensively. 'You should pack now.'

'I need to hear it from your social worker first, so does your mummy and nana,' I replied, and changed the subject.

The girls were restless and couldn't settle to anything. Paula suggested we played something in the garden, but Angie said I might not hear the phone when the social worker called. We organized some activities at the table in the kitchen-diner and at 12.30 we had lunch. Just as we were finishing, Fatima called my mobile. I left the room to take the call.

'Sorry I missed my visit this morning,' she began. 'I've had rather a lot to sort out.'

'Has Selina phoned you?'

'Yes, and her mother. That's what's taken up my time. Mrs Weaks, Selina's mother, has come forward to look after Angie and Polly, but that's not going to happen.' I felt my stomach churn. 'Mrs Weaks believes Ashleigh has made up the allegation against her stepfather and says their relationship has been fraught for some years. She is convinced Tim has done nothing wrong and says both parents have a right to see their children, so she wouldn't stop them from coming into her house if Angie and Polly were there. She can't protect them, so they won't be going.'

'So Angie and Polly are staying with me,' I checked.

'Yes, that's the care plan for the foreseeable future.'

'The girls are going to be very disappointed.'

'They know?' Fatima asked.

'Yes, Selina told them.'

'She didn't mention that to me. She should have spoken to me first. Her solicitor has been in touch and we have agreed to face-to-face supervised contact at the Family Centre twice a week, so that should help soften the blow. I'll email you the details of the contact. I'm due to see the girls anyway so if I reschedule my virtual visit and make it in five minutes' time then I can explain it to them then. I have to make a quick phone call first, but then my next meeting isn't for twenty minutes.'

'All right.'

The girls were still with Paula, so I went into the living room for my tablet and launched the app ready for Fatima's virtual visit. I knew Angie and Polly were going to be bitterly disappointed by what Fatima was about to tell them, but at least they would be seeing their mother in person for a few hours each week.

I returned to the kitchen-diner. 'Your social worker is going to talk to you soon,' I said, sitting at the table.

'When are we going?' Angie asked, still excited.

'You need to listen to what Fatima says.'

Fatima logged in and I propped the tablet on the table so both girls could see her and she them. Paula left the table and went into the kitchen.

'Hi, ladies, how are you?' Fatima began.

'OK,' Angie replied.

'I've spoken to your mother this morning and I think she might have given you the wrong impression. You will be staying at Cathy's for now, but you will be seeing your mother for a few hours each week.'

There was silence. The girls stared at her, unable to digest what they were being told, then Angie asked: 'Aren't we going to Nana's?'

'No. I don't know why your mother told you that,' Fatima replied.

Angie's face fell – her world had just collapsed. Polly began to cry, so I put my arm around her.

'Can we see Daddy?' Angie asked.

'I'm afraid not,' Fatima said, and seemed surprised that Angie had even asked. 'I suppose they're too young to understand,' Fatima said to me.

'Yes.'

Paula had stopped what she was doing in the kitchen and was looking worriedly at the girls.

'Have you seen your sister?' Fatima asked.

'Yes, on Saturday,' I replied, as the girls didn't.

'Ashleigh is doing very well,' Fatima said. 'Try to be happy like she is. You're being well looked after there, aren't you?'

Angie just stared at her. Paula handed me a tissue to wipe Polly's eyes.

'What do you like doing?' Fatima tried asking the girls.

Neither of them replied.

'What do you like to play with? Have you been out somewhere nice?' she asked.

These were questions she would have very likely asked during a normal visit, but of course the girls weren't in any mood to answer her now. They'd just had their hopes of going to Nana's or returning home smashed.

'You go to school soon,' Fatima said, brightly.

'They are,' I replied on their behalf. 'It's a big step for Polly, starting school.'

'Are you looking forward to going to school like your sister does?' Fatima asked her.

Polly rubbed her eyes and hung her head.

'When does the term begin?' Fatima asked me. 'I'll arrange contact for after school when the new term starts.'

'I think it's the second of September, but I'll need to check.'

'OK, email me when you know,' she said. 'Can you give me a tour of your house now, please? I saw it when I placed the girls, so a quick look will do.'

Leaving Paula comforting the girls, I carried the tablet in and out of the rooms, giving Fatima a tour similar to Joy's, only shorter and without going into the garden. I returned to the kitchen-diner where Fatima said goodbye and ended the call.

'I want Mummy,' Polly said, fresh tears forming.

'I want to live with Nana,' Angie said miserably. 'Mummy said we could.'

It was heart-breaking and some of their upset could have been avoided if Selina had spoken to Fatima first. Paula comforted Angie as I took Polly onto my lap.

'You're going to see Mummy for real in a few days,' I told them, hoping this would help. 'That'll be nice, won't it?'

Angie looked like she didn't believe me and who could blame her? It was Monday now and I was hoping they wouldn't have to wait too long to see their mother. Fatima would email the arrangements.

Eventually Paula and I managed to distract the girls from their sorrow by doing a giant jigsaw puzzle they hadn't seen before. Once it was completed they wanted to watch television. They snuggled close together on the sofa holding hands, drawing comfort from each other. It was very touching. My thoughts went to Selina and I wondered how she was coping. As four o'clock approached I left the girls in the living room and steeled myself to make the video call to Selina.

She was there ready as usual but looked utterly wretched, as if the stuffing had been knocked out of her. She'd been convinced the girls would be going to her mother so was as disappointed as they were.

'How are you?' I asked gently.

She let out a heartfelt sigh. 'You know what's happened?'

'Yes, Fatima phoned and told Angie and Polly.'

'How are they?'

'They were upset but they're calmer now and watching some television.'

'Tim says we should sue the social services and the police once we've got Angie and Polly back.'

I didn't know if they had grounds to sue or not.

'Have you heard from Ashleigh?' Selina asked.

'The girls had a video contact with her on Saturday.'

'I've been trying to speak to her but she's not answering her phone. Have you got her carer's number? I'll try her.'

This was difficult. 'You'll need to ask Fatima for it,' I said.

'Why? I only want to talk to my daughter. I don't need to know where she is living.' I assumed she hadn't been given Janet's contact details because of the seriousness of the allegations Ashleigh had made against her stepfather.

'I'm sorry, you will need to ask Fatima,' I said. 'It's good you will be able to see the girls at the Family Centre,' I added positively. 'When you talk to the girls I suggest you concentrate on that.'

'I don't need you telling me how to talk to my children!' Selina snapped, then immediately apologized. 'I'm sorry. I'm not sure how much more of this I can take.'

'I understand. Do you have people to support you?' I asked, as I had before.

'Only my mother. A lot of my friends have fallen away and stopped calling, having heard about Tim. No smoke without fire. Our neighbours are acting weird too. Not that I want to confide in them.'

'I am sorry. Do you feel up to speaking to Angie and Polly right now?' I asked.

'Yes, I need to. It's what's keeping me going.'

I fetched the girls. I felt sorry for Selina, but my priority lay with Angie and Polly.

'We're not allowed to go to Nana's,' Angie said as soon as she sat down.

'Not right now,' Selina said.

'When can we go?' Angie asked.

'Not yet. As soon as possible,' Selina replied. 'But we will be able to see each other soon so I'll be able to give you both a big hug.'

'I want a hug,' Polly said.

'Why can't we go to Nana's?' Angie persisted.

'Mummy made a mistake. Shall we talk about something else?' Selina said. 'Tell me what you've been doing today.'

'Nothing,' Angie said.

'We watched television,' Polly said.

'What did you watch?'

As they talked I saw an email come through from Fatima, subject line: *Contact*. I opened it.

'Selina, sorry to interrupt, but I've just received an email saying the first contact will take place tomorrow. Have you got an email?'

'Let me check,' she said.

As she read it, she finally smiled.

'Yes, one o'clock on Tuesdays and Thursdays,' she said. 'Marvellous. I can't wait. Angie, Polly, we're going to see each other tomorrow.' Her eyes filled, but this time they were tears of happiness and relief.

The rest of the call was positive and largely about them seeing each other tomorrow.

So often in fostering the carer is drawn into the family's crisis, hopes and joys, often more than they'd anticipated. It's inevitable if the children see their parents regularly – which most children do, at least when they first come into care. It didn't matter that it was currently virtual; their feelings were still real.

Angie and Polly had a lot of questions about contact, so once they'd finished talking to their mother I sat them down in the living room and explained about the Family Centre and what they could expect.

'It's like a house with lots of living rooms,' I said. 'I will take you there in my car and collect you after. You may see your mother in the outside play area where there are lots of toys, or indoors in one of the rooms. The room will have a sofa, table and chairs, and plenty of games to play. Other children may be seeing their families in other rooms. A contact supervisor will be with you the whole time to make sure you're all right.'

The Family Centre had been shut during lockdown and had reopened on a very limited basis, with contact taking place outside where possible or indoors in well-ventilated rooms to reduce the risk of transmitting the virus. At present it was largely the decision of the social worker as to whether the children had virtual or face-to-face contact, based on the care plan and any court order in place.

'At the end can we go home with Mummy?' Angie asked.

'No, love, I will come to collect you. You'll see her again on Thursday.'

I was assuming they'd still have video contact on the other days, but I'd check with Fatima first. While the girls seemed a little anxious, I knew from experience that once they settled into the routine of contact they would start to feel more relaxed and hopefully happier. As well as maintaining the bond, it is reassuring for the children to see that their parents are all right, as of course it is for the parents to see their children. Some parents arrive late for contact or don't arrive at all, but I was certain that wouldn't be the case with Selina. She seemed very committed.

Paula was pleased for Angie and Polly too and answered their questions as I had been doing.

'How many sleeps to when I see my mummy?' Polly asked.

'Just one,' Paula said. 'Tonight.'

Later, after dinner, Paula read them some bedtime stories in the living room and then I took them up for their bath and put them to bed.

'Will Daddy be there?' Polly asked, although I'd explained that contact was just to see their mummy.

'No, love.'

'Will I ever see him again?' Angie asked.

What a question! I honestly didn't know. If he was found guilty of raping his stepdaughter he would receive a long custodial sentence, so they might not see him again.

'I don't know when you'll see him again,' I replied. 'There's a lot to sort out. We'll be told in time.'

'Will a police lady tell us?' Angie asked. Polly looked worried. They were having to grow up so quickly.

'Maybe, or maybe your social worker will tell us, but it's nothing for you to worry about. I will deal with it.'

I knew that if their father was convicted, someone was going to have to have a very difficult conversation with the girls, but for now I turned the conversation back to seeing their mother tomorrow.

Once Angie and Polly were in bed and ready to go to sleep I said goodnight, dimmed the light and, leaving their door slightly open, went downstairs to my computer. I'd been answering emails for about fifteen minutes when my mobile rang. It was Janet.

'Hi, Janet. How are you and Ashleigh?' I asked.

'I'm OK – not sure about her, though. I need to run something by you.'

'Sure, go ahead.' I stopped what I was doing to concentrate on what Janet was about to say.

'Ashleigh went to her father's yesterday, and she was supposed to be back this morning. She texted to say she's staying another night and won't be back until tomorrow.'

'Fatima knows she's there?' I asked. I hadn't been told the contact arrangements for Ashleigh to see her father as I wasn't fostering her.

'Yes, she goes there most weekends and can stay the night in the school holidays. But the problem is, she has to go to the police station at ten o'clock tomorrow to make her statement and I'm worried she won't go. I've tried phoning and texting her, but she's not answering.'

'Have you got her father's telephone number?' I asked.

'I don't think so.'

'It could be in the Essential Information Form that Fatima gave you. If it's there I would phone him to confirm arrangements for Ashleigh getting home.'

'Do you think I should? Ashleigh won't like that.'

'She's a minor and in your care. The contact arrangements seem to have suddenly changed so I think it's reasonable to phone him and ask how she's getting home. It's possible she hasn't told him she has the police interview tomorrow. In any event you need to know.'

'I'll look for his number now. What if I haven't got it?'

I thought for a moment. 'If it was me, I would text Ashleigh to say you will collect her either tonight or first thing tomorrow. That should produce a response.'

'Thanks, Cathy.'

'You're welcome.'

We said goodbye and I continued replying to emails. Ten minutes later Janet texted. *All good. Spoke to Ashleigh's father. Nice man. He's going to drop her off here in the morning. She told him she had to go for the police interview.*

Great. Well done, I replied.

Thanks.

I appreciated it was a sharp learning curve for new carers or those returning after a long break, not helped by the pandemic, so I was pleased I'd been of some help.

CHAPTER ELEVEN

A PAINFUL REUNION

As soon as Polly woke on Tuesday morning she asked how long it was until they could see Mummy. Angie counted off the hours.

'Seven,' she announced.

'Yes, that's right, love,' I said. 'It's only six o'clock. A bit early for you to get up yet.' I stifled a yawn.

Polly had also woken during the night, asking if it was time to see Mummy, so I was tired.

'I'd like you to stay in your beds and see if you can go back to sleep,' I said. 'It will make the time pass more quickly.'

'How will the time pass more quickly?' Angie asked. She was an intelligent child. They both were.

'Well, if you go back to sleep until nine o'clock, there will only be four hours until you see Mummy,' I explained.

'I think I'm going back to sleep,' Angie told her sister, and snuggled down.

'So am I,' Polly agreed, and did the same.

When I looked in on them ten minutes later they were both asleep. They slept until eight o'clock, which was good and gave me the chance to shower, dress and have a quiet cup of coffee. Once they were up it was non-stop, even with Paula's help.

By nine o'clock the girls were dressed, downstairs having breakfast and counting off the hours again until they could see their mummy. I needed to buy a few grocery items so I suggested we walk to our local shop where they could also buy a little present for their mother.

'Like we do on Mother's Day?' Angie said.

'Yes, love.'

'Is it Mother's Day?' Polly asked.

'No, but it's nice to give presents to those we love at other times too. I'm sure your mummy will be pleased.'

'I'd like to buy Mummy a new dress like Daddy does,' Angie said.

'I'm afraid the shop we're going to doesn't sell dresses, and anyway we don't know her size or what she likes. I was thinking more of chocolates or a bunch of flowers.'

'Daddy knows Mummy's size and what she likes,' Angie said.

I nodded. Whenever the girls mentioned their father, which they often did, I felt uncomfortable. He'd clearly played a big part in their lives and they loved him, but he had been accused of raping their older sister. While Angie and Polly were aware they were in care as a result of something that had happened between their father and Ashleigh, they didn't know the details or the severity of the allegation. When they mentioned him I usually gave a small nod to let them know I'd heard them, but I didn't feel I could give much more as I did when they talked of their mother.

'Mummy likes chocolates,' Polly said.

'Good, you can choose some for her. Now, let's get ready and go.'

Leaving Paula to get up at her leisure, we headed to our local shop. It was another warm day and as we strolled hand in hand, Polly on one side of me and Angie on the other, we paused to look at flowers in front gardens, a cat on a low wall and birds sitting in trees or on rooftops. I put on my mask before going into the shop and pumped the hand sanitizer onto all our hands. Taking a wire basket, I collected the milk, bread rolls, veg and fruit that we needed, then Angie chose a bunch of flowers to give to her mother and Polly a box of chocolates.

'Daddy likes chocolates too,' Polly said.

'I expect your mummy will share them,' I replied as we headed for the checkout.

Angie then spotted the display of cards. 'Can we buy Mummy a card too?' she asked.

We went over and had a look, but they were all for special occasions like birthdays, new homes and retirement.

'You could make Mummy a card when we get home,' I suggested.

'Yes, I like making cards,' Angie said.

'Me too,' Polly agreed.

'Great.'

I took my mask off outside the shop and cleaned all our hands with my antibacterial wipes, then we continued home.

Paula was up when we arrived and ready to go out.

'A friend from work just phoned and I said I'd meet her if you can manage without me.'

'Yes, of course, love, go. You haven't been out for a while.'

I was pleased Paula was going out. She'd hardly seen her friends that year with all the pandemic restrictions and hadn't been in her job long before being furloughed. I felt for her. Like so many other young people just starting out, her life had been put on hold.

Angie wanted to know where Paula was going.

'Clothes shopping with a friend,' she said.

'Enjoy!' I called. 'See you later.'

Once I'd unpacked the groceries I covered the table in the kitchen-diner with a plastic cloth and got out the box of card-making materials, which contained glitter, different-coloured card, felt-tip pens, glue, sequins and felt shapes. Making cards kept the girls occupied for some time. I helped them as necessary. They made a card each, beautifully decorated, and addressed them to Mummy and Daddy. I helped Polly with the writing. Then I spent the same amount of time as the activity had taken clearing up glitter, which had managed to find its way everywhere, including onto the cat.

I made us an early lunch and then, with the presents and cards for Selina in a large gift bag, we left for the Family Centre at 12.30, arriving at 12.50. I pulled into the small car park at the side of the centre and was struck by how empty it was. Normally it was full when the centre was fully operational.

'There's Mummy's car!' Angie cried.

It was parked on the road outside.

'Where is she?' Polly asked, expecting to see her straight away.

'I expect she'll be inside or in the playground at the back,' I said, getting out.

I opened their rear door, which was child-locked, and helped the girls out. Angie wanted to carry the gift bag. I put on my mask and held Polly's hand as we went up the path to the security-locked main door where I pressed the bell. Last time I'd brought a child here at the end of lockdown I'd been let in the side gate and contact had taken place in the play area at the rear, but I wasn't sure what was happening today. The closed-circuit television camera above us was monitored in the office and a few moments later the door clicked open. I led the way into reception. A member of staff sat behind a Perspex screen with a mask on; the office behind her was empty.

'Contact isn't going ahead,' she said anxiously, standing.

'Why ever not?' I exclaimed.

'A member of staff has just phoned in with possible Covid. We're all having to self-isolate. We're closing again as from now.'

'Oh no. The girls are so looking forward to seeing their mother. Selina is here, isn't she?'

'Yes. She's in the manager's office now.'

'Can't they see each other for a while outside in the play area?' I asked.

'I don't think so. We've been told to close straight away. We only had a few coming today anyway, and the contact supervisor has been told not to come in. In fact, you should go. I might be infectious.'

I took the girls outside and cleansed our hands with my antibacterial wipes.

'Where's Mummy?' Polly asked.

'Aren't we seeing her?' Angie said, close to tears.

I took off my mask and tried to think what to do, and if it was possible for them to see their mother, even briefly.

'Just a minute,' I said. We were on the path that led in and out of the centre. There was no one else around. I could see the member of staff I'd just spoken to through the slats of the blinds at the office window, moving around and getting ready to leave.

Taking my phone from my bag, I called the centre's number.

'It's Cathy, I'm outside.'

'I know, I can see you. All contact has been cancelled. You'll need to speak to the children's social worker.'

'I was just wondering if perhaps they could see their mother for a little while outside in the play area? I could bring them in through the side gate.'

'We don't have a contact supervisor.'

'I could stay with them if their social worker agrees.'

'I'll need to speak to our manager. I'll call you back.'

'Can we see Mummy?' Angie asked. She was still holding the gift bag.

'I don't know yet, love. I'm trying to sort out something.'

'Why can't we see Mummy?' Polly asked.

'Because of the virus,' Angie replied. Children of her age and younger had some understanding of what the pandemic meant.

'Yes, that's right, well done,' I said. 'Someone in the centre may have caught the virus and they're closing so we don't catch it.'

'I need to do a wee-wee,' Polly said, an edge of desperation to her voice.

I guessed they wouldn't let us into the Family Centre to use the bathroom.

'Come on, you'll have to water the plants,' I told her, and took her hand.

Angie came with us and I led Polly behind a large shrub, out of sight of the road and the houses opposite. When she'd finished we returned to where we'd been standing on the path. My phone rang and it was the member of staff I'd just been speaking to in the centre.

'I've asked our manager and I'm afraid we can't let you into the play area as we have to close now.'

'Thanks for trying,' I said.

'We're not seeing Mummy, are we?' Angie said miserably.

'Not in the centre, no.'

Selina was still inside and might not know we were here, I thought. At some point she'd leave and would have to come out of the main door or the side gate. If we stayed here they'd be able to see each other briefly. It would be better than nothing. It wasn't as though they weren't allowed to see each other – just the opposite, in fact. Contact had been arranged, and then cancelled at the last minute due to Covid.

'We'll wait here a moment,' I said, and watched the entrance.

A minute later the door opened and Selina came out, taking off her mask. She'd been crying and clearly wasn't expecting to see us. For a split second she stopped dead and stared in disbelief. Then she realized and cried, 'Angie! Polly!' and ran to them.

Kneeling, so she was at their height, she hugged and kissed them, tears streaming down her face. The girls were crying too and saying, 'Mummy, Mummy,' over and over again. It was painful to watch.

'Oh, my darlings, my precious girls, I've missed you so much,' Selina wept, holding them tightly.

'We've missed you, Mummy,' Angie cried, also in tears.

'I want to go home,' Polly said, her arms wrapped tightly around her mother's neck and her face pressed to hers.

I swallowed my own tears as they poured out their emotion, uninhibited by my presence. Then Selina came to and remembered I was there. Wiping her hand over her eyes, she straightened and looked at me. 'They didn't tell me you were here. They said they were telling you not to come.'

'We arrived a bit early and learnt it was cancelled. I thought rather than go straight home, I would wait so you could at least meet.'

'Yes, thank you, thank you so much, you are kind. I'm so grateful. Just to be able to see and hold them again is wonderful.'

My eyes filled and I knew I'd done the right thing in waiting. Selina hugged and kissed the girls again and then Angie remembered she was holding the gift bag.

'We've brought you some presents,' Angie said, passing the bag to her mother.

'Oh, my loves, seeing you is a present.'

'And cards,' Polly said. 'We made cards.'

She looked in the bag. 'Flowers, chocolates and cards – how wonderful. Thank you so much.' She took them out and read the words in the cards. 'Beautiful,' she said, wiping away fresh tears.

'Will you show Daddy? They're for him too,' Angie said.

'Yes, of course, love.'

Selina was shorter and more petite than I'd expected. I'd never seen her standing before, just seated at a table during the video calls. Her clothes seemed to hang on her and I wondered if she'd lost weight with all the stress.

'Do they know we're here?' she asked, looking at the centre, as if she was doing something wrong.

'I guess so, there's all that CCTV,' I said, nodding towards the cameras.

'Thank you so much for waiting. I suppose you have to go home with them now? They said the centre will be closed for at least two weeks.'

My phone began ringing and I answered it.

'Cathy?'

'Yes.'

'It's Fatima's colleague, Liz. We met when we placed the girls with you.'

'Yes. Hello, Liz.'

'The Family Centre is having to close due to Covid so your contact is cancelled until further notice. Can you video-call their mother instead.'

'I'm at the Family Centre now. We've bumped into Selina on the way out so the girls are just saying hello outside.'

'Oh, I see.'

'It's fine. I was wondering if perhaps we could go for a little walk if I stay with them? They won't let us in the centre. They were due an hour's contact.'

Selina and the girls were now looking at me.

'Just a minute,' Liz said.

I assumed she must have spoken to Fatima, for a moment later, when she came back on, she said, 'Yes, but Fatima says don't let them out of your sight. She still has concerns about Selina's role and doesn't want the girls got at.'

'I'll be careful,' I said. 'Thank you.'

'Let's go for a walk,' I said. 'Fatima has approved it as long as I stay with you.'

'Thank you so much,' Selina said. Then to the girls, 'Say thank you to Cathy.'

I was touched and embarrassed by their gratitude. Some parents are angry when their children are taken into care, but Selina had been destroyed.

CHAPTER TWELVE

A FORBIDDEN HUG

I suggested to Selina we walk to a park I knew that wasn't far away from the Family Centre. She didn't mind where we went as along as it was with the girls. She put their gifts into her car first and we set off along the pavement towards the park. Angie and Polly were holding her hands and I walked just behind them, able to hear what they were saying. Their excitement at being together again was obvious.

'I've missed you so much,' Angie said, over and over again.

'Don't leave us,' Polly said desperately. 'I love you.'

'I love you too, so very, very much, and I've missed you both dreadfully,' Selina replied, her voice full of emotion.

As I walked behind them I noticed Selina was limping and I wondered if it was a recent injury and whether she might not want to walk all the way to the park.

'Are you all right to walk?' I asked. 'It's about another ten minutes.'

'Yes. I'm fine. Don't worry about me. I was knocked over as a child and my leg plays up sometimes.'

'I am sorry,' I said.

'It's OK. I've been offered another operation, but it would mean a long recovery period, and there's no guarantee it would help.' Clearly the girls were used to their mother limping as they didn't comment on it.

Once in the park we went to the children's play area. Both girls wanted to be pushed on the swings. I was going to push one but they wanted their mother to do it, so I stood aside. It was the same on the roundabout and climbing apparatus. I understood and waited close by, watching. They were enjoying their time together and none of them mentioned the reason they were here or what had happened. It was a warm afternoon, and presently Polly said she was thirsty.

'I haven't packed any drinks,' I said. 'I wasn't expecting to be in the park. But there is a café just at the brow of that hill over there,' I said, pointing.

'We'll go with Mummy to get a drink and you can stay here,' Angie said, resenting my presence.

'I will need to come,' I said to Selina. 'Fatima asked me to supervise contact.'

'Yes, that's fine. You come.'

We all went to the café. Outside was a kiosk selling drinks and ice cream. Selina insisted on paying. We had a cold drink each and the girls had ice creams too. As I watched Selina taking the money from her purse to pay I thought how frail and vulnerable she looked. Small in stature, she had the manner of someone beaten down by events. I couldn't equate this fragile, broken woman with someone who would protect a paedophile husband at the expense of her children. But, of course, you can never tell. Fostering had taught me that.

We sat on the grass to have our drinks and ice creams. Selina took a photo of the girls having theirs. There were many other families in the park; the schools were on holiday and many workers were still furloughed or had had their hours cut.

'It feels unreal,' Selina said, looking around. 'All these people going about their lives, and I'm trapped in a living nightmare.'

'I have nightmares,' Angie said, hearing the word but not really understanding the context.

'Not often,' I said.

'She normally sleeps well,' Selina says.

'Yes. They wake sometimes but I always go to them,' I reassured her.

She saw me glance at my watch.

'We'll have to go back soon, won't we?' she said quietly.

'I'm afraid so. We'd better keep to the hour.' In fact, it would be over an hour by the time we'd walked back to the Family Centre.

'Do you think they'll let us do this again on Thursday?' Selina asked. I'd been thinking the same.

'I'll ask Fatima,' I said. 'There might be a problem if it's raining, though.'

'I'll bring their waterproofs from home,' she replied.

I smiled. Of course she wouldn't let a bit of rain stop her from seeing her children, assuming Fatima agreed.

Once the girls had finished their ice creams we began a slow walk back towards the Family Centre. It was only then Selina mentioned Tim.

'He didn't do it, you know,' she said, quietly to me. 'I know I'm not allowed to talk about it at contact, but he didn't. He was very firm with Ashleigh, perhaps too firm.

But she was getting out of control and her father doesn't discipline her. He just has a good time and leaves the rest to us.'

'I can't really comment,' I said.

'I know. If I could just talk to Ashleigh, but they won't let me. The social worker thinks I'm covering up for Tim. There is nothing to cover up. Tim has offered to move out if it helps but there's no point. They won't let Angie and Polly return while I'm under suspicion. I've told the police all I know, but their investigation is taking forever. The solicitor says they have evidence, but he doesn't know what it is yet.'

As she confided in me I felt the nice time we'd had in the park evaporate and her desperation return. Soon she'd have to say goodbye to the girls. I hoped she didn't do something silly and try to snatch them.

'At this rate they are going to forget me,' she said dejectedly as we drew nearer to the centre.

'They won't,' I reassured her. 'Perhaps you have a photograph I could put in their bedroom, so they can see you as they go off to sleep and first thing in the morning. I find it helps.'

'Yes, of course, I'll bring one on Thursday.'

'Assuming we can get together then,' I pointed out. 'If not, give it to Fatima and she'll pass it on to me. I'm still taking photos of the girls for you.'

'Thank you,' she said, but without much enthusiasm. Of course photographs of her children would be a poor substitute for having them with her.

As the Family Centre came into view Polly said to her mother, 'Can I come home with you?'

'Not today, love,' Selina replied bravely.

'Why not?' I want to come with you,' Polly said, and gripped her mother's arm.

'I want to come home,' Angie said. 'Take us in your car. Please Mummy.'

'I can't, love, honestly,' Selina replied.

Their desperation and anxiety grew and by the time we arrived outside the centre both girls had worked themselves into a state and Selina was fighting back tears.

'I really can't take you home,' she said, again. 'I would if I could, but I'd be in a lot of trouble.'

'Like Daddy is,' Angie said.

'No, not like that. I just can't.'

'It's his fault we can't come home,' Angie said. 'His and Ashleigh's. I hate them both!'

It was too much for Selina and she burst into tears. Covering her face with her hands, she wept.

'I'm sorry, Mummy,' Angie immediately said, feeling bad for upsetting her mother. Polly looked very worried and clung to her mother.

I lightly rubbed Selina's back. 'It's OK, take your time.'

Then to the girls I said, 'We'll wait until Mummy feels better, then we'll get into my car and go. You'll video-call her tomorrow like you usually do.' It was all I could offer at present.

I continued lightly rubbing Selina's back, trying to comfort her, as the girls looked on anxiously. It had given them a shock, seeing their mother so upset.

'I'm sorry, Mummy,' Angie said again, while Polly clung desperately to her arm.

'It's not your fault,' Selina said, and finally raised her head. She wiped her hands over her tear-stained face. 'We're going to have to be brave. Do what Cathy says and

118

we'll speak tomorrow.' Then to me she said, 'Just take them.'

'I can't leave you like this,' I said, and passed Selina a tissue from the packet I kept in my bag.

Normally goodbyes like this take place in the Family Centre. The carer collects the children from the room and leaves ahead of the parent(s). They can stay in the room to recover, where the contact supervisor and other staff members are on hand to support them if necessary. Goodbyes are never easy, but this was more painful than most and it was all my responsibility. I glanced towards the car park. It was empty now except for my car.

As Selina wiped her eyes and tried to compose herself I wondered if it would be better if she left first or if we should, but neither seemed right. She took some deep breaths and seemed to recover a little.

'When you feel up to driving, I suggest you help me get the girls into my car, then get into yours and we'll drive away together.'

She nodded. 'Whatever you say. Let's do it now then.'

'I don't want to go with her,' Angie said, scowling at me.

'You must help me,' Selina said to her daughter.

'Why can't we come home with you?' Angie asked.

'Because you need to stay with me for now,' I said, feeling Selina needed help.

'Because of Daddy and Ashleigh,' Angie said sourly, which we both ignored.

With the promise to video-call their mother tomorrow, we went to my car where Selina helped me get the girls into their seats. As we leant in to fasten their belts Polly wrapped her arms tightly around her mother's neck, not wanting to let her go, and Angie smacked me over the head.

'Ouch,' I said.

'That was naughty,' Selina said. 'You should say sorry.'

She didn't, but it didn't matter; at least the girls were in their seats with their belts on. Selina said goodbye and we closed the doors.

'Are the child locks on?' she asked me.

'Yes.'

The girls were looking pitifully at their mother through the side window, so to avoid further upset and a prolonged goodbye I said to Selina, 'If you get into your car, we'll all leave together. As soon as I get back I'll email Fatima about Thursday.'

'Thank you,' she said, and hugged me.

I didn't move away. We weren't supposed to hug anyone outside our own household for fear of spreading coronavirus. However, she and the girls had been hugging and kissing all afternoon so if she did have the virus it was likely she had already passed it on to them, and they were living with me. I hugged her back, for if ever a woman was in need of a hug it was Selina.

'Look after them,' she said and, moving away, wiped a tear from her eye.

'I will. Drive carefully. We'll call you at the usual time tomorrow, and hopefully see each other again on Thursday.'

'Yes.'

She walked to her car as I got into mine. The girls had given up their fight to go with their mother and were just sitting holding hands and staring sadly out of the window.

'Let's wave to Mummy,' I said, fastening my seatbelt.

I started the car and drew up to the exit of the car park. Selina approached in her car. 'Wave,' I told the girls.

They waved as she drove slowly past. I pulled out and followed her car down the road. 'Keep waving,' I said. Whether Selina could see them or not in her rear-view mirror I didn't know, but waving was helping to distract the girls from their sorrow.

When we came to the T-junction at the end of the road Selina indicated to turn right. We needed to go left.

'Final wave,' I said.

They put all their effort into waving as Selina completed the turn. I breathed a sigh of relief. The first contact for children in care is often the most difficult and then they gradually get into the routine. I hoped this would be true for Angie, Polly and their mother. They didn't need any more upset.

The girls were quiet during the journey home. Paula wasn't back yet from shopping with her friend so I let the girls watch television while I emailed Fatima. I gave a brief résumé of contact, said it had gone well and asked if we could do the same on Thursday. At four o'clock she phoned from her mobile. Paula was home by then and looked after the girls while I talked to Fatima in another room.

'I got your email,' she began. 'Not sure about Thursday is the answer. Did you stay with them the whole time?'

'Yes.'

'What about when Angie or Polly needed the toilet?'

'They didn't, but had they wanted to I would have gone with them.'

Silence.

'I've supervised contact before,' I pointed out.

'All right, we'll see how it goes this Thursday. You'll meet outside the Family Centre?'

'Yes.'

'Let me know straight away if anything is said about the girls' father and Ashleigh.'

'I have been doing, but other than that they argued a lot there hasn't been anything to tell.'

'What about contact with Ashleigh?' Fatima asked.

'It was short. I included it in my log notes.'

'I saw. Janet needs to supervise Ashleigh better. I'll tell her, and email the new contact arrangements for Angie and Polly to all parties.'

'Thank you.'

We said goodbye.

When Fatima said she was going to tell Janet to supervise Ashleigh better I assumed she would offer a few diplomatic words based on her observations, not blame me, but that's what happened.

CHAPTER THIRTEEN

FEELING LOW

'You'll see Mummy again on Thursday, just two more sleeps,' I was able to tell Polly and Angie, which helped.

An hour after Fatima's call confirming contact, Janet telephoned, not at all happy with me.

'Cathy, I'm hurt you saw the need to tell Fatima I needed a lot of support.'

'I didn't,' I said.

'I've just had my supervising social worker on the phone. She's making an extra visit tomorrow. It seems I've been getting it wrong.'

'How so? I haven't said that.'

'I apologize for giving your phone number to Ashleigh, but I thought she was old enough to make the call. It seems I need to be more vigilant and stricter all round with her.' Janet then referred to instances I'd covered in my log notes and emails to Fatima, which out of context sounded as though I'd been highly critical of her. 'It's not easy looking after Ashleigh. She's got her own mind and wants her independence.'

'I appreciate that, and she must also be very trauma-tized from what happened. I am sorry my words have been taken out of context. I just write what happens in my log and email updates as honestly and objectively as I can.'

I apologized again and patched it up with Janet as best I could. But I was annoyed with Fatima and felt she could have handled it far more sensitively. It meant that in future I needed to be careful what I wrote in my log notes and emails to her. It played on my mind and the following morning I telephoned Joy and related what had happened to her. She took the matter very seriously and asked if I wanted to put in a formal complaint.

'No, but I don't want this happening again,' I said. 'I'll be thinking twice about what I write in my log notes and emails.'

'That's not on. Are you happy for me to have a quiet word with Fatima then?'

'Yes.' I knew Joy could be relied upon to be discreet.

'Leave it with me. Apart from that, how are you all? I see you are going to facilitate contact in the community while the Family Centre is closed.' Fatima would have copied Joy into the email confirming this.

'Yes, that's right. It's better for Polly and Angie to see their mother properly rather than just online.'

'Absolutely. Younger children are struggling with virtual contact.'

We talked for a few minutes longer about the girls' general wellbeing and then Joy wound up by saying she'd speak to Fatima as soon as they were both free. I opened an email that had arrived from Fatima confirming arrangements for contact on Thursday and 'until further notice'. There was another email from Fatima advising me of Angie and Polly's review, which was scheduled for

28 August. As with other reviews and most meetings at present, it would be held virtually.

Children in care have regular reviews, the first within four weeks of the child being placed. The child's parent(s), social worker, teacher, foster carer, the foster carer's support social worker and any other adults closely connected with the child meet to ensure that everything is being done to help the child, and that the care plan (drawn up by the social services) is up to date. As usual with a child's review there was a form for me to fill in, which I would do tonight, and a form for each of the girls, which I printed out ready to fill in when the opportunity arose.

Although Angie and Polly were obviously pleased to have seen their mother the day before and were looking forward to seeing her tomorrow, being together had stirred up a lot of memories and sharpened the pain of not being with her.

'What's Mummy doing?' Angie asked regularly throughout the morning.

Clearly I didn't know, but she wanted reassurance so we talked about the things she might be doing, which seemed to help. Angie asked the same question as we sat down to lunch.

'I expect she's having her lunch,' I suggested.

'Is Daddy having his lunch with her?' Polly asked.

'Possibly. What usually happens in your house?'

Angie thought for a moment. 'If Daddy is home he has dinner with us, but not lunch because he's at work.'

'That makes sense. Does Ashleigh eat with you?'

'Sometimes,' Angie replied.

'Only sometimes?' I queried.

'Other times she has food in her room.'

'Mummy takes it up on a tray,' Polly added.

'Why doesn't Ashleigh eat with you?' I asked.

'When Daddy is there and they've had an argument she eats in her room,' Angie said.

'I see. Is that often?'

'I think so,' Angie replied, and Polly nodded.

A picture of their home life was starting to form. I knew it was important for a family to have their main meal together whenever possible and foster carers are expected to do this. As well as making sure the children eat well, it is a social meeting point where a family can get together and share their news. Often it is the only time in the day a busy family can come together. But if there is animosity between family members it can also be very uncomfortable. The more Angie and Polly told me of the relationship between Ashleigh and her stepfather, the more concerned I became. I would note the girls' comments in my log, and I assumed Janet would be doing the same if Ashleigh talked to her about life at home. What emerged could even contribute to care proceedings – at this stage it was impossible to know.

It was raining outside so that afternoon I took the opportunity to get the girls to fill in their review forms, turning it into an activity. I brought them to the table where I gave them a form each, crayons and a pencil. I explained a little about the review. I would explain more nearer the time as they would be present for at least part of it. Angie could read some of the questions and I helped her with the words she didn't know. Polly needed hers read to her. The two forms were identical. The first question was: *Do you know why you're in care?*

'Because of Daddy and Ashleigh,' Angie said, and Polly nodded.

Although I was there to help I shouldn't change their replies. I helped Angie spell 'because'. She knew how to spell the other words.

'I can't write,' Polly said, frowning.

'I know, love. I'm going to write it for you. What shall I put?'

'Same as Angie.'

With the paper angled so Polly could see, I wrote, *Because of Daddy and Ashleigh.*

The next question asked what the child liked about living with their foster carer. Angie looked at me as though she would have liked to have written, *Nothing.* Polly was watching carefully for her reaction.

'I like your cat,' Angie said at last.

'Excellent. Write it down,' I encouraged.

'I like your cat,' Polly said.

'Great.' I wrote it on her form.

'Shall I put his name?' Angie asked me.

'Yes, if you wish.'

'How do you spell Sammy?'

I told her.

The next question asked what the child didn't like about living with their foster carer, and again Angie threw me an old-fashioned look.

'You can be honest,' I said. 'I don't mind. It's your review. I am just here to help you.' Older children fill in their own forms.

'I don't like not being at home,' Angie said, which I thought was quite tactful.

I helped her with the spelling.

Polly said, 'I want to go home.' So I wrote that on her form.

The next question asked, *How do you feel most of the time?* There was a selection of emoji faces ranging from a big, smiling happy face, to a moderate smile, neutral, moderately unhappy and crying.

'You can draw a circle around the face that you feel like most of the time,' I explained. 'Then colour them in if you wish.'

Angie picked up a crayon and carefully drew a circle around the moderately unhappy face. Polly copied her sister as best she could, then they spent a little while colouring in the faces.

Some of the questions – for example, what had gone well for the child since their last review? – weren't relevant, so I just wrote, *N/A. First review*, on Polly's form. Angie copied it, and I explained that N/A stood for 'not applicable'.

I helped Angie read out the next question. *Who is your social worker?*

'Fatima,' she said, and I helped her with the spelling.

'The same as Angie,' Polly said. I wrote 'Fatima' on her form.

Would you like to see more of them? the next question asked. Angie shook her head and wrote, *No*, in big letters, without any help.

'Why not?' I asked.

'She took us from home and made us live here,' Angie replied.

'You can put that if you want,' I said, and helped her with the spelling.

Polly had lost interest and was now crayoning on the paper, which didn't matter.

Who are your friends? was the next question.

'Belle and Jasper,' Angie replied. 'They are in my class.' She knew how to spell their names.

'Polly? Do you have a friend at nursery?' I asked.

'Daisy,' she said.

As I wrote I said, 'When you go back to school we can try to arrange a playdate.' I was sure the girls would still be with me when school returned at the beginning of September, and it would help them settle with me if we began thinking ahead. At present they believed they would return home shortly, and I knew that wasn't going to happen.

I helped Angie read out the next question as Polly swapped crayons and continued drawing lines. *If you have a problem, who do you tell?*

'Mummy,' Angie said.

'Mummy,' Polly repeated.

'We'll write that down then. I also hope while you are living with me you can tell me if you have a problem so I can sort it out,' I reminded them.

Angie ignored me while Polly nodded, although she probably didn't know what she was agreeing to.

Do you have any questions about what will happen in the future? the penultimate question asked.

'When can we go home?' Angie asked.

'Write it down,' I told her. She did, and then asked, 'What's the answer?'

My heart went out to her.

'That you will stay with me until the problems at home are sorted out,' I replied with an encouraging smile.

Polly didn't have any questions so we moved on to the last question, which asked if there was anything the child would like to add.

'I want to go home,' Angie said.

'Me too,' Polly said, then threw me a really cute grin.

On the last page was a line for the child to sign their name. Angie carefully printed hers and Polly drew a blue curly line that, with a bit of imagination, could have spelt Polly. Beneath that was space for the name of any person who'd helped the child complete their form. I wrote my name on Polly's form, but Angie told me firmly I didn't need to write it on her form as she'd done it all by herself. I praised both girls and said I'd send off the forms so they'd arrive in plenty of time for their review.

Paula came down from her room and together we organized various activities at the table until it was time to video-call their mother. I was hoping Selina would be feeling a bit brighter as she'd seen the girls the day before and would be seeing them again tomorrow. As usual I went into the front room to make the call, leaving Angie and Polly with Paula. Selina appeared on screen but was so deep in thought she didn't immediately see me. She was staring distractedly to her left and looked utterly miserable. Then she saw I was there and snapped to.

'Are you all right?' I asked.

She shook her head. 'Not really. Tim spoke to his solicitor again this afternoon to see if there was any news. He said it will be months before the police complete their investigation and he sees all the evidence. But it's not looking good. Tim was at home with me the evening when Ashleigh says it happened, but we can't prove it. We didn't see anyone and didn't phone anyone. Angie and Polly were upstairs asleep in their beds. It's just Ashleigh's word against ours and they are believing her. I even phoned Trevor, my ex, and asked him to talk some sense into Ashleigh, but he doesn't want to get involved and believes her too.' She shook her head despairingly. 'If only we could prove Tim was here.'

There wasn't much I could say. I felt sorry for Selina, but it was qualified. She had never doubted Tim and seemed blinkered to the possibility that the allegation might be true – that her husband had raped her eldest daughter.

I fetched the girls and Selina rallied a bit as they talked about going to the park yesterday and going again tomorrow, as well as what they'd been doing today. When they'd finished the girls watched some television and then we all had dinner together. When it was nearly their bedtime Paula read to them and then I took them up to bed. Once they were settled I returned downstairs to my computer where I logged into the council's website and completed my review forms for Angie and Polly. Each form took me about half an hour, even though some of the questions weren't relevant. They asked about the children's health, education, hobbies and interests, contact with family and friends, general wellbeing and if the child's cultural and religious needs were being met.

I then joined Paula in the living room where we watched the news. Like many, since the start of the pandemic we'd been watching the news more regularly for updates on the coronavirus. There was a piece about feeling depressed as the number of those suffering from depression was rising sharply. Some had suffered mental complications as a result of contracting Covid, but others were depressed, anxious and unable to sleep, largely as a result of isolation, unemployment and fear of the unknown. Some were turning to alcohol and drugs.

I looked at Paula. 'Are you OK, love?'

She shrugged. 'Not always. I know there are a lot of others far worse off than me, but sometimes I feel low.' Her eyes filled.

'Oh, love.' I went over and, putting my arms around her, held her close. 'You need to talk to me more and tell me when you're feeling down. What is it that's making you feel like this, do you know?'

'Nothing in particular. My life seems to be going nowhere and I'm worried about my job.'

'You're still furloughed?'

'Yes, but that can't continue forever and the company may have to make some employees redundant.'

'If you are one of them then you'll find another job. It may take time, but the main thing is you stay healthy.'

'I know.'

We talked for about an hour. As well as concerns about her job, Paula admitted she'd been thinking a lot about Nana and was missing her even more now. I think the pandemic was making us all reflective and think about those we'd lost. She seemed brighter after our chat and promised to tell me if she was feeling low in future, but I could have kicked myself. I'd been so busy with Angie and Polly that I hadn't seen what was going on under my nose. I phoned Adrian and Lucy to make sure they were coping and also texted a few friends who lived alone. Before going to bed I checked on Paula again and she reassured me she was fine and would confide in me in the future if she had any worries.

CHAPTER FOURTEEN

VIRTUAL REVIEW

On Thursday morning I received a text message from Janet: *Ashleigh not happy. Police interviewed her boyfriend. Is that usual?*

Yes, I replied.

Even though it's her stepfather who's abused her?

Yes, as part of their investigation.

Thank you for your help xx

So I assumed I'd been forgiven.

When Paula got up I asked her if she'd slept well and she said she had. I'd be keeping a closer eye on her now I knew she had bouts of feeling low. One of my friends had replied to my text that she was 'pissed off' so I telephoned her and we had a good chat.

That morning was about keeping Angie and Polly occupied until they could see their mother again at 1 p.m. We had lunch at 12 and I left at 12.30. Despite arriving early at the Family Centre, Selina's car was already there. As soon as she saw us she got out. As I finished parking she opened my rear car door.

'Mummy! Mummy!' the girls screamed, delighted.

She helped them out and cuddled them.

'We'll go to the park again, shall we?' I suggested.

'Yes, I've got their waterproofs just in case,' she said.

I had also brought rain clothes from my spares for the girls and an umbrella as rain had been forecast in some areas. We set off along the pavement with the girls holding their mother's hand and me walking just behind. Selina's limp seemed even more pronounced today and at one point she paused and flexed her back.

'Are you all right?' I asked.

'Yes. I've asked the doctor for some stronger painkillers. Some days are worse than others.'

She made light of it and we continued to the park. It wasn't as busy as last time, maybe because the weather wasn't so good, but that didn't stop the girls enjoying their time with their mother. Most of the conversation was between them and Selina; I was there to supervise so I stood unobtrusively to one side. Selina had brought little cartons of drinks for the girls – 'Their favourites,' she told me.

'I'll get some,' I said.

The hour flew by, the rain held off, and on the way back to the car Selina talked to me about the girls' likes and dislikes and also their bedtime routine. That she was able to talk about this when she hadn't before suggested she was starting to accept that her children were in care and likely to remain so for the time being. However, when I mentioned school, she said, 'That's a long way off,' and changed the subject.

As we approached her car she said, 'Just a minute, I'll get the photograph you wanted.'

The girls and I waited on the pavement as she opened the passenger door and took out a wrapped parcel. 'It's in a glass frame so be careful,' she said, handing it to me.

'I will. I'll put it in their bedroom.' I tucked it carefully into my shoulder bag.

Polly began getting into her mother's car.

'You're coming with me, love,' I said gently.

Selina eased her out and Angie gripped her mother's arm.

'I want to come with you,' she said.

'I know but you can't, not yet,' Selina replied.

'When can I?' Angie asked, desperation creeping in.

'Shortly, when things have been sorted out,' Selina said, trying to stay strong.

'But I want to go home now,' Angie persisted.

'So do I,' Polly said, and began to cry.

I could see that Selina was on the verge of tears too.

'Let's take them to my car together like we did last time,' I suggested to her.

She took their hands and we went to my car where I opened the rear doors. Of course the girls didn't want to come with me, they wanted to go home with their mother, but between the two of us we persuaded them into their seats and fastened their belts. Selina then spent some time leaning in, kissing and hugging them, before saying goodbye and closing the car door. I said goodbye to her and then, as before, we both drove off together. I encouraged the girls to wave as their mother's car turned right. They were upset, but marginally less so than last time. As I drove I reassured them we would video-call their mother tomorrow and then they would see her again next Tuesday.

'How many sleeps?' Polly asked, her voice trembling.

'One sleep until the video call and five to when you see her again.' Which even to my ears sounded a long time away and must have seemed an eternity to a young child.

'Why can't we see Mummy every day?' Angie wanted to know.

'Your social worker has set the days,' I replied. 'When we get home you can choose where to put Mummy's photo,' I added, trying to distract them.

'In our bedroom,' Angie replied.

'Yes, on a shelf so you can both see it from your beds,' I said.

I continued to distract them from their upset with talk of the photo and other things. Once home they were eager to see the photo and I unwrapped it. I suppose I'd been expecting a picture of their mother, but it was a family group. Ashleigh, Selina and a man I assumed to be Tim sitting on a sofa with Angie and Polly.

'That's our home,' Angie said, and I smiled.

I could tell from the ages of the children it was a recent photo. I looked at Tim and wondered. Of course Selina would send a family photo. I guessed most of the pictures they took were of the children or the family all together, as mine were. Selina probably didn't have any photos of just her, and why shouldn't she send one that included Tim? She didn't believe he'd done anything wrong. Even so, it was a bit of a shock coming face to face with him. Of average height and a slender build, he had fair hair and an arm around the girls.

We went upstairs to the girls' bedroom where I got them involved in choosing the best position for the photo so they could both see it from their beds. I'll admit I felt uncomfortable having a photograph of Tim in their room – it was as though I was allowing a paedophile in – but it would stay there for now. In time, if and when Tim was convicted, I could replace it with photos of their mother and Ashleigh. I assumed by then Selina would want nothing to do with him.

On Friday Paula and I took Angie and Polly to an adventure park, which they enjoyed and helped them temporarily forget about missing their mother. I made sure we were home by four o'clock to video-call her. Their conversation that afternoon was subdued and they kept talking about when they could meet again. I thought Selina was really struggling and I wondered if she'd had more bad news from their solicitor. She didn't want to share whatever it was with me and once they'd finished talking she logged off.

On Saturday morning – the designated time for contact with Ashleigh – I was expecting her or Janet to call. I kept my mobile phone with me but as the morning passed and I didn't hear from either of them I wondered if they'd forgotten, so I phoned Janet.

'Ashleigh doesn't want to speak to her sisters,' Janet said.

'Oh, really?' I said, surprised. 'Why not?'

'I don't know. She won't tell me and I can't force her to talk to them.'

'No, of course not. Call me if she changes her mind. Hopefully she will feel like speaking to them next Saturday.'

'Maybe, although she goes all defensive if I try talking about them or her family.'

'How is she generally?' I asked.

'Difficult to say. She's only here for her meals.'

'Where is she the rest of the time?'

'Out with friends, boyfriend, and she's been seeing more of her father.'

'Fatima knows?'

'Yes.'

Angie and Polly weren't in the same routine of speaking to Ashleigh as they were with their mother and didn't miss her call, so I didn't tell them. They had enough to cope with at present without being told their older sister didn't want to talk to them.

We spent most of the afternoon in the garden until it was time to video-call their mother. Selina appeared less down and preoccupied than she had the day before and managed to think of some topics to talk about.

'Daddy sends his love,' she finished by saying, as she did sometimes.

'Is he there?' Angie asked.

'No, love, he's out.'

Which is what Selina always said and Angie now accepted.

So the pattern of our lives continued during the following week – with days out, video calls to their mother and two more contacts. On both occasions we went to the park where Selina spent her time with her girls. I watched and sometimes lent a hand; for example, by pushing a swing, which the girls were more accepting of now. Saying goodbye was that bit easier for the girls too. They were getting used to the routine of contact, but also, sadly, their bond with their mother was gradually loosening as they spent the larger part of their week with me. I noticed they were also talking less about their father. If Selina noticed, she didn't say. I think the poor woman was at her wits' end and was just about holding it together. At Tuesday's contact the following week she was limping less, though, and said her doctor had prescribed stronger painkillers and recommended she had the operation. She also said her doctor had been shocked to learn her children were in care. The social services had asked her doctor to provide a report, and he reassured her that he'd told them he'd seen nothing to suggest the girls were being abused. He'd been their family doctor since Angie and Polly had been born. Selina also mentioned the review, which was the following day, and said she'd been advised to attend, although Tim hadn't been invited.

'It's as though he's already been found guilty and shut out of the children's lives,' she said. 'But as the review is virtual he'll be there, off-screen. Whatever they say.'

At the end of the contact Selina gave me a bag containing new school uniforms for Angie and Polly.

'I was going to get these on Friday,' I said.

'I wanted to do it,' she replied. 'I left it as long as possible as I was hoping the girls would be home and we could go shopping together, but realistically that's not going to happen.' Her eyes filled and she blinked back tears. 'I think I've got their sizes right.' She sniffed. 'If not, I can change them.'

My heart went out to her. She was being so brave. I could picture her going to buy the school-wear for the children she no longer had.

'Thank you,' I said. 'I'll take plenty of photographs.'

'Yes, please, especially of Polly's first day. My mother was appalled I won't be there for her on her big day.'

I nodded sympathetically, as I appreciated that a child's first day at school is a huge milestone and Selina wouldn't be there to see it.

On Wednesday I logged into the virtual review five minutes before it was due to start while Paula kept Angie and Polly amused in the living room. I knew the review would want to see the girls at some point, but at their age they wouldn't be expected to be present for the whole review, which usually lasted an hour. Virtual reviews had largely replaced in-person reviews during the pandemic, but they retained the same format. As I logged in the IRO (Independent Reviewing Officer) who would chair and minute the meeting said hello. Then I sat in the gallery of images waiting for everyone to arrive. Selina was there and I noticed she kept glancing to her right. I wondered if it was Tim she was looking at.

The IRO asked Fatima if we were all present and she confirmed we were, then he opened the meeting. He welcomed us, said it was the first review for Polly and Angie Fletcher, and asked us to introduce ourselves. Introductions are normal at most social services meetings, whether we know each other or not.

'I'm Jeff Planter, the Independent Reviewing Officer,' he began. As a person spoke their image in the gallery highlighted.

Fatima went next. 'Fatima Hadden, social worker for Polly and Angie Fletcher.'

'Joy Philips, supervising social worker for Cathy, foster carer.'

'I'm Cathy Glass, Polly and Angie's foster carer.'

'Selina Fletcher, mother of Polly and Angie,' she said tightly, her gaze again shifting to her right.

'Thank you,' the IRO said. 'The school hasn't sent anyone?' he checked with Fatima.

'No, the schools don't return until next week. I have the girls' reports from last term.'

'Welcome everyone,' the IRO said. 'And a special welcome to Selina. I'm glad you felt able to attend.' Selina gave a stiff nod. 'Cathy, I take it that Polly and Angie are there somewhere?'

'Yes, my adult daughter is looking after them. They're playing in another room. Shall I fetch them?'

'We'll leave them playing for now and speak to them later,' he said. 'So, let's begin. We are here to make sure that everything is being done as it should to help the girls while they are in care. However, I should say that we can't change any court order. Selina, everyone will have a chance to speak, but if you have any questions please feel free to interrupt.'

She gave another stiff nod and then said, 'There is no court order.'

'No, a Section 20,' the IRO confirmed. He would have had access to information like this before the review.

'As long as you know,' Selina said. I thought there was a feistiness about her today that I hadn't seen before.

The IRO continued. 'Thank you everyone for completing the consultation forms. I have read them, and they will remain on file and form part of this review. Cathy, let's start with you. Could you tell us how the children are settling in?'

I looked at the gallery of images and began.

'Angie and Polly are delightful to look after. They are intelligent, articulate, and have good self-care skills. They have a strong bond with their parents and were very distressed when they first arrived. They are more accepting now and have some understanding of why they can't live at home at present. My adult daughter Paula, who is furloughed, helps with their care and together we make sure they are kept occupied. We have had days out, spent time in the garden and have arranged activities like painting and dough modelling. Angie and Polly are included in family outings and have met my other daughter Lucy and her family, and my son, Adrian, and his wife. I have emailed the school with my details in preparation for them returning next week.'

'They are going to the same school?' the IRO asked.

'Yes. Angie will be in Year Two when they return and Polly in Reception. Polly already attends the nursery there so the school is familiar to her.'

'Good,' the IRO said, typing the notes he was taking. 'Please continue.'

'Both girls are healthy. They are up to date with their vaccinations, and dental and health checks. They don't have any allergies or require any medicine. They haven't had any illnesses since they've been with me. Now they are more settled they are eating and sleeping well.'

'Any accidents?' the IRO asked. It was a standard question. He would have a checklist of matters to be covered in the review.

'No. Polly sometimes takes a tumble on the grass while playing, which gives her a shock, but she's not hurt.'

'Normal for a child her age then,' the IRO said.

'Yes.'

'Thank you. And contact? How is that going?' the IRO asked.

'Well. The girls see their mother twice a week for an hour. I have been asked to supervise contact, so we meet outside the Family Centre and have been going to a local park. Prior to that contact was online because of the pandemic.' I was acutely aware that Selina was present, but I was talking honestly and saying what I would have said anyway.

The IRO nodded and typed. I was about to continue when Selina said, 'Contact is going to be increased.'

Fatima's image highlighted as she spoke. 'Yes, we've agreed contact will be three times a week for an hour.'

I was going to ask which days and if I was still required to supervise but Fatima spoke again. This time there was an edge to her voice. 'Selina, I need to ask, is there someone present in the room with you? You keep looking away as if there might be. If there is, they will need to leave straight away for this review to continue. The instructions that were sent to you made it clear that online reviews should be held in a private place and are only for those who have been invited.'

Selina's eyes flashed angrily. I could see she was deciding what to say for the best, as was I. She'd placed me in an awkward position by telling me that Tim would be there.

Thankfully the IRO's manner was more conciliatory than Fatima's had been.

'I suggest we pause for a moment so you can check you're alone,' he said to Selina. 'You'll appreciate we follow the same guidelines for virtual reviews as for those held in person.'

Selina's gaze shifted off-screen and she seemed to track someone's movement. Then we all heard a door close.

'I'm alone,' she confirmed, tightly.

'Thank you. Cathy, please continue.'

CHAPTER FIFTEEN

REGRETTABLE

I took a breath and refocused on contact. 'Do we know yet what days the new contact will be?' I asked.

'Monday, Wednesday and Friday at four o'clock,' Fatima said. 'None tomorrow but start the new arrangements this Friday.'

'And you want me there?' I checked.

'Yes.'

'And the video calls remain as they are now, on the other afternoons?' I asked.

'Yes!' Selina said vehemently, before Fatima had a chance to reply. 'Thanks to our solicitor!'

She glared at Fatima so I assumed there'd been a heated exchange between their lawyer and Fatima, resulting in the additional contact.

I continued. 'Angie and Polly look forward to seeing their mother very much and enjoy their time with her. They are sorry to part, but Selina and I have a little routine going – we take the girls to my car together where she says goodbye, and then we drive off at the same time.'

'This is where?' the IRO asked.

'Outside the Family Centre. That's where we were told to meet.'

The IRO nodded as he made a note.

'The girls will be delighted they are seeing their mother for an extra day,' I said. 'Video calls can be difficult for children their age, although Angie and Polly look forward to them and are coping much better now.'

'The contact is with their mother only?' the IRO asked.

'Yes. They are supposed to have phone contact with their older sister, Ashleigh, but that's only happened once.'

'Why?' Fatima asked. I'd emailed her updates, but I supposed she was responsible for so many families with different contact arrangements it was difficult for her to keep track.

'Ashleigh hasn't wanted to talk to the girls. I don't know why. I phoned her foster carer, Janet, but she didn't know either, so we'll try again next Saturday.'

'I need to speak to Janet,' Fatima said, making a note. 'Don't worry, Cathy, I won't say it was you.' So I assumed Joy had spoken to her about passing on information.

'Do the children have a close relationship with each other?' the IRO asked.

'Polly and Angie do,' I replied. 'They are very close. But from what I've seen not so much with their older sister.'

Selina's image highlighted as she spoke. 'They used to be close but not in recent years when Ashleigh began seeing more of her father. That's when things started going wrong. I'm sure he's the cause of all this.'

'Thank you,' the IRO said sagely. This wasn't the place

to start a discussion about the relationship between Ashleigh and her natural father. 'Cathy, is there anything else you would like to add?'

'I don't think so. The girls are a pleasure to look after. I appreciate how difficult it is for them, but they are doing remarkably well.' I always tried to focus on the positives in a review.

'And you will be taking the children to and from school?' the IRO checked.

'Yes.'

'You have a copy of the care plan?' he asked.

'Yes.'

'And you can keep the children for as long as is necessary?' It was another standard question.

'Yes.'

'Thank you.' He then spoke to Joy. 'As Cathy's supervising social worker is there anything you would like to add?'

Joy sat upright in her chair as she spoke. 'My role is to supervise, support and monitor Cathy in all aspects of fostering,' she began for Selina's benefit. 'Cathy is one of our most experienced foster carers and can be relied upon to give a high level of care to all the children she looks after. We are in regular contact by phone and email. I also visit her every month – virtually, at present – when we discuss the children she is fostering. In between she keeps me updated and will ask for help if necessary. I know the whole family and they welcome the children they look after unreservedly.'

'No complaints then?' the IRO asked, as he was expected to.

'None.'

'Thank you, Joy. Selina, I thought I'd ask Fatima, as the girls' social worker, to speak next and then you. Is that all right?'

Selina gave a stiff nod.

Fatima began by giving the dates the children were brought into care, the reasons, and the type of care order. She didn't really say any more than I already knew as she continued speaking dispassionately, confirming the care plan was up to date and the children would remain in care pending the outcome of the police investigation and social services assessments. She referred to the girls' school reports, which showed Polly had settled well into nursery, and Angie was above average in her class. But as she talked I could see that Selina was becoming increasingly agitated and struggling to hide her anger. The IRO confirmed a couple of legal points with Fatima and then asked, 'Any complaints?'

'Plenty from Mr and Mrs Fletcher,' Fatima replied dourly. 'Especially around removing the girls from home and not letting them live with their maternal grandmother.'

'Why couldn't they go there?' the IRO asked.

'There were safeguarding concerns in respect of Selina's mother allowing contact. The children are in care under a Section 20, but if necessary we will apply to court for an Interim Care Order.'

Selina was unable to control her anger any longer. 'Just you try!' she cried. 'We'll go to the press. Our solicitor is going to sue you once we have the girls back. You have no idea the damage you've done to this family! And if you make the girls have medicals without our consent, we'll have you prosecuted for abuse!'

Clearly a lot had gone on I didn't know about, and my advice to Selina to try to work with the social worker now seemed risible. I hadn't been told to take the girls for a medical as I had with some other children I'd fostered. Selina was about to continue when Tim suddenly appeared, either having not left the room or having returned. I recognized him from his photograph.

'This meeting is a bloody farce!' he shouted angrily. 'How dare you sit there and discuss my children without me. You should be ashamed of yourselves! You can minute that we're leaving!' Their images vanished and the box where Selina should have been went blank.

There were a few moments of stunned silence and then Fatima remarked, 'They are very angry and it isn't helpful.'

'You'll speak to them after this meeting?' the IRO checked.

'I'll try,' Fatima said.

'Cathy, I take it the children didn't witness this?'

'No, they are still with my daughter in another room.'

'Good.' Then he spoke to Fatima again. 'I believe we have Ashleigh's review tomorrow. Will Mrs Fletcher be attending?' This didn't affect me, so I hadn't been notified.

'No,' Fatima replied. 'Neither of the parents have been invited. Mr Fletcher, because of the allegations Ashleigh has made against him, and Ashleigh didn't want her mother there.'

The IRO nodded, then spoke to me again. 'Cathy, is Mr Fletcher ever present when the children video-call their mother?'

'No, not as far as I'm aware. I've never seen or heard him during the calls and I'm with the girls the whole time.'

The IRO then spoke to us all. 'It's a pity Mrs Fletcher didn't feel able to stay, but I worry she felt it was acceptable to allow Mr Fletcher into the review given the seriousness of the allegations made against him. That's one of the problems with these virtual meetings. You don't have the same control as you do with meetings held in person in a room. When we first started online reviews some parents were using their phones in public places. One social worker conducted meetings containing highly sensitive material outside a coffee shop, using their Wi-Fi. You could see and hear the people on the next table and those passing in the street. I understand he lived in a flat-share so it was difficult to get privacy at home. I'm sure he wasn't the only one struggling. We then set out guidelines for virtual meetings and they seem to be running much better now. However, they do rely on the cooperation of all parties, as we've just seen.'

Joy and Fatima agreed. The IRO confirmed with Fatima that a copy of the minutes of the review would be made available for the parents, which was normal. Then he asked me to bring Polly and Angie into the review. I'd already explained to them what would happen, but they were expecting to see their mother.

'Your turn now,' I said, going into the living room. 'I'm afraid Mummy had to leave early so you'll see her later when we video-call her.'

'Not now?' Angie asked, as she and Polly stood, leaving the toys they'd been playing with.

'No, you'll see her as normal at four o'clock,' I replied, making light of it.

They came with me and sat together on the chair in front of the monitor. Angie looked a bit disgruntled and Polly wary.

'Where's Mummy?' Angie asked.

'She's had to go, love,' I said again. 'You'll speak to her later. Look, there's Fatima.' I leant over their shoulders to point at the screen.

'Hi, girls!' Fatima waved.

'And there's Joy, my social worker,' I said, pointing again. She too waved.

'And that's Jeff Planter, who is in charge of this meeting.'

'Hello, Angie, Polly. Welcome to your review,' he said.

The girls stared at them but didn't say anything.

'What have you been doing today?' the IRO asked.

They didn't reply so I suggested, 'Playing.'

'What have you been playing?' he tried.

'With puzzles and building bricks,' Angie muttered moodily. I guessed her pique was due to her mother not being there.

'Polly, do you like puzzles and building bricks too?' the IRO asked.

She nodded.

'What else do you like doing?'

Both girls remained quiet and Polly gave a little shrug.

'Baking cakes,' I prompted.

'That's nice,' the IRO said with a smile.

'Playing in the garden,' I prompted again. 'Feeding the ducks in the park.'

I felt it was turning into a one-person show with just me doing the talking. 'Watching television,' I also suggested.

As I tried to encourage the girls to talk I heard a bleep, then the IRO looked down at his keyboard so I assumed a message had come in. 'What else do you like to do?' he asked the girls, but there was no reply. 'Are you both well?' he tried.

They nodded.

'What do you like to eat?'

'Chips,' Polly said. I hoped the review didn't think that was all I gave them.

'Fish fingers and chicken nuggets,' Angie added. It wasn't getting any better!

'With salad or veg?' I asked them hopefully.

Joy knew what I meant and laughed. 'Don't worry, I know you feed them well,' she said.

'My daughter likes peas when she has chicken nuggets and chips,' the IRO said, trying to engage them. They just looked at him. 'Thank you for completing your consultation forms,' he said.

The girls hadn't a clue what he was talking about.

'Those forms I helped you with,' I reminded them. 'You coloured them in. They asked what you liked and didn't like about living with me.'

'I remember,' Angie said, tersely.

'I have those forms, thank you,' the IRO said. 'I have read them and noted what you said. I think you feel a mixture of happy and sad.'

Angie gave a small nod and Polly copied her.

'You're going to school next week. Are you looking forward to that?' he asked.

'I don't know,' Angie said, while Polly shook her head.

I heard the bleep again, but the IRO didn't seem bothered by it. 'You'll see your friends again,' he said.

Angie nodded.

'Is there anything you would like to ask me about being in care and living with Cathy?'

I saw Angie hesitate and then she said, 'Why can't we go home?'

'Has your social worker explained to you why you are in care?'

'Yes,' Fatima said. 'But I will again.' Then, addressing the girls, she said, 'Do you remember we talked about keeping you safe and how it was best for you both if you lived with Cathy for now?'

Angie gave a tight nod, a bit like her mother did.

'Do you have everything you need there?' the IRO asked.

To my surprise Angie replied, 'No.'

'What do you need?' he asked.

'Mummy's iPad. I play games on it,' she said, with the same sulky expression.

'They have a tablet from home they play games on,' I said.

'But I like to use Mummy's so we have one each.'

'I have one they can use,' I said. 'But it hasn't been mentioned until now.'

'Is that all right if you use Cathy's?' the IRO asked.

Angie gave a reluctant nod.

'Good. Do you have any other questions?' the IRO asked.

Angie shook her head and Polly copied her.

'If you do, or if you have any worries, you can talk to your social worker or Cathy. Who is your social worker? Do you know?'

Angie pointed to Fatima's image and Polly did the same.

'Thank you for talking to us,' he said. 'You can go and play now or stay. It's up to you. We're nearly finished.'

Both girls slid from the chair and I saw them into the kitchen-diner where Paula was. I returned to the front room. The IRO was talking to Fatima, from which I learnt that Selina or Tim had tried to re-enter the review but the IRO had stopped them. Those were the bleeps I'd heard. He said it was regrettable, but he'd felt he had no choice as Mr Fletcher could have reappeared when Angie and Polly were in the review. He wound up by thanking us for attending and set the date for the next review in three months' time.

I logged off and closed the app.

Selina hadn't done herself any favours. What on earth had she been thinking of? We were due to video-call her at 4 p.m. and I hoped she wouldn't try to let Tim in. If she did, I'd have to quickly end the call, which would be very upsetting for the girls. I now wondered if Tim had been in the room during any of the previous video calls. Selina always said he was out if the girls asked, but was that true? And while part of me thought it was what any loving father would do, wanting to see and hear the daughters he missed so dearly, another part of me, from years of fostering, said that if he'd been sexually abusing Polly and Angie – which was possible – then he could have an ulterior motive. I shuddered at the thought.

CHAPTER SIXTEEN

DESTROYING ME

After the review I went to find Paula and the girls.

'Angie says their mother wasn't at their review,' Paula said as soon as I entered the living room.

'That's right. We'll video-call her at four o'clock as usual.' I threw Paula a knowing look to say I would explain later.

But Angie wasn't satisfied and wanted answers. 'Why wasn't Mummy there? You said she would be.'

'I am sorry, love. I got it wrong. We'll speak to her later instead.' Better I took the blame than tell Angie and Polly their father had appeared, which wasn't allowed, then became angry so that both parents had left and the IRO had refused to let them return. An older child would very likely have been present for the whole of their review and would have witnessed the scene. Thankfully Angie and Polly didn't have to know.

I changed the subject. 'It's a nice day so we can go to the park after lunch. In the meantime, you can play some games on my tablet.' I explained to Paula that Angie had mentioned having to share a tablet at her review.

'I don't want to play on your tablet,' Angie said, disgruntled. 'I want Mummy's. It's better than yours.'

This was probably true, although I suspected it was more about it being mine rather than her mother's. She'd seen me use it many times and not once had she asked to play a game on it.

'I want to play on your tablet,' Polly said, perhaps feeling sorry for me.

'OK, love.'

'I will too then,' Angie said sulkily.

'You don't have to, love. You can have the one from home.'

Paula fetched both tablets and sat with the girls in the living room while I made us some lunch. After we'd eaten we took the children's scooters from the shed and went to our local park. Angie could scoot well – she had a scooter at home – but Polly was still learning. Polly was now over her disappointment at not seeing her mother at the review, but Angie was still grumpy. I was hoping that once she'd seen and spoken to her later she'd feel better. On the way home my mobile rang: it was Fatima.

'I'm changing the video calls to phone contact,' she said. 'Starting from today. I've told Selina. She's not happy, but they've only got themselves to blame for breaching the trust I placed in them and allowing Tim to attend the review.'

'The girls will be disappointed,' I said.

'I appreciate that, but it can't be helped. They'll be seeing their mother three times a week from next week, and they can still phone her on the other days, which is more contact than most children in care have at present. Put your phone on speaker and monitor the calls. If Tim is there, end it straight away and tell me. Also, if their mother says anything untoward, I want to know. She shouldn't be talking to Angie and Polly about the allegations Ashleigh has made against her stepfather.'

'I understand. Do I have Selina's mobile number?' I asked as we walked.

'It should be on the Essential Information Form but I'll send it to you again. Do you want me to tell the girls?'

'No, we're out at present so I'll tell them when we get home.'

'Who was that?' Angie wanted to know as I returned my phone to my bag.

'Your social worker – I'll explain once we're home.'

'Why can't you tell us now?' Angie asked.

'It's private and better said at home.' I knew it would be upsetting for them.

Once home we wheeled the scooters down the side way to put away later and went into the house through the back door. Angie looked at me expectantly.

'You'll be seeing your mother three times a week,' I said positively. 'And instead of the video calls we'll be phoning her on the other nights.' The inflection in my voice suggested this was all good news, but Angie wasn't fooled.

'We won't be able to see her if we phone her,' she said.

'That's true, but I'll have the phone on speaker so you'll both be able to talk to her and hear her like the video calls.'

'Why can't we see Mummy on your computer like we usually do?' Angie asked.

'Because your social worker says it's better to phone her for now.'

'You don't have to do what she says,' Angie said, her face setting.

'I do, love.'

'Why?'

'She's your social worker and in charge.'

'No, she's not. My mummy and daddy are,' Angie said crossly. 'I don't like her and I don't like you.'

Paula could see Angie was working herself into a lather.

'Let's cook,' she suggested. 'How about we make flap-jacks?'

'Yes,' Polly agreed.

'Thanks, love,' I said to Paula. 'Angie, are you going to help?'

She gave a sullen nod and went with Paula into the kitchen. Once they were settled I took the opportunity to reply to some emails and enter Selina's number in my phone. I then helped clear up the kitchen as the flapjacks cooked.

At four o'clock I left the girls in the living room and went into the front room to phone their mother. I had no idea how she'd be after the upset at the review, so I wanted to speak to her first. I set my phone to private number before making the call.

'Who is it?' she asked, answering straight away.

'Cathy. How are you?' It's so much easier to gauge someone's mood if you can see their face.

'We're not going to take this any longer,' she said, clearly upset and angry. 'We've been speaking to our legal team. They have been in touch with the police and social services. There's no evidence against Tim. The medical report shows Ashleigh had sex that night, which was a shock for us. We thought she was out with a friend. But there was nothing to connect it to Tim. Neither was there any trace of his DNA or semen on her underwear or the bedsheets the police took away. They found some fibres from him on her clothes, but no more than you'd expect from living in the same house. Ashleigh's statement is flimsy and vague, and doesn't give any details about what is supposed to have happened. So it proves Tim didn't abuse Ashleigh.'

'Does it?' I asked. 'I really don't know.' I think Selina was looking for confirmation.

'Yes. There is no evidence against Tim apart from what Ashleigh is saying. Not that I ever doubted him. Of course he wouldn't abuse a child. Any child. Once the investigation is complete and Angie and Polly are home, we'll sue the police and social services.' Which Selina had said before.

I'd heard other angry parents with children in care say similar, but whether they pursued it I didn't know. Selina had never doubted Tim's innocence, but as far as I could tell nothing had changed. The children were in care, Ashleigh was claiming her stepfather had raped her and the police hadn't finished their investigation yet. I think the only difference was that rather than going to pieces as she had been doing, Selina was now channelling her anger and upset into being more proactive. Whether it achieved what she hoped remained to be seen.

'Don't mention any of this when you speak to the girls,' I said to her.

'I won't. And thanks for what you said at the review.'

'What was that?' I asked, taken aback.

'You said nice things about Angie and Polly and how you liked looking after them, and that they have a strong bond with their parents. Parents, that includes Tim. It shows we've done nothing wrong. And it was nice of you to say they look forward to seeing me and that you appreciate how difficult it is for all of us.'

I was stunned by how much this had meant to Selina.

'I was only telling the truth,' I said.

'Still, it was nice of you. Everyone else is against us.' I heard her voice catch.

'I can see why you might think that, Selina, but really the social services are acting in the best interests of the children.'

'We'll have to disagree on that one,' she said tersely.

'Shall I put the girls on now?'

'Yes, please.'

'Fatima told you the phone would be on speaker?' I checked.

'Yes. I can't stand that woman. I know you'll say she's only doing her job, but I find her manner harsh and insensitive. Not for one moment has she given Tim the benefit of the doubt and considered that Ashleigh might be lying. She even thinks I could be involved.'

I could see why Selina might feel that way, but Fatima *was* 'only doing her job', which involved protecting vulnerable and abused children. In my experience, if a child or young person makes a serious allegation as Ashleigh had done then they are believed and appropriate action is taken, which often includes removing the child and siblings from home.

'I'm sure I don't need to say this, but you know you mustn't let Tim talk to Angie and Polly?' I checked before I took my phone to the girls.

'Yes, but there is nothing stopping him from listening,' she said.

I didn't comment, nor did I ask if he'd been in the room during the video calls. Better I didn't know, as I had a duty to inform Fatima.

Selecting speaker on my phone, I went into the living room.

'Mummy's on the phone,' I said.

I sat on the sofa with Angie on one side and Polly on the other and held the phone between us. Paula left to get on with something else. 'Say hello to Mummy,' I encouraged.

'Hello, Mummy,' Polly said quietly.

'Hi, love, how are you?'

'I love you.'

'I love you too. Is your sister there with you?'

'Hello, Mummy,' Angie said sullenly.

'What's the matter?' Selina asked. 'You sound a bit down.'

'I wanted to see you on the computer.'

'I know, I wanted to see you too. This is just for now. I'll see you both again properly on Friday. Then three times next week.' I thought Selina was doing well considering the emotion she must be feeling. 'What have you been doing today?' she asked them.

'We went to the park,' Polly said.

'Great. What did you do in the park?'

'Went on swings,' Polly dutifully replied.

'What else have you been doing?'

'We made flat jack,' Polly said.

'What are those?' Selina queried.

'Flapjacks,' Angie corrected.

'Oh, I see. That sounds fun. Did you help make them, Angie?'

'Yes.'

'Have you eaten them all?'

'No,' Polly said.

'Can I have one?'

The girls looked at me and I nodded.

'Yes,' they said together.

'And we'll bring one for Daddy too,' Angie added.

Selina gradually encouraged Angie out of her bad humour and she managed to keep the conversation going, upbeat and positive for about twenty minutes. Then Angie grew mournful and just kept telling her mother how much she loved and missed her and wanted to go home.

'I think it's probably best if we wind up now,' I suggested to Selina.

'Yes,' she agreed. 'I don't like to hear her unhappy. I'll speak to you both again tomorrow,' she told the girls. 'Then we'll see each other on Friday. Don't forget those flapjacks.'

'We won't,' Polly said.

Angie and Polly said goodbye and Polly blew a kiss down the phone. As soon as we'd finished we went straight into the kitchen and put four flapjacks into an airtight container ready for Friday. 'Two for Mummy and two for Daddy,' Angie said.

The following day I took the girls shopping for the last of their school clothes. Selina had bought their uniforms, but I needed to buy school shoes and PE kits. I also bought them more casual clothes, nightwear and under-wear. Selina hadn't sent any more of their personal possessions since they'd arrived, always assuming they would be going home soon. Paula came too and bought herself some jeans. We had lunch in a café in the shopping centre, which Angie and Polly enjoyed.

That afternoon when we phoned Selina she asked Angie and Polly what they'd been doing, and Angie told her we'd been shopping and bought school shoes and PE kits. Selina went very quiet and from then on seemed to struggle to make conversation. At the end she asked if she could speak to me alone, so I took my phone out of the room.

'Don't tell any of the other parents at school that Angie and Polly are in care,' she said. I assumed this was the reason she'd gone quiet.

'I won't.'

'What will you tell them?'

'If anyone asks, I'll say the girls are staying with me for a while. That's all.'

'They're sure to find out,' she said anxiously. 'The school knows, so it will get out somehow.' Some parents worry about this and find having children in care embarrassing, others don't. 'It's best if you have nothing to do with the other parents while you wait in the playground before and after school,' Selina continued. 'Especially those parents whose children are friends with mine. They're the ones who are likely to ask you. One has been texting me to see if we can meet up before school starts next week. I've said I'm too busy.'

'Selina, from what I've read on the school's website there won't be much opportunity to socialize in the playground because of the pandemic restrictions. School start and end times are being staggered so only one class arrives and leaves at a time. Parents have to wait two metres apart to collect their children and then leave straight away.'

'Oh, yes. I read that too,' she said, brightening a little. 'And parents have to wear a face mask while they wait.'

'That's right. Try not to worry. Even if another parent does approach me, I am very good at deflecting prying questions.'

'When all this started I never in my wildest imagination thought Angie and Polly would still be in care now. I thought what Ashleigh said would have been cleared up long ago. But my nightmare goes on and on with no end in sight.'

'I know these investigations can take time,' I said.

'Do you know how long?'

'Months, not weeks.'

'I'm losing my children, Cathy. I can feel it. They're slipping away. Time is passing. I'm not there for them. We're drifting apart. I'm no longer surprised I can't hear them in the house or that their beds are empty. I'm adjusting to my children not being with me and it's destroying me.'

I felt so sorry for her, but she was right. 'You're adjusting in order to cope,' I said. 'For a parent to lose a child is horrendous, truly the stuff of nightmares, so you have to adjust to function. The children do too. I think you are all coping remarkably well.'

'We shouldn't have to cope at all!' Selina snapped, her anger and frustration returning. 'The damage that is being done to me and my family is irreversible. Even Tim and I are arguing now.'

'I am sorry.'

'So am I! See you tomorrow,' she said curtly, and ended the call.

CHAPTER SEVENTEEN

ADAPTING AS CHILDREN DO

On Friday morning I received an email from Fatima confirming the new contact arrangements: supervised community contact on Monday, Wednesday and Friday, meeting point at the Family Centre. Phone calls on the other days. This Friday we were to meet as usual at one o'clock, then from Monday at four o'clock, to allow us time to get there from school, which returned for the autumn term on Tuesday.

I could appreciate why Selina didn't want other parents to know her children were in care as playground gossip can be vicious, but in practice there was going to be very little opportunity for anyone to approach me. To minimize the risk of transmitting the virus, parents and carers had been told not to mingle in the playground or outside the school – a favourite congregation point – but to collect their children quickly and leave the area. If anyone in a household tested positive, then their child had to be kept off school. Also, parents were being told not to arrange playdates. Sad, but a necessary precaution.

I'd emailed the school with my contact details and received an acknowledgement from the school secretary, forwarding an email that had originally been sent to

Selina and Tim. It included arrangements for the first day of the new school year and the classes the girls were in. The classes seemed to be named after birds: Angie was in Raven and Polly in Robin. As Polly was starting school she would be attending mornings only for the first week to get her used to it, so I had to collect her at 12. From then on she would be full time and would need to be collected at 3.20. Her class went in at 9 and Angie's at 8.50 and I had to collect her at 3.10. It sounded confusing, but I guessed it had all been carefully worked out. I didn't know the layout of the school, but I assumed someone would be on hand the first day to direct us to where we had to go. Parents and carers of children starting school would have been invited to an introductory meeting before the end of last term, but I hadn't been looking after the girls then.

Satisfied that I was as ready as I could be for the following week, I concentrated on making the most of our last few days before the school routine took over. The weeks were going to be busy once the term began as the girls had contact straight after school three times a week. I booked tickets for the cinema on Saturday – just for me and the girls as Paula didn't want to come. It was showing a children's film and tickets had to be booked in advance as numbers were limited due to the social distancing measures they had to put in place. I then booked tickets for a theme park on Sunday when Paula would be coming. It had the same requirements – to book in advance because tickets were limited. I phoned Lucy and Adrian to see if they wanted to join us there. Lucy did and booked their tickets, but Adrian and Kirsty were already going out.

We had an early lunch on Friday and, with Angie holding the box of flapjacks, I drove us to the Family Centre for 1 p.m. Selina's car was already there and she came over as soon as I drew into the car park.

'For you and Daddy,' Angie said proudly, presenting her mother with the box.

'You remembered! Thank you. We'll enjoy these,' she said.

She hugged and kissed both girls and then left the box in her car while we went to the park. As usual they walked just in front of me, although I could hear what they were saying. 'Have you spoken to Ashleigh?' Selina asked them at one point.

They turned to look at me as they weren't sure.

'No,' I replied. 'We're due to phone tomorrow.'

Nothing more was said until we were pushing the girls on the swings, when Selina said quietly to me, 'Have you heard that Ashleigh is going to be moved?'

'No,' I said, surprised. 'Are you sure?'

'Yes. The social services told us. They are obliged to tell us. I don't know the details, just that she's going to be moved from her present carer as she's unhappy there. I wondered if you'd heard any more.'

'No, nothing. I was hoping she was going to talk to Angie and Polly tomorrow. Where is she going, do you know?'

'No.'

'What a pity she's having to move,' I said. 'It's so unsettling. I wonder what's gone wrong.'

Selina shrugged. 'I'm afraid I can't feel too much sympathy for her as she's brought all this on herself.'

I didn't reply. Selina had made it sound as though

Ashleigh had instigated what had happened, when in fact she was the victim of shocking abuse.

We stayed in the park and the hour flew by, then we returned to our cars where Selina and the girls said an emotional, but not traumatic, goodbye, and I said we'd phone tomorrow.

I was puzzled and concerned to hear that Ashleigh was moving, assuming it was correct. Sometimes parents misunderstand the situation, although that was usually when the child or young person told them. The looked-after child didn't like something at the foster carer's and told their parents they were leaving. Then it was sorted out and they were happy to stay. But this had come from the social worker. Janet had returned to fostering after a long gap and in response to a recruitment drive as there was a shortage of foster carers. I wondered what had gone wrong.

Once Angie and Polly were in bed I telephoned Janet to see how she was and to check phone contact could go ahead the following morning. It was important the girls kept in touch. It had been mentioned at their last review and the IRO would expect to know it was happening at the next review.

'Janet, it's Cathy, Angie and Polly's carer.'

'Hello.'

'How are you? I understand Ashleigh might be moving?'

'She's already gone. She went out this morning and refused to come back. I'm packing her bags now, although I've no idea when they'll be collected.'

'Oh dear. What happened?'

'She told that social worker a pack of lies about me,

and now I've discovered thirty pounds is missing from my purse. I doubt I'll foster again, not after all of this.'

She was clearly upset, and immediately I felt guilty and thought I should have done more to support her, although she hadn't asked for help.

'What lies?' I asked.

'To be honest I really don't want to talk about it. I'm seeing my supervising social worker on Monday to discuss it and I'm busy packing Ashleigh's things right now.'

'I am sorry. You know where I am if you want to talk.'

'Yes.'

Even though Janet hadn't wanted to talk, it was obvious that the placement had ended badly, which was a great pity for both Janet and Ashleigh. Sometimes placements don't work out and the child has to be moved, but even then good endings are important as they allow everyone involved to move on without recrimination or guilt. Janet was clearly very unhappy about whatever had happened, and I assumed Ashleigh would be feeling the same. I was now in two minds about the phone contact the following morning. Had the social services still been open I would have phoned Fatima, but there was only the duty social worker on call for emergencies. I had Ashleigh's mobile number from when she'd phoned me – the one time Ashleigh had spoken to her sisters since they'd all come into care. What to do for the best? I wondered. Foster carers are constantly faced with dilemmas like this.

* * *

By the following morning I'd decided to call Ashleigh's mobile. It would be away from the girls, so if she answered and wanted to talk I'd put them on. If she didn't, the girls would be none the wiser. I'd told Angie and Polly we were going to the cinema and a theme park that weekend and they were looking forward to it. Mid-morning, I left them with Paula and went into the front room to make the call. Ashleigh must have stored my number in her phone as she answered with, 'Hello, Cathy.' But her voice was flat.

'Hi, love. How are you?' I asked.

'OK.' She didn't sound it.

'I understand you've left Janet's.'

'Yes, I'm staying with my dad for now.'

'I see. I'm sorry it didn't work out with Janet, but your dad's looking after you all right?'

'Yes.'

'And Fatima knows you're there?' I checked.

'Yes.'

'Good. You have phone contact this morning with Angie and Polly. Would you like to talk to them?'

'Yes.' Unlike the last time I'd spoken to Ashleigh, when she'd been upbeat and seemed to be coping well, she now sounded very low. But she was living with her father and had said he was taking care of her.

I took the phone to the girls, told them Ashleigh wanted to speak to them, then, engaging the speaker, I sat between them, holding the phone. 'Say hi,' I prompted.

'Hi, Ashleigh,' Angie said.

'Hi. What are you doing?'

'We're going to the cinema today,' Angie replied.

'I'm going too,' Polly added.

'That's nice.'

'Paula's not coming,' Angie told her. 'Cathy is taking us.'

'Have you seen Mum?' Ashleigh asked.

'We saw her yesterday. We see her three times a week now,' Angie said, and my heart ached for her.

'And we phone her,' Polly added.

'Is she still angry with me?' Ashleigh wanted to know.

Angie looked uncomfortable and then said, 'I think so.'

I stepped in. 'Your mum is doing all right. Obviously she's worried and upset but she's coping.'

'I wish I could see her,' Ashleigh said, which took me aback. Until now Ashleigh hadn't wanted anything to do with her mother, I'd assumed because she was angry with her for failing to protect her from her stepfather.

'Does she know you want to see her?' I asked.

'I don't know.'

'Tell your father and your social worker,' I said.

'Do you think Mum wants to see me?' Ashleigh asked.

'I would think so, but you need to talk to Fatima.'

'I'm sorry for what happened,' Ashleigh said.

'It's not your fault, love. You have nothing to be sorry about. You were a victim.'

'I mean because Angie and Polly had to leave home. I wanted to go, but they shouldn't have been made to leave too.'

'It's normal practice,' I said, 'but they're doing all right.' I threw Angie and Polly a reassuring smile as they were looking concerned. I tried to get the conversation onto a lighter note.

'Tell Angie and Polly what you are doing this weekend? They'd like to know.'

'Not much,' Ashleigh replied. 'Listening to music, I guess. Dad might get my clothes tomorrow from Mum.'

'Can you go to the cinema?' Angie asked.

'Don't know,' Ashleigh replied despondently.

'We're going out on Sunday too,' Angie said. 'Paula's coming.'

But Ashleigh wasn't interested. 'When are you next seeing Mum?' she asked.

'Monday,' Angie replied.

'Tell her I miss her,' she said, and Angie looked confused.

'Talk to your social worker about seeing your mother,' I said.

'OK. Dad wants me now, I have to go.'

'All right. We'll phone again next Saturday,' I said. Then I told the girls to say goodbye.

'I think Ashleigh is unhappy,' Angie said as the call ended.

'I know, love, but don't you worry. I'll tell the social worker. Now, let's have some lunch and then we're going to the cinema,' I said, and our day got back on track.

The animated Disney film I took the girls to see was a great success. It was slightly odd having to sit so far away from others – rows of seats had been taped off to maintain social distancing – but I didn't have to wear my mask once seated, which was good. I found that after a while they became rather hot and uncomfortable. The girls were young enough not to have to wear them.

For the duration of the film Angie and Polly were transported to a magical fairy-tale land of colourful characters singing emotive songs, where a fast-paced dramatic narrative saw good triumph over evil. So was I. There's nothing quite like a good fantasy to lift the spirits and take us to a place far away from the humdrum of daily life. It was much appreciated after the year we'd had of coronavirus and lockdowns.

On the way out Angie said she'd been to the cinema before with her mother when Polly was too young to go and had stayed at home with their father. I guessed from what she said it had been about a year ago when Polly had been three. If this was Polly's first trip to the cinema, which it appeared to be, she'd done well. She hadn't been scared when the lights had dimmed and had sat still throughout. I said we'd go again when there was another suitable children's film showing. Our cinema often showed children's films on a Saturday, but some of them were aimed at older children.

Naturally, when we phoned Selina that afternoon Angie and Polly told her of our trip to the cinema. She seemed pleased for them and asked questions and took an interest in what they were saying. Her mood changed when Angie said they'd spoken to Ashleigh that morning and she was at her dad's.

'I know, he told me, gloating,' Selina said, seeming to forget the girls were there.

'What's gloating?' Angie asked.

'It doesn't matter,' Selina replied. 'What else have you been doing?'

'We're going on rides tomorrow,' Angie said. 'Ashleigh is unhappy and wants to talk to you.'

It went quiet on the other end of the phone.

'I told Ashleigh to talk to her social worker,' I said.

'Yes, good,' Selina replied. But her tone, short responses and the lack of conversation that followed said she was preoccupied. Presently she wound up. 'Well, have a good day tomorrow.'

'We may be a bit late phoning,' I said. 'We've got half an hour's drive and I want to make the most of the day.'

'That's OK. Phone when you get back,' she said. 'Bye.'

'Bye, Mum,' the girls chimed.

On Sunday we left the house at 9 a.m. to go to the theme park and met Lucy, Darren and Emma in the car park. Everyone was very excited, especially Darren. He recounted tales of when he used to visit the park with his mates as a teenager, but he hadn't been for years. We loaded the picnic bags onto Emma's stroller and then made our way to the main entrance. We had to socially distance in our groups to go in – Paula, the girls and me, followed by Lucy, Darren and Emma. Once we were inside the grounds, large signs by the paths told us to keep two metres apart, to wear masks indoors (for example, in the washrooms) and to use the hand-sanitizer pumps that were positioned throughout the park. We'd also brought our own sanitizing gel and anti-bacterial wipes.

There was a notice apologizing for some rides being closed as it was impossible to socially distance on them. The cafés and restaurants were open, but numbers were limited as only alternate tables were in use. I'd seen this on their website. Darren remarked how much it must have cost businesses like this one to become Covid safe, in addition to the revenue they would have lost during lock-down.

We headed first to the area for young children, which contained small rides that gently swayed, turned and rose a little into the air, as well as sand and water play and so forth. After a while it became clear that Angie, Polly and Emma would happily stay here all day so I suggested to Darren, Lucy and Paula that they went on the adult rides while I looked after the little ones. It was no sacrifice as I don't like roller-coasters or other 'exhilarating' rides. They only took a little persuading and were gone for over two hours, although they texted to make sure we were all right. They returned on an adrenalin high, having been suitably scared and thrilled.

We ate our picnic lunch sitting on the grass, and then spent the afternoon on family rides that we could all enjoy. It was after five o'clock when we left the park, exhausted but having had a great day out. Angie and Polly had been the happiest I'd seen them. They'd mentioned their parents a few times – 'I wish Mummy and Daddy could come with us.' But not having them with us didn't spoil their enjoyment as it had when they'd first come to live with me. They were adjusting and adapting as young children do.

When we phoned Selina they told her of our day out. She didn't say much, just that she was pleased they'd had a nice time and that she'd see them tomorrow. Perhaps she'd felt the pain of not being able to share in the outing, but as a foster carer I couldn't not do something that would benefit the children because of the effect it might have on the parents' feelings. The children had to come first.

CHAPTER EIGHTEEN

SCHOOL

Fatima and Joy had both arranged a virtual visit for Monday morning, before the schools returned on Tuesday. Joy's visit was at 10 a.m. and I used my tablet so I could show her around the house as she would expect. She wasn't aware that Ashleigh had left Janet's care as she wasn't her supervising social worker. I told her what I knew, and she expressed concern that Ashleigh had simply taken herself off and gone to her father's without discussing it with Janet and Fatima first. We continued with the other business of the meeting and discussed Angie and Polly's routine, their development, general health and wellbeing, contact and, finally, my training, which was up to date. Joy then wanted to see Angie and Polly, so I took my tablet to them. They were more used to her now, albeit virtually, and answered her questions. I then showed Joy around the house before we said goodbye.

At 11.30 I logged in for Fatima's visit – away from the girls at first. She'd spoken to Janet and Ashleigh, and Ashleigh's father, that morning.

'Ashleigh may not be allowed to stay there,' she said. 'Her father will need to be assessed if he's offering her a permanent home, which isn't clear at present. We can't have our young people just taking off when they feel like it. I've told Ashleigh that.'

'Why did she leave Janet's?' I asked.

'In my opinion Janet struggled right from the start. Although she claims Ashleigh didn't want to be there and made life difficult for her. She said she wanted to live with her father. According to Ashleigh, Janet wasn't nice to her and didn't make her feel welcome. Janet is vegetarian and refused to cook her meat. She was only allowed a short shower each day rather than a bath, to save hot water. She wasn't given her allowance on time. There's a whole list of things. Janet's supervising social worker is going to see her at some point this week.'

'I believe it's today,' I said. 'Selina told me on Friday during contact that Ashleigh was leaving as she was unhappy, so I phoned Janet. She didn't go into detail, but she was obviously upset. She said Ashleigh had told lies about her and that money had gone missing from her purse.'

'I don't know about that. I'll leave it to her supervising social worker to deal with. So how is contact between Selina and the children going?'

'Generally good.' I continued to say that they enjoyed their time together in the park, and that saying goodbye was easier now for all. I said that Selina didn't discuss the allegations Ashleigh had made against her stepfather with the girls.

'And contact with Ashleigh?' she asked.

'They spoke on Saturday morning while Ashleigh was at her father's house. She didn't want to talk for long and seemed unhappy. She said she wanted to see her mother.'

'Yes, she told me that, but it's not going to happen at present. There was an incident yesterday afternoon involving her father and stepfather. It seems her father went to Janet's to collect Ashleigh's belongings and then continued on to Selina's house to get some more of her things. Selina refused and there was a scene between him and Ashleigh's stepfather, resulting in a neighbour calling the police, although they'd gone by the time they arrived.'

'Ashleigh saw all of this?' I asked, dismayed.

'It seems so. She was waiting in the car.'

'Dear me. She was already feeling bad and blaming herself for Angie and Polly having to leave home. She didn't understand why that was necessary, so I tried to explain.'

'Ashleigh didn't tell me that, although she didn't say much at all. She sounded down but given all that's going on it's hardly surprising. I'll speak to her and her father again when I have the chance.'

We then continued with Fatima's 'visit' by discussing Angie and Polly, much the same as Joy and I had, culminating in her seeing the girls and then looking around the house.

Later, I thought about what Fatima had said in respect of Janet struggling right from the start. If that was so then her supervising social worker should have spotted it and put in more support. Perhaps Janet hadn't liked to admit she needed help, and the problem with virtual visits is that they can miss so much. A good supervising social worker visiting a carer in person would have stood a much better chance of seeing signs of problems early. Virtual visits were limiting and gave a snapshot rather than an in-depth assessment. I wondered how many other fast-tracked foster carers were struggling, as well as families considered at risk who were being monitored by the social services. Since the start of the pandemic most of these visits had been virtual.

That afternoon, when we met Selina for contact, we took our usual route to the park. Although it was only the beginning of September a chilly wind was blowing from the north-east, suggesting autumn wasn't far away. The girls did most of the talking, telling their mother about our weekend and going to school tomorrow. At one point I heard Angie say, 'Ashleigh said she's sorry and she misses you.'

'Did she?' Selina replied, without any real feeling. And Angie talked about something else.

But once we were in the park and the girls were playing Selina said quietly to me, 'Did you hear what happened yesterday? Ashleigh's father got into a fight with Tim.'

'Fatima mentioned there'd been an incident when we spoke this morning, but that was all.'

'She didn't tell you what happened?'

'Not the details.'

'Trevor came looking for trouble. He arrived without any warning and demanded I get Ashleigh's belongings, then said, "Is that pervert in the house?" Tim heard – he was standing out of sight. He told Trevor to take it back. He wouldn't and they started pushing each other, then they were in the front garden, fighting. I had to separate them. As Trevor left he shouted to me that it was right I'd lost my children as I was living with a paedophile. Ashleigh was in the car. I think she was crying. The police arrived after Trevor had gone and Tim said it was a misunderstanding and he didn't want to press charges. I thought you should know in case Ashleigh says anything when you phone her. It wasn't Tim's fault. Trevor came looking for trouble.'

I gave a small nod, acknowledging I'd heard her, but I couldn't share her indignation. Ashleigh's father had been wrong going to their house and provoking Tim, but who could blame him? As far as he was concerned his daughter had been horrendously abused by her stepfather. I think I'd have been very angry too. What parent wouldn't? In matters like this I never take sides and just concentrate on the children I'm looking after, as I'm expected to.

When it was time to say goodbye Selina said she'd be thinking of Angie and Polly tomorrow as they went to school and looked forward to hearing all about it when we phoned.

'I'll take plenty of photographs,' I reassured her. Although I appreciated this would only be small recompense for her not being there.

That evening after dinner I started the girls' bedtime routine earlier than usual as we had to be up smartly in the morning and out of the house for school. They were a bit anxious about their first day back. I said that was normal and their friends would be feeling the same way, and that I didn't know the school so they would need to show me where to go, which got Angie talking about the layout of the building. Their school-wear, including their PE kits, was ready in the wardrobe. Prior to Covid, children took their PE kit to school and changed before and after the lesson, but I'd read on the school's website that in line with current guidelines the changing rooms were closed so pupils should go to school in their PE kit on the days it was timetabled. It was one of many precautions being taken by schools to minimize the spread of coronavirus. As well as staggered start and finish times, breaks would be staggered too, so only one class was in the playground at a time, and there would be no school assemblies or functions for parents to attend until further notice.

Later, as Paula and I sat in the living room, she said she'd had an email from work saying she could return to the office in two weeks' time. She was delighted. So was I, as it seemed her job was secure. There would be extra measures in place to make the office Covid safe, and if any employee had been shielding or felt unsafe returning to the office they should contact their departmental manager. We both felt as if life was gradually returning to normal.

Paula told me to wake her as she wanted to see the girls off to school in the morning. Without the routine of work her body clock had slipped into holiday mode and she'd been getting up later and later. She recognized she would need to change before she returned to work. I told her how grateful I was for all her help.

The following morning I was up and dressed just after seven o'clock and then I woke the girls at 7.30. Once they were in their school uniforms and before they had breakfast I got them to pose in the hall with their school bags over their shoulders so I could take some photographs. They looked adorable – Polly's school bag was nearly as big as she was!

'Why are you taking photos?' Polly asked, although I'd already explained.

'To show Mummy because she can't take us to school,' Angie said bravely.

After breakfast I took them to the bathroom to brush their teeth. I'd woken Paula and she came out of her bedroom in her dressing gown. She said how smart they looked. When it was time for us to leave Paula saw us off at the door. It was 8.30, and if I'd timed it correctly we should arrive at school for Angie to go in at 8.50. Parents and carers had been asked not to arrive early, and if they did to wait in their cars, not outside the school gates. Angie's class went in at 8.50 and Polly's at 9, so I was assuming I'd have to wait in my car for the ten minutes in between.

The girls were quiet as I drove, probably feeling a bit nervous about their first day back, but as we pulled into the road and the school came into view they began to relax.

'There it is! That's where we have to go in,' Angie cried, reassured by the familiarity.

I drove past the building and parked further up the road, put on my face mask, then opened the rear door to let the girls out. Holding hands, we began along the pavement towards the main entrance gate. It was only as we got close that I happened to glance across the road and saw what looked like Selina's car parked a few cars up. Perhaps it wasn't them, I thought, but it was the same make and colour. A bit further along I was able to see Selina in the passenger seat and Tim in the driving seat. My stomach clenched. I hoped they didn't get out and approach the girls. I'd encountered parents of children I was fostering outside schools before, because they knew that's where they'd be. While I understood the parents' need to see their children, it's unsettling and disruptive for the child, and in this case Tim wasn't allowed contact with the girls at all. Thankfully Angie and Polly were concentrating on going in and didn't see the car. Once we were through the gates the road was no longer in view. I hoped this wasn't going to be a regular occurrence.

'You're holding my hand too tightly,' Polly said, pulling a face.

'Sorry, love.' I relaxed my hold. I hadn't realized I'd tensed my hand so much on seeing the car.

I concentrated on where we had to go. We were now in a large, tarmacked playground with doors to classrooms leading off. Other parents seemed to know which classroom they needed, but I didn't have a clue where ours were. Angie and Polly were looking a bit lost too. Then a lady wearing a mask came over, said hello to Polly and Angie, and asked me if she could help.

'I'm Cathy Glass, foster carer. I'm not sure where to go.'

'Welcome. I'm the Deputy Head here. Remind me what classes the girls are in this year and I'll show you where to go. Also, the Head would like to see you for a few minutes if you have the time.'

'Oh, yes, sure. Now?'

'Please, if you're free.'

'Yes. Angie is in Raven class and is due to go in now. Polly is in Robin class, but her start time is nine o'clock,' I said. 'I had to bring them together.'

'That's not a problem. We're making exceptions for parents with more than one child in the school. They can go in at the same time, but I'm afraid you won't be able to see them into the classroom; you'll have to leave them at the door. This way.'

We went with her across the playground and to one of the open classroom doors. 'Angie Fletcher is here with her carer,' she said, poking her head in. Then to Angie, 'You can go in now.'

I was able to say a quick goodbye and Angie disappeared into the room.

'Now for Robin class,' she said to Polly. 'You were in our nursery last year.'

Polly didn't say anything as we went to another open classroom door.

'Goodbye, love, see you later,' I had time to say before she too disappeared inside.

'At the end of school parents wait over there,' the Deputy Head said, pointing to an area marked off near the main entrance. 'The children will be brought out a class at a time. Once you have collected the first child please leave the playground and then re-enter when it is time to collect the second child.'

'All right,' I said, a bit worried I might do something wrong. It was all so different from when I normally took children to and from school.

'I'll take you to the Head now.' We retraced our steps across the playground. 'How are Angie and Polly?' she asked. 'We were shocked to learn they were in care.'

'They're doing well,' I said. 'Gradually settling in.'

'And we've got your contact details?' she checked.

'Yes, you should have. I emailed the school.'

She showed me in through a door that led to reception. Reception was closed to parents at present.

'Please wait here and I'll tell the Head you've arrived.'

I waited in the corridor that overlooked the playground, with the empty reception area to my left. Prior to Covid restrictions, school receptions were often very busy at the start and end of school; now, it was eerily silent. So too was the playground. Normally children would have played outside before the start of school. Now, lone masked parents arrived with a child and, having taken them to their classroom, immediately left.

The Deputy Head reappeared and showed me up a flight of stairs to the Headmistress's room. A name plaque on the door told me she was Elizabeth R. Hambridge. I went in.

'Thank you for making the time to see me,' she said from the other side of the room. 'Do sit down.'

She was wearing a mask and I kept mine on as we were supposed to. We sat opposite each other on socially distanced chairs in the area to the right of her desk. It was a large room, but the window was wide open to allow in plenty of fresh air.

'I won't keep you long, but I wanted to meet you,' she began. 'If there is anything the school can do to help Angie and Polly, please tell me or their teachers.'

'Thank you, I will.'

'How are they?'

'Settling in. Doing well, considering.'

'Do they see their parents?' she asked.

'They see their mother three times a week for an hour after school and have phone contact on the other days.'

'They don't see their father?'

'No.'

It was difficult to read her expression behind the mask but her next words needed no explanation.

'We were all totally shocked when we found out Angie and Polly had been removed from home. They were the last children we would have expected to be in care.'

'You're aware of the reason?' I asked.

She nodded. 'Their social worker has been in touch, so have the police. They asked about the parents and Angie and Polly. They wanted to know if either of the children had given us any cause for concern. They haven't. I've spoken to both their teachers from last year. Neither of the girls showed any worrying behaviour – I would have been immediately alerted if they had. I'm struggling to believe this has happened.' She paused. 'Have they said anything to you?'

'Some things about their home life, which I have passed on to their social worker. But nothing in respect of the allegations Ashleigh has made.'

'We don't know Ashleigh,' the Head said. 'She didn't come to this school. But the parents were liked and respected here. Mr Fletcher was an active member of the Parent Teacher Association and was often found running a stall or game at fundraising events.'

While the Head seemed to think this helped show he was of good character, I knew there could be another reason. If he was a paedophile then school fundraising events would have afforded him plenty of opportunity to be near children.

'It's very worrying,' Elizabeth Hambridge said. 'You start to wonder who you can trust. He's been removed from the PTA now, of course.'

'He's not allowed any contact with the girls,' I said. 'I saw the parents' car parked outside the school just now.' She immediately looked worried. 'The girls didn't see it and their parents didn't get out. I'm hoping it's a one-off, but I'll have to inform their social worker.'

'I'll alert the staff. We have a few other children in care so we're aware of the issues involved.'

The Head repeated that if there was anything the school could do to help Angie and Polly I should let her know, then she thanked me for my time and saw me from the premises. The gates were security-locked now as all the children were in. She came with me to the pavement, where we both looked up and down the road. Selina and Tim's car had gone.

CHAPTER NINETEEN

WON'T END WELL

I returned home. Paula was dressed and, having cleared away the breakfast dishes, was now busy on her laptop. With a coffee in hand, I logged on to my computer to check my emails. I would update my fostering log at the end of the day. I hoped I wouldn't have to include another sighting of Selina and Tim at school, or worse – a confrontation. If they approached the children, I'd be in a very difficult position and would have to phone the social services as an emergency and even the police.

I thought about the girls a lot that morning, wondering how their first day was going. I left the house at 11.30 to collect Polly, and Paula came with me. The school's instructions had said that only one parent or carer was allowed in the playground to collect a child so Paula would wait in the car. She was as much a part of the girls' lives as I was and wanted to come while she had the chance. Once back at work she wouldn't be able to join me on the school run.

To minimize the risk of contamination being brought home from school, the advice was that children should change their clothes on arriving home and have a bath or shower. The virus was thought to live on surfaces for some hours so anything they touched before washing should be thoroughly cleaned. That would be virtually impossible with young children, and foster carers had accepted there was a risk of catching the virus from the children they looked after. For this reason, some carers with underlying health conditions or with someone in the family who was considered at risk had stopped fostering during the pandemic. Understandable, but it had added to the shortage of foster carers. Given that Paula, my family and I were all well with no underlying health conditions and were following the guidelines, we felt it was a calculated risk that we were willing to accept.

I'd told Paula I'd seen the girls' parents in their car outside the school that morning and, like me, she was a bit apprehensive that they would be there again. As I pulled into the road the school was in I kept a keen look-out, but I couldn't see them or their car. The road wasn't as congested as it had been earlier as only the Reception classes were leaving at present.

'They're not here,' I told Paula as I parked.

'Good.'

A few parents were already forming a socially distanced queue on the pavement by the main gates. I waited a couple of minutes, then put on my mask and joined them, leaving Paula in the car. The pavement had been marked out at two-metre intervals so those waiting knew where to stand. At exactly 12 the electronic gates opened and we filed in, then stood on the spaced markers in the area the Deputy Head had pointed out earlier, waiting for our children.

On the other side of the playground the door to Polly's classroom opened and her teacher came out. Despite her mask, I recognized her from her photograph on the school's website. All staff members were shown there. She was accompanied by a teaching assistant and together they led the children in an orderly procession towards us. They looked so small and cute in their new school uniforms – bought slightly big so they would last. They had to wait a little way from us and then one by one, as the children spotted their parent or carer, the teacher or TA allowed them to come to us. Polly looked a bit lost and I wasn't sure she had recognized me behind my mask from a distance, so I gave a little wave. She spotted me and told her teacher, who looked over and then sent Polly to me. Like other children were doing, she greeted me with a hug, which was nice.

'Hello, love. Have you had a good morning?' I asked. My voice was slightly muffled behind the mask.

'I've done some drawings,' she said. 'They're in my bag.'

'Great. We'll look at those as soon as we get home.'

I held her hand to leave the playground and to cross the road to the car. Before we got in I cleaned her hands and mine with anti-bacterial wipes and then fastened her seatbelt. Paula was in the front passenger seat.

'How are you?' she asked with a smile.

'I've made you a picture,' she said.

'Wonderful. Did you see Angie?'

She shook her head.

'They're keeping the classes separate,' I reminded Paula. Then to Polly I said, 'You'll see Angie later when school ends.'

She was quiet during the journey home, but I'd found before that often when a child first comes out of school they need time to adjust before they begin to talk about their day. Once home, Paula made us some lunch while I took Polly upstairs and gave her a quick bath and changed her clothes. I put her school uniform in the washing machine. During lunch she talked about school and it seemed to have gone well, then we sat in the living room. Tired from the morning, Polly wanted to be read stories.

I had to leave at 2.40 to collect Angie so I left Polly with Paula. Again, I approached the area outside the school with some unease. It was busier now the rest of the school was coming out at ten-minute intervals. Cars were arriving and others leaving, and some were parked, but I couldn't see Selina and Tim's car. The socially distanced queue for Angie's class was forming along the pavement so, putting on my mask, I joined it, again looking out for their car. At exactly 3.10, the time Raven class was due to come out, we were allowed into the playground to stand on the socially distanced makers. It was the same procedure I'd followed at lunchtime when I'd collected Polly, although the Deputy Head was also in the playground now, making sure everything was running smoothly. She saw me and nodded. When Raven class came out Angie spotted me straight away and told her teacher, who allowed her to come to me.

'Where's Polly?' Angie asked.

'At home with Paula. Have you had a good day?'

'Yes.'

I held her hand as we walked to my car and, before getting in, I wiped her hands and mine with the antibacterial wipes.

'We had to wash our hands a lot in school,' she said.

'It's to help keep everyone well.'

'I know. Our teacher said. When are we phoning Mummy?'

'At four o'clock.'

Angie was more talkative than Polly had been, and as I drove she told me she'd been playing with Jasper, whom she'd previously mentioned as being one her friends. Once we were home, there was just enough time to give her a quick bath and change her clothes before we had to phone her mother. In fact, we were a few minutes late and I apologized.

'Sorry, it was a bit of a rush,' I said.

'Have Angie and Polly washed and changed their clothes like they're supposed to?' Selina asked.

'Yes. Polly at lunchtime as soon as we got home, and Angie just now. I'll put the phone on speaker so they can hear you,' I said.

'Before you do – I know you saw us this morning.'

'Yes, I did.'

'Our solicitor said it was all right for us to wait there as long as we didn't approach the girls.'

'My worry is that Angie or Polly could see you and want to talk to you. What will you do then?'

'We won't make it a regular thing, but it was Polly's first day at school and we didn't want to miss it.'

'I understand. I'll put the girls on.'

I'd have to include that I'd seen them outside the school in my log notes, but it wasn't for me to lecture Selina. Their solicitor had advised them it was all right to wait outside the school, and if Fatima felt differently then it was for her to deal with.

Angie did most of the talking, mainly about school. I think Polly was still a bit overwhelmed by it all, but she did answer her mother's questions. Then after a while Polly said she needed to go to the toilet, so we said goodbye and we'd see her tomorrow outside the Family Centre. I'd be taking the girls there straight after school and was assuming we'd go for our usual walk to the park. However, when I next checked my emails I saw one from Fatima, subject line: *Fletcher Contact*. It said that from tomorrow supervised contact for Angie and Polly would be in the Family Centre and I should take them there for 4 p.m. and collect them at 5 p.m. It continued by saying that the transmission rate of the virus had sufficiently fallen to allow this, and measures had been put in place to make the centre Covid safe. I wondered what Selina would make of this. I assumed she hadn't known when we'd phoned or she would have mentioned it. To me, it seemed like a step backwards. Usually, supervised contact in the Family Centre develops into community contact in preparation for the children going home. This was the reverse.

A second email arrived with the subject line *Fletcher Contact*, this time from the Family Centre. It gave the guidelines we were to follow when using the centre. All adults were to wear a mask while indoors; young children were exempt. Contact would take place outside in the play area when the weather permitted. The rooms would be well ventilated so children should wear warm clothes and keep their coats on when necessary. Hand sanitizer would be provided at the entrance and in all the rooms. The kitchen would be closed, but parents or carers could bring a small snack and drink for the children to have during contact. The washrooms would be open as usual.

That evening I explained to Angie and Polly that, starting from tomorrow, when they saw their mother it would be in the Family Centre – the building we usually parked outside of – or in their playground at the rear. Upbeat and positive, I reminded them of what to expect if they were inside: 'It's like a house with living rooms and plenty of toys to play with.'

'Why can't we go to the park?' Angie asked.

'Because your social worker wants you to use the Family Centre,' I said. 'Lots of children I've fostered in the past have seen their parents there and they had great fun. I'll take and collect you. It will be fine.'

But quietly I thought it was a pity that the contact arrangements had changed during their first week at school. Readjusting to the routine of school after the long summer holidays, and in Polly's case transitioning from nursery to school, and coming on top of a disrupted year of schooling due to lockdown, was enough to cope with at present. The decision couldn't have had anything to do with me seeing the parents outside the school as I hadn't written up my log notes yet, unless the school had informed the social services. I wouldn't have enough time to come home and bath the children and change their clothes after school before taking them to the Family Centre and I wondered if Fatima was aware of this when she'd made the decision. I would phone her tomorrow to check. As I continued to reassure the girls about the Family Centre, not once did either of them ask if they'd be seeing their father there too, as they would have done in the early days. They just assumed they wouldn't.

* * *

The following day after I'd taken the girls to school – Selina and Tim's car wasn't there – I returned home and phoned Fatima. I pointed out that the girls would be going to the Family Centre straight after school and I wouldn't have a chance to bath or change their clothes as the school was advising.

'It's not proven how long the virus can survive on clothes,' Fatima said. 'Wash their hands and use the hand sanitizer and it should be fine.'

'All right.'

'You wouldn't have had time to take them home and bath and change them anyway, even if contact had remained in the community,' she added. Which was true, although it was generally accepted that the virus was less transmissible in the fresh air. Fatima then said something I thought was very telling.

'I had to weigh up the small risk of the children or their mother passing on the virus with keeping Angie and Polly safe. I didn't have the best childhood and I know from personal experience how devious abusers can be when they want to get at a child. Supervised contact in the Family Centre will be safer for them.'

I wondered how far Fatima, and indeed other social workers, were motivated to follow a career in child protection because of an abusive childhood, then possibly allowed their decision-making to be influenced by their past.

It wasn't long before I was leaving the house again to collect Polly from school. Paula came with me and would wait in the car. There was no sign of Selina and Tim as I parked. I joined the mask-wearing queue and we filed into the playground. When Polly came out she saw me straight away. She was carrying a colourful drawing, which she said was for Paula. Like yesterday she wasn't very talkative but recovered once home and had had a bath and something to eat and drink.

After lunch she wanted to be read to and, while snuggled between Paula and me fell asleep for about twenty minutes. Both girls had been in bed by seven o'clock and had slept well, but Polly was still young and I think adjusting to school was exhausting. I can remember how tired my children were when they first started.

When it was time to leave to collect Angie, Polly wanted Paula to come so I explained that it wasn't possible today as we'd be going straight to the Family Centre to see their mummy. She hugged Paula goodbye and wanted a kiss before we left. Both girls had become more tactile and affectionate towards us – wanting to give and receive hugs and kisses. It had happened naturally and gradually over the weeks as they'd slowly relaxed and bonded with us. I'd found before in fostering that you can't force affection onto the child, even though you'd love to cuddle them; you have to take it a step at a time and at their pace.

I parked in the road by the school and let Polly out of the back seat. We then held hands as we waited in the socially distanced queue forming on the pavement. I automatically looked up and down the road for any sign of Selina and Tim's car, but realistically she should be on her way to the Family Centre now. It crossed my mind that if Tim had his own car he could be sitting here now, watching us, as I didn't know what his car looked like. 'How many cars do you have at home?' I lightly asked Polly as the queue began moving forward.

She looked thoughtful for a moment and then said, 'Two.'

I didn't pursue it by asking what colour her father's car was, as it could have made her anxious. We continued into the playground and stood on the markers. Raven class came out and their teacher sent the children to those waiting. Angie was pleased to see Polly and gave her a big kiss.

'Are we going to see Mummy now?' she asked me.

'Yes, love.'

As I drove, Angie talked to Polly about school. She'd seen her at morning break through her classroom window. I thought it must be comforting for Polly to know her big sister was looking out for her.

It was five minutes to four as I drew into the car park at the Family Centre. Selina's car was already there. I put on my face mask and opened the back door to let the girls out, making sure they kept their jackets with them. As we crossed the car park we could hear children's voices coming from the play area at the rear of the building, so I assumed that at least some contact was happening outside. We went up the path to the security-locked main door where I pressed the buzzer. Presently a member of staff appeared at the side gate.

'Angie and Polly Fletcher to see their mother, Selina,' I said.

'Yes, they can come in,' she said. 'They'll be outside today. I'll take them.'

It was clear I wasn't going to be allowed in, so I quickly gave the girls the packets of drinks and bananas I'd brought as a snack and said goodbye.

'See you later,' I added, with a smile. They were looking rather serious as this routine was new to them.

I didn't see Selina so had no idea what she thought about the new contact arrangements – that was, until I collected the girls at five o'clock. I pressed the bell and was told through the intercom to wait outside and Angie and Polly would be brought out to me. The play area was quiet now, but I heard Angie's voice ask, 'Is it time to go?'

Selina replied, 'Yes.'

A minute later the member of staff I'd seen earlier appeared at the side gate and let Selina and the girls out.

'Everything all right?' I asked Selina, but she didn't reply.

Head down, she took the girls to my car and only once they were in their seats did she turn to me.

'Our solicitor said there's no reason why contact couldn't have stayed as it was unless you had raised concerns.'

'No, not at all,' I said, taken aback. 'I felt it was going well.'

'In that case the social worker has it in for us,' Selina replied angrily. 'This is completely out of order. Now I'm not allowed to see my children without a supervisor writing everything down, and Tim hasn't seen them for weeks! We've cooperated with the police and social services and it has got us absolutely nowhere! We'll be trying a different approach.'

She didn't say what that was, but I had a feeling this wasn't going to end well, and I was right.

CHAPTER TWENTY

COURT

On Thursday when I phoned Selina for contact she seemed guarded in what she said to the girls. She didn't want to speak to me before or after the call. She didn't have to. The phone contact was for her and her daughters, although in the past she'd sometimes wanted to talk. I sensed there was something going on.

The following afternoon, shortly after I arrived home from collecting Polly from school, Fatima phoned and said contact was cancelled that afternoon.

'Selina is unlikely to be back in time to go to the Family Centre,' she said. 'Phone her instead, but later, around six.'

'All right. Why?'

'We're about to go into court. I'm applying for a care order. Tell Polly and Angie they can see their mother on Monday as usual and phone her.'

'I will.'

'I have to go,' she said hurriedly, and ended the call.

I knew this wasn't good. At present the girls were in care under a Section 20 (of the Children Act), which was a voluntary agreement between the parents and the social services and didn't require a court order. It relied on cooperation and trust, which now seemed to be in short supply on both sides. For whatever reason Fatima had decided to apply to court for a care order. It didn't make any difference to fostering the girls, but if the court order was granted it would remove parental responsibility from Selina and Tim and place it with the local authority. It would then require another court order to return the girls home.

However, that was for the lawyers to argue and the judge to decide. I sometimes have doubts about the appropriateness of the adversarial nature of our child-care proceedings, but until a better solution is found, that's what we have. I now had to tell Polly she wouldn't be seeing her mother that afternoon, and it was going to be difficult. I felt the girls had benefited from seeing their mother compared to the virtual contact we'd had before. I'd said so when asked and in my log notes.

I waited until Polly had eaten her lunch before I told her.

'Your social worker has said we will phone your mummy rather than see her today,' I said, phrasing it as sensitively as I could.

She looked at me and blinked as she did sometimes when considering something.

'Why?' she asked at length.

'Because your mummy has to go to an important meeting and won't get back in time. We'll phone her later and then at the weekend. You'll see her again as usual on Monday,' I emphasized.

'I miss Mummy,' was all she said, and looked sad.

Later, when I collected Angie from school, Polly stayed at home with Paula so as soon as Angie came out she knew something was amiss.

'Where's Polly?' she asked, frowning. 'You're supposed to bring her with you and then we go to see Mummy.'

'We're going to phone Mummy instead today,' I said, and taking her hand I headed out of the playground.

'Why?' she demanded. 'We see Mummy today.'

'Fatima telephoned and said your mummy has to go to an important meeting with her and others, and she won't be back in time. We'll phone her later. You'll see her on Monday.'

'It's not fair,' she said angrily, and snatched her hand away.

'I know it's disappointing, love, but it can't be helped.' I opened the car door.

'I hate you,' she said, getting in. 'I want to go home! Now! Take me home!' she screamed, and lapsed into a full-scale tantrum.

I got into the back seat of the car beside her and closed the car door. I couldn't drive with her like this and she needed comforting. She kicked the seat in front, screamed, cried and called me all the names she could think of. I'd never seen her so upset and angry, but I wasn't surprised. All her pent-up emotion had to come out eventually. Most foster carers and many parents have been on the receiving end of their child's anger at some time.

I sat with Angie, talking to her gently and trying to soothe her. I tried to hold her, but she pushed me away. Eventually, after many minutes, her anger peaked and then receded. Finally, she dissolved into tears. She allowed me to dry her eyes. 'I know it's difficult for you, love. You're doing very well. Now let's go home. Polly will be wondering where we are.'

Satisfied she was calmer, I got into the driver's seat, started the engine and headed for home, every so often glancing in the rear-view mirror to check on Angie. She was gazing mournfully through her side-window, her cheeks red and her eyes ready to spill more tears. I felt so sorry for her. One change in arrangements and another disappointment had been enough to tip her over the edge. Polly was a different character, and two years younger reacted differently. I thought it was a pity the social services hadn't gone to court on a day when there wasn't contact, but then I didn't know the circumstances leading to their decision. Perhaps it couldn't have waited. Foster carers are often left second-guessing the reasons behind decision-making.

I parked on the driveway and let Angie out. 'Are we going to phone Mummy now?' she asked forlornly.

'Not just yet, love – about six o'clock, so after dinner.'

'Why can't we phone her now?'

'She's in an important meeting until later,' I said. I saw no need to go into the details, given her age.

I opened the front door and let us in. We took off our shoes and coats and then went into the living room where Paula was playing with Polly. Seeing her sister looking so miserable, Polly left what she was doing and gave her a big hug. It was really touching. Then, taking her hand, she led her in a motherly fashion to the sofa. 'Would you like to watch television?' she asked her. It broke my heart.

Angie nodded, so they sat with Paula watching children's television while I went into the kitchen to prepare dinner. As I worked I wondered how Selina and Tim were faring in court; I assumed he would be there too. These were child-protection proceedings, so separate from any criminal charges he might face, although the judge would be aware of the allegations Ashleigh had made. It was the reason the children were in care.

As the dinner cooked and the girls watched television, I caught up with some work on my computer, then called Paula, Angie and Polly to the table. Polly ate well, but Angie picked at her food and kept looking at the clock on the wall.

'Come on, eat up,' I encouraged her. 'I won't forget to phone, but it's not six o'clock yet.'

She ate a little more. 'Why can't we phone now?' she asked. It was 5.40.

'Because I don't think Mummy will be free yet. Fatima said six o'clock.'

Both girls ate a little pudding and then Paula took them into the living room to play on the tablets while I cleared up. At exactly six o'clock I stayed in the kitchen and called Selina, but it went through to voicemail. I left a message: 'Selina, it's Cathy. I hope you're all right. Fatima told me to call you about this time for phone contact, so I'll try again in about fifteen minutes.'

Angie must have been clock-watching for she came in. 'It's time to phone Mummy,' she said.

'I have, love, but she's not answering yet. I've left a message and will phone her again shortly.'

'Try her again now,' Angie said.

'In a few minutes. You go and play for a while.'

'I don't want to play,' she muttered moodily, but returned to Paula and Polly.

Fifteen minutes later I tried Selina again and this time she answered. 'Are you free to talk to the girls?' I asked.

'Yes,' she replied tightly. 'Put them on.'

I went into the living room and sat on the sofa between the girls, with my phone on speaker. Paula left to do something else.

'Hello, Mummy,' Angie said in a small, plaintive voice.

'Hello. Is Polly there too?'

'Yes,' Polly replied.

'Why couldn't we see you?' Angie asked in the same small voice.

'Because we were in court,' Selina replied. 'You know Daddy and I want you to come home very much, so we went to court and told the judge.'

'We can come home?' Angie asked, her face lighting up.

'No,' Selina replied, and sounded close to tears. 'People are telling lies about us, so you have to stay there for now.' I had no idea what 'lies' she was referring to and I guessed this was a simplified version. Even so, the girls didn't need to hear this. They were both looking very anxious and sad.

'Selina, maybe change the subject,' I suggested.

'Why? They need to know what's going on and that none of this is our fault. Ashleigh told lies about your father and the social worker believed her. That's why you were taken from us. We've cooperated but it's not helped, so our solicitor gave notice to the social services to say we were bringing you home. But the social worker took us to court and told the judge you'd be in danger if you came home and he granted them a court order, so you have to stay there, even though your daddy offered to move out …'

'Selina, please. Stop,' I said, interrupting. I took the phone off speaker and stood. 'Wait here,' I told Angie and Polly, who were now looking very worried and close to tears.

I went into the hall with the phone to my ear. I could hear Selina crying and cursing the social worker on the other end.

'Selina, the girls can't hear you,' I said. 'Have you got someone there with you?' She sounded in a dreadful state, and I was concerned for her.

She continued to sob, close to hysterical. I poked my head around the living-room door to check on the girls. They were on the sofa where I'd left them, looking lost and afraid. 'It's all right, don't worry. I'll be with you in a minute,' I told them.

I stepped back into the hall. It had gone quiet on the other end of the phone and then a man's voice came on.

'Cathy, this is Tim Fletcher. Are you still there?'

'Yes, I'm here,' I said, trying to keep my voice steady.

'It's probably better if you phone tomorrow. We've had a very difficult day and Selina is very upset.'

'Yes, of course. I am sorry. I hope she feels better soon. Please reassure her Angie and Polly are all right. I'll phone her tomorrow at the usual time.'

'Thank you. And while I have the chance, I'd like to thank you for looking after my daughters. I appreciate none of this is your fault any more than it is ours. I would say please give my love to my daughters and tell them I miss them, but you probably wouldn't be able to pass that on. Thanks anyway.' He ended the call.

I stood for a moment, thrown, my heart pounding. Polite, sensitive and respectful. The last time I'd seen him – virtually, at the review – he'd been very angry. Now there was no bitterness and he had thanked me for looking after his daughters. However, he was right when he'd said I couldn't pass on his message. It would be seen as a form of contact, which he wasn't allowed.

As I stood there I had to remind myself that paedophiles don't fit a norm and can often come across as friendly and courteous – in fact, 'normal' – despite their demonic acts.

I returned to the living room.

'What's the matter with Mummy?' Angie asked.

'She's a bit upset right now. We'll phone her again tomorrow.'

'Is it our fault?' Angie asked. So often children feel they are to blame.

'No, love, it's because you can't be with her.'

'Does she still love us?' Angie asked. I swallowed hard.

'Yes, very much.'

'Does Daddy love us?' Angie asked.

'Yes.'

'She said we could go home.'

I then explained in child-friendly language that they would be staying with me for now because their social worker and the judge wanted to make sure they were safe. They didn't say much about what their mother had actually said about court and so on – I think it was all a bit beyond them. They had just heard her upset.

However, at bedtime, as I settled Angie and Polly into their beds ready to kiss them goodnight, Angie said, 'Did Ashleigh tell lies about Daddy?'

'I hope not.'

'She and Daddy used to argue a lot, and that made Mummy and Daddy argue.' She'd said similar before.

'That must have been very upsetting for you to hear,' I said.

'Yes. I don't like arguments.'

'No, love, neither do I.'

I sat with them until they dropped off to sleep. Normally I said goodnight and came out and they fell asleep, but they'd been unsettled. Polly fell asleep first, while Angie took longer. She closed her eyes but every so often she frowned as if remembering something. I assumed it was about their mother being upset on the phone. Then she mumbled, 'Mummy and Daddy were arguing on the night we had to leave home. About Ashleigh.'

'It's all right, love,' I said, stroking her forehead. 'No one is arguing now. You're safe. Try to go to sleep.'

'I don't like arguing,' she murmured groggily and then fell asleep.

I kissed her cheek and quietly left the room.

Now Angie and Polly felt more secure with us they were regularly letting go of snippets of information from home. The picture that was building was of a financially comfortable household with generally good parenting but scarred by distressing scenes between Ashleigh and her parents. It seemed that when Ashleigh was present there was an atmosphere in the house, especially between her and her stepfather. Angie had once said that there were no arguments when Ashleigh was out, and she thought she should live with her nana or father as she wanted to. It was sad she'd heard all that at her age.

CHAPTER TWENTY-ONE

VOICES IN THE NIGHT

On Saturday morning I telephoned Ashleigh for the girls' contact, but it went through to voicemail. I left a message saying I hoped she was well and to call me when she was free to talk to Polly and Angie. The girls didn't ask about calling Ashleigh, so I didn't tell them I'd phoned, although I noted it in my log.

The weather had turned warm again, as it can in the UK in September, so we arranged to meet Adrian and Kirsty, Lucy, Darren and Emma with picnic lunches at a local beauty spot. It was very picturesque with a small stream where tiny fish darted in shallow, clear water and bugs hopped across the surface. We dropped in leaf boats and watched them float away. There was also a play area for children. I really appreciated having all my family together again and hearing their news. Adrian was still working from home, Kirsty was in school again, and Lucy and Darren were part-time at the nursery where they worked. They only had about 60 per cent of the children who normally attended. Although we were out of lockdown, following government advice, many were still working from home to minimize the transmission of the virus, so parents didn't need the same amount of day care.

It was a lovely afternoon. We didn't leave until 4 p.m., which meant it was 4.30 before I telephoned Selina. I wondered how she'd be after yesterday. She answered in a flat voice.

'Sorry we're late,' I said. 'We've been out for the day.'

'It's all right,' she replied.

'I was going to ask you if we could make the phone calls at five o'clock in future? It would help when we go out at weekends and also wouldn't be such a rush after school.'

'Yes.'

'Thank you. I'll let Fatima know. Contact at the Family Centre will stay the same. I'll put the girls on now.'

I sat on the sofa between Angie and Polly with the phone on speaker. Paula was in the kitchen unpacking the picnic hamper.

'Why were you upset?' Angie asked her mother.

'Because I miss you so much,' Selina replied.

Angie looked like she didn't know what to say.

'Tell Mummy what you've been doing,' I suggested.

'We've had a picnic and played,' Angie said.

'Yes, and we've got a cat,' Polly added as he strolled into the room, meowing loudly.

'I can hear him,' Selina said. 'What's his name?'

'Sammy,' Polly said.

The conversation was back on course. After some talk about our cat, Selina asked how school was going and the girls had plenty to say, especially about all the hand-washing. Selina sounded subdued but wasn't upset; she didn't mention the court case or trying to get the girls home. After about twenty minutes, as they ran out of things to say and began to wind up, Selina asked, 'Have you spoken to Ashleigh?'

'No,' Angie said, glancing at me.

'She didn't answer this morning,' I explained. 'So I've left a message suggesting she phones us.'

'OK. I just wondered,' she said.

Ashleigh didn't return the call over the weekend, so I'd try again next Saturday if I didn't hear from her in the meantime. We had a relaxing day in the garden on Sunday. It was warm enough for the padding pool. Then on Monday we began our weekday routine again. Polly was now full-time and would be staying at school for the whole day, including lunch. My heart clenched as I took her in that morning. She seemed so small and vulnerable to be staying all day.

'Bye, love, see you later,' I called as she disappeared into her classroom. Angie's class had already gone in.

I hadn't been home long when I took a call from Helen Greenwood.

'I'm the Guardian ad Litem for the Fletcher children,' she said. 'Does that term mean anything to you?'

'Yes.'

The Guardian ad Litem is appointed by the family court for the duration of the care proceedings. They are qualified social workers but independent of the social services and work within the organization known as CAFCASS (Children and Family Court Advisory and Support Service). They have access to all the files and see all parties involved, including the children, their parents, the foster carer and social services. They report to the judge on what is in the best interests of the children and usually the judge is guided by their view, which may uphold the social services' care plan, but not always. As they'd only been to court on Friday I was surprised to hear from her so soon. Even more so when she said, 'Good. I'd like to see you this afternoon.'

'The children are at school and they have contact straight after,' I said.

'We mustn't disrupt that, so how about tomorrow?'

'This is in person and not a virtual meeting?' I checked.

'Yes. I need to see them at least once.'

'Tomorrow is fine. We arrive home from school around four o'clock.'

'Excellent. I'll be there for four then. Perhaps you'd like to tell me about Polly and Angie now while we have the chance, so I can make some notes.'

'Yes. Where to start?' I said, thinking aloud. Her call had caught me unprepared.

'You presumably know why Polly and Angie are in care?' she asked.

'Yes.'

'So how have they adjusted to being in care?'

'They were devastated to have to leave home to begin with,' I said. 'They really missed their parents, but they're more settled now.'

'They missed both parents?' she asked.

'Yes. In the early days they asked for both Mummy and Daddy, but they don't mention their father so much now. They haven't seen him since they left home.'

'So you would say they had a strong bond with both their parents?'

'Yes, they did have.'

'Do they still ask for their mother?'

'Yes, but not as much. I think because they know they will see her or speak to her on the phone every day.'

'And how is that going? You had been supervising contact until recently.'

'I still supervise the phone contact. I thought the community contact was going well. To be honest I'm not sure why it was stopped. The girls enjoyed going to the park.' I then spent some time talking about contact.

'So from what you've observed how would you describe Polly's and Angie's relationship with their mother?'

'Close. Loving. Normal.'

'And what about their relationship with their older sister, Ashleigh? I shall be seeing her and her father later this week, although at present she is saying she doesn't want to see me.'

'I haven't met Ashleigh's father or spoken to him. I phone Ashleigh's mobile for contact, but she doesn't always answer. She phoned me the first week. I think I'm right in saying that she's only spoken to Angie and Polly twice since they all came into care, but I'd have to check in my log notes.'

'No need. That's fine. When was the last time they spoke to each other?'

'The Saturday before last. Ashleigh sounded down. She was at her father's and asked about her mother and if she was still angry with her. I spoke to her and reassured her as best I could. She said she wanted to see her mother, so I told her to tell her father and her social worker. She also said she was sorry that Angie and Polly had had to leave home.'

'I see. What did she think was going to happen?'

'That only she would leave.'

'Interesting,' Helen said, thoughtfully. 'How would you describe the relationship between all three girls?'

'Polly and Angie are very close but not so close to Ashleigh. I assume partly because of the age gap.'

'Any other reasons you can think of?'

'Well, based on what Polly and Angie have been saying, there seems to have been friction between Ashleigh and her parents, especially between Ashleigh and her stepfather, usually about coming-home times, boyfriends, schoolwork and so forth. It created a bad atmosphere.'

'By friction you mean arguments?'

'Yes. Polly and Angie have overheard many heated arguments. Angie told me it was better when Ashleigh was out.'

'That's sad.'

'It is. I can only repeat what Angie and Polly have told me, but it seems that Ashleigh was so unhappy at home she wanted to live with her nana or father. I've included what the girls have said in my log notes. You can access those?'

'I can,' Helen replied. 'Has Selina confided in you?'

'She offloads sometimes. She is very supportive of Tim and believes he has done nothing wrong. She says Tim was only doing what any responsible parent would do by putting boundaries in place.'

'Has Selina talked about Ashleigh's allegation of rape?'

'She doesn't believe it happened. She is completely behind Tim and says he would never harm any child.'

'She said similar in court. Mr Fletcher offered to leave the family home temporarily if it meant that Polly and Angie could return. But the social services voiced concerns that Selina would allow Tim access to the girls. The judge agreed with them and granted the care order.'

'Selina was very upset when we phoned her on Friday after the court case.'

'She was very upset in court. The judge had to pause the proceedings to allow her time to compose herself. I'll be seeing both Mr and Mrs Fletcher tomorrow morning. How are Angie and Polly doing in school? I believe the new term has just started.'

'It's their second week back,' I said. 'Polly was doing half-days last week so this is her first full week. She attended the nursery there last year. Both girls seem to be doing well. Angie can read and write and tell the time. Polly is learning. Elizabeth Hambridge is the Head and she asked to see me on the first day back, mainly to say if there was anything they could do to help support the girls I should let them know. She said they were shocked when they learnt the girls were in care. The parents were well liked and respected, and Tim was on the PTA. The police had spoken to the Head and wanted to know if either of the children had given them cause for concern, which she said they hadn't.'

'I'll be speaking to the Head later this week,' the Guardian said. 'Have Angie and Polly given you any cause for concern? Any disclosures or signs of sexual abuse?'

'No. None.'

'So as far as you are concerned the children have received some good parenting?'

'Yes. Absolutely.'

'Why were the video calls to their mother stopped?'

'I don't know. Fatima had concerns. I suppose for the same reason contact was put into the Family Centre, although I hadn't raised any issues.'

'Why do Polly and Angie think they are in care?' the Guardian now asked.

'Because of something Ashleigh said about their father. I've talked to them about having to make sure they are safe. They heard an argument on the night they had to leave, so they think it was to do with that.'

'Ashleigh had to leave her foster carer. Do you know why?'

'Not the details. You will have to ask Fatima. But I think it was quite acrimonious. Ashleigh accused Janet of not looking after her properly and Janet has accused Ashleigh of lying and taking money from her purse.'

'Do you have the carer's phone number? I'd like to talk to her.'

'Yes.' I read it out from the contacts list in my phone.

'Thank you. It's a difficult one, this.' She gave a small sigh. 'There isn't much evidence against Mr Fletcher apart from what Ashleigh is claiming, which are very serious allegations. It seems the family was divided even though they'd been together some years – Mr Fletcher's birth children and his stepdaughter, Ashleigh. If he isn't prosecuted, do we return Angie and Polly home?'

I thought it was a rhetorical question and one she wasn't really expecting me to answer, so I stayed quiet.

'If the decision is made not to return the children home, would they stay with you?' she asked.

'They could, although it would be for the social services to decide.'

'Thank you for your time. See you tomorrow around four o'clock.'

'Yes.' We said goodbye.

'That was a long phone call,' Paula said, appearing in the living room.

'It was the Guardian ad Litem.'

'I'm going out. Making the most of my last week of freedom before I start work and meeting up with some old school friends.'

'Great. Have a nice time.'

I stayed where I was, staring into space and deep in thought. I heard the front door close as Paula let herself out. Then I stood and made myself a much-needed coffee, which I carried into the front room. There was something I needed to check. I took my fostering folder from the locked drawer of my desk and opened it at the start of the Essential Information Form, then looked at my handwritten log notes. I was right. Selina had told me that Ashleigh was out and Tim was at home with her the night Ashleigh claimed he'd raped her but had said they couldn't prove it as there were no witnesses. Angie had told me she'd overheard her parents arguing that night. If she was right, surely that confirmed Tim was home?

I returned my fostering folder to the drawer and got on with some other work. Angie, Polly and Ashleigh were never far from my thoughts, but I wanted to confirm a few details with Angie before I telephoned Fatima.

That afternoon Angie came out of school looking serious. 'Are we still seeing Mummy?' she asked, remembering the cancellation on Friday.

'Yes, love. As soon as we have Polly we'll go straight there.'

She immediately brightened and we went to my car to wait the ten minutes before Polly's class came out. Angie had a new reading book and wanted to show it to me. I sat with her on the back seat and she turned the pages.

'Very good,' I said. 'You can read it to me later. Angie, there is something I want to ask you. You remember you told me you heard your mummy and daddy arguing the night you had to leave home?'

'Yes.'

'Was Ashleigh home?'

'No, she was out. That's why they were arguing.'

'And you definitely heard Mummy's and Daddy's voices?'

'Yes. Ashleigh had an argument with Daddy at dinner and left. She slammed the door, which made Daddy more annoyed. Then Mummy and Daddy began arguing and it went on all evening, even after we were in bed.'

'What about?'

'Ashleigh. It's always about her,' she sighed.

'Do you know roughly when you last heard your parents' voices?'

'Half past one,' she said, without hesitation.

'Really? How can you be so sure?'

'I have a clock in my bedroom. Their voices woke me up and I looked at the clock and saw the time.'

I knew Angie could tell the time. 'What were they saying? Could you hear them?'

'They were still arguing about Ashleigh because she hadn't come home and it was very late. She wasn't answering her phone. Then it went quiet and I fell asleep. When I woke up the police were there and Mummy was crying and Polly and me had to leave.'

'Thank you, love. That's helpful. Now it's time to collect Polly and then see your mummy. I wonder how Polly got on with her first full day at school?'

CHAPTER TWENTY-TWO

GUARDIAN AD LITEM

Sometimes foster carers have to play detective to get to the truth. I didn't know if Angie had remembered events correctly, but I instinctively felt she had. In which case, what she'd overheard was surely significant and I needed to tell Fatima.

Angie came with me into the playground and Polly rushed to us, smiling, with an armful of paintings. Her teacher was looking over and gave me a thumbs-up, signalling Polly had had a good day.

'I've made pictures for you, Mummy and Paula,' Polly said, pleased with herself.

'They're lovely, thank you. We'll put them on the front seat so they can dry without smudging. You enjoyed your first full day at school then?'

She nodded happily. I opened the rear car door and they clambered into their seats. I fastened their seatbelts and then set off for the Family Centre. They were both quiet during the journey – I think exhausted from being at school, as young children often are – although every so often Polly gave a little chuckle of delight as though she was happy. It was lovely to hear.

'I like school,' she said.

'Wonderful. You can tell Mummy all about it.'

I parked in the car park at the Family Centre. Selina's car was already there. Polly spent a while choosing which painting she was going to give to her mother, then we went up the path to the security-locked main door. As before a member of staff came to the side gate and took the girls in, so I didn't see Selina at the start of contact. Having said goodbye and that I'd see them in an hour, I returned to my car. An hour wasn't really enough time to make it worth my while going home, so I'd put the time to good use by phoning Fatima. My thoughts were still buzzing with what Angie had told me – I was sure it was significant.

'Have you got a minute?' I asked Fatima as she answered.

'Why? What's wrong.'

'Nothing, but I need to run something past you.'

'Go ahead. I've got all of five minutes.' So I guessed she was very busy.

'Angie has told me that she heard her parents arguing on the night she and Polly were taken into care. She said Ashleigh and her daddy argued at dinner, then Ashleigh left, slamming the front door as she went. Angie then heard her parents arguing about Ashleigh during the evening and that night. The last time was at one-thirty in the morning. There is a clock in her room and I know she can tell the time.'

There was silence on the other end of the phone and then Fatima said, 'Sorry, am I missing something here?'

'Well, from what I know of that night, Ashleigh is claiming she was with her stepfather and that he raped her. Selina says he was at home with her, and that is what Angie is saying too.'

Another silence, then: 'I see what you're getting at. But even if Angie has remembered all this correctly, which is a big if at her age, it doesn't account for the other times Ashleigh is saying her stepfather sexually abused her.'

'Oh, I see. I hadn't realized there were other times.'

'Plenty. But include what Angie said in your log.'

'I will.'

I ended the call, feeling a complete fool.

I went for a short walk to clear my head and then returned to the Family Centre at 5 p.m. to collect the girls. It was the same procedure as last time. I was asked to wait outside, then a member of staff let Selina and the girls out of the gate. Selina was holding the picture Polly had given her. She said a brusque hello to me and, concentrating on the girls, took them to my car. I stood to one side as she helped them into their seats and fastened their belts. Leaning in, she kissed them goodbye, then straightening closed the door.

She was about to walk away when I said, 'We've got the Guardian ad Litem coming tomorrow straight after school, so it may be a bit after five o'clock when we phone you.'

'Fine,' she said curtly, and returned to her car.

I guessed I wasn't her favourite person right now, but as a foster carer you get used to being on the receiving end of parents' anger and frustration, as do social workers.

Selina drove out of the car park just ahead of us and the girls waved until she turned right at the end of the road and we went left.

'Everything go well?' I asked them, glancing in the rear-view mirror.

Angie gave a small nod but that was all. Polly was rubbing her eyes as if tired. I assumed that if there'd been a problem during contact the supervisor, who was supposed to be with them the whole time, would have dealt with it, and if it was something I needed to know I would be told eventually. Feedback on contact is useful for foster carers as it helps them better understand the child's behaviour and meet their needs, but it's not always forthcoming.

Paula was home by the time we arrived, having had an enjoyable day with her friends. Polly and Angie brightened up when they saw her, but I took them upstairs to bath them and change their clothes first. Paula then played with them while I made dinner. After we'd eaten she read to Polly while I heard Angie read her school-book. Polly hadn't been given a school reading book yet. Angie also had a piece of maths homework that needed to be done online, and we used her tablet from home.

Paula helped me get the girls ready for bed. They were exhausted, having had school followed by contact. Contact for children is often emotionally draining. They fell asleep very quickly.

With a mug of tea each, Paula and I watched the evening news. It included an update on vaccine trials taking place in the UK and other countries. Mass testing was being increased and in some areas the R number – the indicator of the number of people being infected – was rising, although it was still very low so there was no immediate cause for concern in the UK at least. Every day the news included the numbers of those who had died from Covid in the last twenty-four hours and those who'd tested positive. Although these figures remained low, even one preventable death was too many and we were reminded to follow the guidelines: hands, face and space. To wash our hands regularly, cover our faces in enclosed public spaces and stay two metres apart.

I took the opportunity to tell Paula the Guardian ad Litem was visiting tomorrow. She understood her role from having had other Guardians visit the children we'd fostered. I hadn't told Angie and Polly yet and would do so the following morning.

'Helen is a nice lady the judge has asked to visit us,' I said as I drove to school the next day. 'She will want to know how you are both doing, so she'll ask you some questions.' I'd already explained what a judge and court were.

'Is she going to see Mummy?' Angie asked.

'Yes.'

Having seen the girls into school I went home, where I completed another foster-training module online, then in the afternoon I caught up with the housework. When I collected Polly and Angie from school I reminded them of the Guardian's visit.

'You told us that already,' Angie said testily.

Once home, I had just enough time to give them both a quick bath and put them in fresh clothes before the doorbell rang. We were still upstairs so Paula let the Guardian in and showed her into the living room. 'I think I'll stay up here,' Angie said sullenly.

'I think you will come down to talk to her,' I replied positively, and taking her hand we all went downstairs together. I took a face mask from where I kept some on the hall stand and we went into the living room.

'This is Angie and Polly,' I said.

'Hello. Nice to meet you, I'm Helen,' she said with a smile. She had her mask just under her chin.

'Do you want me to put this on?' I asked her, referring to my mask.

'Not if you are happy without. We can socially distance and perhaps open the patio doors a little? I find it easier to talk to children without it on.'

'That's fine with me.' I opened the patio doors wide enough to let in some fresh air.

Helen was of average height and build, I guessed in her fifties, and dressed smart-casual in navy trousers and a printed blouse. She had short brown hair and an easy manner that I thought the children would respond to.

'Has Cathy told you why I'm here?' she asked, returning to her seat. The girls were standing a little way from her, close to me.

Polly nodded and then said, 'I had school dinner today,' as if it was the main event.

'Lovely, and what did you have to eat?' Helen asked, while Angie watched her suspiciously.

'Can't remember,' Polly said, with a chuckle.

'I expect it was something nice,' Helen said. 'Did you have school dinner too?' she asked Angie, trying to put them at ease.

'Yes,' Angie replied.

'And what did you have?'

'Macaroni cheese,' Angie said.

'Lovely.'

'I had that too,' Polly added.

'Would you like a drink?' I asked Helen.

'No, thank you.'

'I want a drink,' Angie said.

I fetched the girls a tumbler of water each; they usually had a drink when they returned from school. Having said hello to Helen, Paula went upstairs to her room.

'Do you want me to stay?' I asked Helen. Guardians usually did, but some liked to spend time alone with the children, and we'd spoken at length yesterday on the phone.

'I think it might be nice for Angie and Polly,' she replied. 'Would you like Cathy in the room while we talk?' she asked them.

Both girls nodded so I sat on the sofa. Polly came and sat on my lap while Angie sat beside me. The Guardian was in the armchair opposite us. She didn't have a note-pad or laptop.

'Can you tell me why I'm here?' she asked them gently.

'To tell the judge about us,' Angie replied, as she might answer a question in class.

'That's right,' Helen said. 'Has Cathy explained my role?'

They looked at her blankly.

'As best I could,' I replied.

Helen smiled. 'I'm what's known as Guardian ad Litem, or Guardian for short. I report to the judge about how you are doing and where you should live in the future.'

'Do you tell the judge we can go home?' Angie asked perceptively.

'I advise him on this,' Helen replied. 'Would you like to live at home again?'

'Yes,' Angie replied, but without the anxiety that would have accompanied any mention of home when they'd first come to live with me. They were used to being in care now.

'So, tell me what it was like living at home with Mummy, Daddy and Ashleigh,' Helen said.

It was a big question and Angie took some moments before she replied. 'It was nice most of the time,' she said. 'I want to go home.'

'Me too, but I want Cathy to come,' Polly said, and kissed my cheek.

I gave her a hug. Helen smiled. 'That's nice. So you liked being at home and you like living with Cathy too. Do you know why you had to live here?'

'Because of Ashleigh,' Angie said.

'In a way,' Helen replied. 'But she isn't to blame for what happened. How did you feel most of the time when you lived at home? Happy, sad, frightened or something else?'

'Happy,' Angie said. 'But I didn't like the arguments.'

'Tell me about those,' the Guardian encouraged.

'Daddy and Ashleigh were always arguing and then Mummy and Daddy argued because of Ashleigh.'

'Why do you think that was?'

'Because Ashleigh was naughty,' Angie replied.

'In what way?'

'Not sure,' Angie said, with a shrug. Polly was sitting very still on my lap, watching Angie and letting her do most of the talking.

'Were you ever naughty at home?' Helen asked.

'Sometimes,' Angie admitted.

'What happened when you were naughty?'

'Mummy told me off,' Angie said, in a quiet voice.

'Did Daddy tell you off?'

'Sometimes.'

'Were you slapped?'

Angie shook her head.

'How were you punished? What happened when you were naughty?'

'We had to say sorry and promise not to do it again,' Angie replied.

'That seems reasonable,' Helen said. 'Were you usually happy the other times?'

'Yes,' Angie said.

'Do you think Ashleigh was happy?' Helen asked.

'No,' Angie said, and Polly shook her head.

'Why do you think that was?' Helen asked.

Angie shrugged and Polly copied her.

'Do you think your Mummy and Daddy treated Ashleigh the same way they treated you and Polly?'

Angie looked thoughtful. 'No. Because she's older.'

'Ashleigh is a big girl,' Polly said, feeling she should add something.

'I understand,' Helen said. 'Did Ashleigh and your daddy spend time together alone, perhaps in a bedroom or out in his car?'

'I can't remember. She didn't like Daddy. She has her own daddy. A different one.'

'That's correct. Your daddy is Ashleigh's stepfather,' Helen said. 'Who used to take you to the toilet at your house?'

'I go to the toilet by myself,' Angie said, a little indignantly.

'So do I,' Polly added, although she still needed help sometimes.

'And when you were little and needed help with the toilet, who used to go with you then?' Helen asked. I knew what she was getting at, but the girls looked at her blankly. 'You probably don't remember,' Helen said when neither of them spoke. 'What about bath-time? You still need help bathing. Who helped you wash at home?'

'Mummy or Daddy,' Angie replied. 'More Mummy because Daddy was at work.'

'I understand,' Helen said. 'While you were living at home did anyone touch you in a way that made you feel unhappy or hurt? Or asked you to touch them?'

The girls didn't appear to understand the question.

'Do you know what your private parts are?' Helen asked.

Polly giggled while Angie nodded, embarrassed.

'They do,' I confirmed.

'Has anyone touched you there?' Helen asked.

I felt sorry for the girls having to answer these questions, although the Guardian was handling it sensitively.

'No,' Angie replied. 'We're not allowed to touch other people's private parts, which is why they are called private.'

'Yes,' Helen said. 'What about you, Polly? Has anyone ever touched or hurt your private parts?'

Polly shook her head.

'When you had a bath at home who used to wash your private parts?' Helen asked.

'Me,' Angie said.

'Me,' Polly said.

'That's correct,' I said. 'They have been taught how to wash themselves.' It's usual for children their age. 'I wash their hair and upper bodies and they do the rest.'

'Thank you. They didn't have a medical when they first came into care, did they?' she asked me.

'No.'

'It's too late now,' she said, meaning that if there was any evidence of abuse it would have gone by now.

'There were no visible marks on their bodies,' I said.

She nodded and looked at the girls. 'You have a grand-mother – your mother's mother?'

'Yes,' I confirmed when they didn't. 'They refer to her as Nana.'

'I believe they used to see her regularly,' Helen said. 'Have they had any contact with her since they came into care?' she asked me.

'No.'

'Do they talk about her?'

'When they first arrived they did, but not so much now.'

'She's put herself forward to look after Polly and Angie if it's found they can't return home.'

'I think she offered before,' I said.

'That's correct,' Helen said, and then turned her attention to the girls again. 'Would you like to live with your Nana?'

'Don't know,' Angie said, while Polly looked confused.

'Tell me about your school. Cathy says you're doing well. Do you have friends at school?'

'Yes,' Angie replied.

'Me too,' Polly said.

'I'm hoping they will be able to invite their friends here for playdates before long, but at present we've being advised against it.'

'Because of Covid?' Helen asked.

'Yes.'

'Thank you for answering all my questions,' Helen said to the girls. 'Is there anything you want to ask me?'

'Are we going to live with Mummy and Daddy?' Angie asked.

'I don't know yet. That will be for the judge to decide. If you can't go home, would you like to live here or at your Nana's?'

Angie shrugged and Polly copied her, then kissed my cheek again.

'She's become very close to you,' Helen commented.

'Yes.'

Angie and Polly hadn't answered Helen's question about where they would like to live in the future and Helen now said, 'There's no need for you to worry, the adults will decide what's best for you.'

She talked to them for a while longer about their hobbies and what they liked to do in their spare time, then thanked us for our time and said if she needed to see them again she could do a virtual visit. I saw her out. It was impossible to know what her recommendation to the judge would be; maybe she hadn't decided yet and was still gathering information.

CHAPTER TWENTY-THREE

ASHLEIGH'S FATHER

It was nearly 5.30 p.m. by the time the Guardian ad Litem left. Paula came downstairs when she heard the front door go and began dinner while I phoned Selina.

'Sorry, the Guardian has only just gone,' I said, taking the phone to the girls.

Selina didn't reply so I sat on the sofa between Angie and Polly with the phone on speaker.

'We told the guardian lady we wanted to go home,' Angie said.

'Good,' Selina replied, but that was all she said on the matter. Maybe she'd been advised not to discuss the Guardian's visit with the children.

Selina sounded exhausted and there were long silences as she tried to make conversation. Angie and Polly were tired from a day at school and the Guardian's visit so weren't very responsive. Angie in particular was irritable. Polly kept rubbing her eyes.

'I don't think you're really in the mood for talking to me today,' Selina said, after about ten minutes.

'They're probably tired and hungry,' I said.

She ignored me but said to the girls, 'Have your dinner and we'll see each other tomorrow.' They said goodbye.

I left the girls watching television while I helped Paula finish making the dinner. After we'd eaten I listened to Angie read her schoolbook – the school expected children of her age to be reading at home every night. Paula played with Polly and then around seven o'clock we took them upstairs to get ready for bed. Paula kissed them both goodnight and left while I stayed behind. Polly, who was cuddling up to her pink rabbit, fell asleep almost immediately, but Angie looked deep in thought. I could tell the signs now when something was bothering her. I sat on the edge of her bed with the light on low. Her soft-toy rabbit was on the pillow beside her.

'Do you think we will live with Nana?' she asked me quietly after a few moments.

'I don't know, love. It's possible. Would you like to live with her?'

'I think so. Would Mummy be there too?'

'I don't know.'

'Would Polly come with me?'

'Yes.' I could be certain of that, as the girls wouldn't be split up.

'Do you think we will ever go to our old house again?' Angie asked.

'I honestly don't know, love, but try not to worry. It will all work out in the end and the adults will make the decisions.' So often children in care take on responsibility far beyond their years, so it doesn't hurt to remind them that they don't need to worry.

'Sometimes I can't remember my old home very well,' Angie said. 'I can remember some of my toys, but I have to think hard to remember other things, like the bathroom and garden. I had a bike when I lived there.'

'I know, love. You use the ones here now.'

Apart from the bags the girls had arrived with, nothing more had come from home. I had bought the clothes they needed, and they used the toys I had accumulated over all my years of fostering, of which there were many. If they were still with me for their birthdays and Christmas, I could buy them bikes of their own if that's what they wanted.

We talked for a while longer and then gradually Angie's eyes began to close. I kissed her goodnight and came out of their room. On my way downstairs I heard my mobile ringing from where I'd left it in the living room. I ran to answer it.

'Cathy?' a woman's voice asked.

'Yes? Speaking.'

'It's Janet. Ashleigh's carer.'

'Oh, yes, sorry. I've had a busy day.'

'I won't keep you, but I just had to tell you this. You won't believe what's happened.' She sounded a lot brighter than the last time I'd heard from her, when she'd been angry and upset with Ashleigh. 'You remember all the trouble Ashleigh caused me?'

'Yes,' I said tentatively, sitting on the sofa, not sure where this conversation was going.

'She phoned two hours ago asking if she could come and live with me again! Can you believe it? After all the lies she told about me!'

'I see,' I said, immediately concerned. 'I thought she was living with her father.'

'She was. But they had an argument and she thought she could just come back here! The cheek of it!'

'What did you say?'

'I told her there was no way she was setting foot in my house again after all the trouble she'd caused me and stealing from my purse. I had a right go at her and she burst into tears. I'm sorry, but she really upset me. I doubt I'll foster again because of her.'

'She sounds very confused,' I said. 'Where is she now?'

'I don't know. From the sound of it she hasn't got anywhere to go so maybe she's back with her father.'

'Have you told Fatima?' I asked.

'No. Why? Do you think I should? It's not like I'm fostering her.'

'I think she should know. It's too late tonight but phone either Fatima or your supervising social worker in the morning. It sounds like Ashleigh needs help and it also throws a different light on what she was saying about you.'

'How do you mean?'

'Well, it can't have been that bad living with you if she's asking to come back.'

'Yes, that's what I thought. I'll phone them in the morning.'

'I'll give Ashleigh a ring to make sure she's OK and has somewhere to stay,' I said. 'Do you have her father's number? In case she doesn't answer her phone. Trevor, isn't it?'

'Yes, Trevor Masters. I might have. Do you want it now?'

'Yes, please.'

'Hang on. I'll have to find it.'

I waited. Strictly speaking, Ashleigh wasn't my problem, but now I knew there'd been issues at home I couldn't just forget and walk away. I needed to make sure that she at least had a bed for the night, and then Fatima could deal with the rest tomorrow. If Ashleigh wasn't at home and her father didn't know where she was, or I couldn't get hold of either of them, I'd call the emergency duty social worker and tell him.

'Yes, I've still got his number,' Janet said, coming back on the phone. She read out Ashleigh's father's number and I made a note.

'Thank you.'

'I must say I feel a lot better knowing my home was good enough for Ashleigh to want to come back to,' Janet said.

'Yes, it sounds like something bad has happened at her father's that's made her desperate to leave. I'll phone her now.'

Saying goodbye, I immediately phoned Ashleigh's mobile, but it went through to voicemail as I thought might happen. I left a message. 'Hi, love, it's Cathy, Angie and Polly's carer. Can you ring or text, please, to let me know you're all right? I'm worried. Janet's just called me and said there's been a problem at your father's. I just want to make sure you're OK and have somewhere to stay.'

I finished that call and phoned her father. He answered straight away with a rather gruff 'Hello?'

'Is that Trevor?' I checked.

'Yes, who is it?'

'Cathy Glass, you don't know me, but I —'

'I do know you,' he interrupted. 'You're the foster carer for Ashleigh's half-sisters.'

'Yes, that's correct,' I said, slightly surprised he knew.

'Ashleigh's mentioned you,' he said. 'She was supposed to live with you but ended up with that other woman, Janet.'

I immediately felt guilty. 'Yes, I'm sorry. I couldn't take all three.'

'No matter. She's here with me, which is what we wanted all along.'

'Is Ashleigh with you now?' I asked.

'Yes, but why do you want to know?' he asked.

'Janet just called me and said there'd been a problem and Ashleigh was upset. Ashleigh phoned Janet and asked to stay there.'

I heard him sigh. 'It's sorted now. Ashleigh can overre-act.'

'So Ashleigh is with you?' I double-checked.

'Yes.'

'I just called her mobile and she didn't answer.'

'She's here, in the same room. Do you want to speak to her?'

'Please. Just quickly. If that's OK?'

I heard him say, 'It's your sisters' foster carer on the phone, wanting to know if you're all right.'

Ashleigh came to the phone and said a small, 'Hello.'

'Hi, love, I just wanted to make sure you're safe and well. Janet phoned me and said you were upset earlier.'

'I was, but I'm better now.'

'Are you sure?'

'Yes.' Her voice sounded flat.

'You've sorted out the problem with your father?'

'Yes.'

'You know you can call or text me if you are not safe.'
I didn't know anything about her father, although I
assumed Fatima had visited him and run checks.

'I'm OK. My phone is in my bedroom on charge.'

'All right, love, as long as you are safe. It would be nice
if you could speak to Angie and Polly before too long.'

'I will,' she said, in the same flat voice. 'I'll put Dad
back on.'

Trevor came back on the phone. 'Satisfied?'

'Yes. Sorry to interrupt your evening. I'm glad
everything has been sorted out. What was the argument
about, if you don't mind me asking? Ashleigh sounds
rather down.'

'School,' he replied. 'When Ashleigh came to live with
me she had to change schools. She doesn't like the new
one and hasn't been going. I leave the house before her to
go to work and she's been telling me she's been going to
school. Even going to her bedroom in the evening suppos-
edly to do her homework. The Head of Year called me
today and told me she hasn't been in at all this week and
only two days last week. I was angry with Ashleigh and
told her off. I said if this was going to work she needed to
be honest with me and go to school. She clearly didn't
like it and must have phoned Janet.'

'Thank you for explaining,' I said, reassured.

'You're welcome. Anything else?'

'No. Thanks again.' We said goodbye.

Mr Masters had sounded reasonable and had acted as
most responsible parents would and told Ashleigh off.
The matter had been dealt with and Ashleigh was home
now. However, I was still concerned for her. She'd
sounded very low, probably as a result of her father telling

her off, and the abuse she'd suffered at the hands of her stepfather. I assumed she'd been offered counselling, but that was between her, her father and her social worker to arrange. I'd felt guilty when Mr Masters had said Ashleigh was supposed to have come to me, but I really couldn't have coped successfully with all three children. Sometimes in fostering we have to say no, difficult though it is.

That evening as I wrote up my log notes I included Janet's phone call and my subsequent conversations with Ashleigh and her father. I also emailed the details to Fatima, copying in Joy, including that while Ashleigh had reassured me she was all right, she had sounded down.

Unsettled by the Guardian's visit and all the talk of home, Angie and Polly woke in the night, although, unlike when they'd first arrived, they were more easily settled.

'I told the Guardian I wanted to go home,' Angie mumbled, half asleep. 'Tell Mummy.'

'She knows, love, it's OK,' I soothed. 'Now back off to sleep.'

Wednesday was contact and Selina shunned me at the end as she had on Monday. It was the same when we phoned her on Thursday. She didn't speak to me, only the girls. She blanked me again on Friday, but as she took Angie and Polly to my car I saw tears welling in her eyes. I honestly didn't know what to say to help. She clearly didn't want to confide in me.

'Take care,' was all I said.

She didn't reply and returned to her car.

We left the car park with Selina's car just behind us. As I glanced in the rear-view mirror I saw her wipe her eyes. The girls had swivelled round in their seats to wave goodbye and Angie saw it too. 'Is Mummy crying?' she asked.

'I don't think so,' I said, feeling a little lie was justified to save them from worrying. 'She's probably got something in her eye.'

'I don't like it when Mummy cries,' Angie said. 'She was upset in contact and the supervisor made her better.'

I thought Selina wasn't coping and this seemed to prove it. I hoped she was getting the support she needed.

CHAPTER TWENTY-FOUR

MY UNEASE GROWS

'We've had a complaint,' Fatima said when she telephoned me on Monday morning. 'From the Fletchers' solicitor.' My heart fell as I guessed it was about me, for why else would she be telling me? 'Among other things, it seems Mrs Fletcher is concerned that you are encouraging her children to call you Mummy and have told them they will be living with you permanently.'

'Not true,' I said. 'I have reassured the girls that they will stay with me for the time being, but I have never encouraged them to call me Mummy. They call me Cathy. Sometimes Polly forgets and calls me Mummy and I always correct her.' Current fostering guidelines discourage children from calling their carers Mummy and Daddy, as it's felt it would be confusing for them as they have their own parents.

'It seems that Polly called you Mummy during contact last week and it upset Mrs Fletcher,' Fatima continued. 'Perhaps you could remind the girls to call you Cathy and reassure Selina when you see her.'

'I can try, although Selina wants nothing to do with me at present.'

'Why?'

'I don't know. She's upset and wants her children back, I guess.'

'She thinks they're too settled with you,' Fatima said.

'It's usually considered good if children settle with their carer,' I replied, a little peevishly.

'Quite so, but remind them you aren't their mother. There's other things in the letter but they aren't to do with you.'

'You got my email about Ashleigh?' I asked.

'Yes. Janet phoned me too. I need to speak to Ashleigh and her father as soon as I have the chance. Is Ashleigh having sibling phone contact?'

'No. I tried again on Saturday, but she didn't answer her phone. I left a message asking her to call when she wanted to speak to Angie and Polly. I can't do any more.'

'Couldn't Ashleigh have talked to them when she spoke to you? Last Tuesday, wasn't it?'

'It was late. Angie and Polly were asleep in bed. Ashleigh and I didn't talk for long. I just confirmed she was safe and at her father's and that was it.'

'All right. Leave it with me.'

Not the best start to the week, I thought. I could understand why Selina was unhappy, although clearly I had little control over how the girls referred to me during contact.

It was Paula's first day back at work after being furloughed, so I texted her at lunchtime asking how she was getting on. She replied with a thumbs-up emoji and wrote, *Not many here. Others still working from home. See you later. Love P xxx*

That afternoon on the way to contact I reminded Angie and Polly that I was their foster carer, not their mother.

'We know that,' Angie said disdainfully.

'Good. I just wanted to check. So you call me Cathy, don't you?'

'Yes,' Angie replied.

I glanced in the rear-view mirror at Polly. 'OK, love?'

She nodded and I left it at that. I wasn't going to make an issue of it; they had enough to cope with, as most children in care do.

I didn't see Selina at the start of contact, only at the end. She was cool with me, but once she'd seen the girls into my car and closed the door I said to her, 'Fatima tells me Polly has been calling me Mummy. I know that must be upsetting for you. I correct her if she does it at home. She knows the difference.'

'Does she?' Selina replied sceptically, and walked away.

In the car going home Angie told me that Polly had called me Mummy again at contact.

'Do you often talk about me during contact?' I asked.

'Sometimes, about the things we do,' Angie replied, looking as if she had done something wrong.

'It's all right, love. I just wondered. Don't worry.'

It must have been another smack in the face for Selina. As well as Polly referring to me as Mummy, they'd been talking about their life with me. Also, Selina would have noticed the girls were parting from her more easily now and were wanting to spend less time on the phone, preferring to be off playing. It was only to be expected as they were with me the larger part of the week. It didn't mean they loved her any less, although I'm sure that's how it must have appeared to her.

'Will Paula be home from work now?' Angie asked as I drove.

'Not sure, but she won't be long.'

They enjoyed spending time with Paula, and I was sure they must have talked about her too during contact, but that wouldn't have had the same effect on Selina as talking about me would. Paula wasn't in the role of mummy but older sister, so Selina was less likely to take offence.

Paula arrived home fifteen minutes after us, and the girls were so pleased to see her. They hugged and kissed her as she came in. Over dinner she told us of her day and how the office had been changed to make it Covid safe, with desks two metres apart and hand sanitizer on all of them, and they had to wear masks when moving around the office.

Although Paula had been at work all day and doubtless was looking forward to relaxing, she still found time to play with the girls and kiss them goodnight once they were in bed.

It was now the middle of September; the nights were drawing in and the evening air was chilling. With the school run, contact three evenings a week, running the house, writing, seeing the rest of my family and everything that came with fostering, the week flew by. I didn't know how the police investigation into Tim Fletcher was going – there was no reason for me to be told unless it affected the girls – so for me, nothing much changed. Selina arrived early for every contact and brought snacks and drinks for the girls but didn't speak to me. Then, towards the end of September, something happened that was to play on my mind and caused a feeling of unease I couldn't shake off.

Angie and Polly sometimes argued, as siblings do. It was usually over a toy they both wanted and the dispute was easily settled. One day they were watching television in the living room after school, while I made dinner, and I heard Polly scream. I rushed in to find her rubbing her arm and looking hurt.

'Angie hit me,' she said accusingly, her bottom lip trembling.

'No, I didn't!' Angie retorted. 'You're such a liar, just like Ashleigh.'

I calmed them both down and then got to the bottom of what had happened. Polly hadn't been interested in the television programme that Angie wanted to watch and had kept talking over it and standing in her line of vision, so eventually Angie had given her a push. Nothing major – Polly, tired from a day at school, had overreacted. I told Angie to apologize, reminding her we didn't hit, push or slap others, which she knew.

But the incident played on my mind. Not the actual pushing, but what Angie had said to Polly in the heat of the moment – 'You're such a liar, just like Ashleigh.' Was Ashleigh a liar? If so, what exactly had she lied about? I guess we all tell little untruths sometimes; for example, if a friend asks us, 'Do you like my new dress?' and we say, 'Yes,' rather than hurt their feelings. But most of us tell the truth about important matters where the conse-quences can be far-reaching.

I went off to sleep that night thinking about Angie's comment and woke the following morning with the same thoughts, my feeling of unease growing. Before we left for school I took Angie to one side and said, 'You remember yesterday when you were annoyed with Polly you said she was a liar like Ashleigh. What made you say that about Ashleigh?'

'She used to say things that weren't true.'

'Like what?'

'About Daddy being horrible to her.'

'You mean the reason you had to leave home and come here?'

'Yes, and other times she told lies.'

'What other times, love?'

'She was always telling Mummy that Daddy treated her differently from us and it was unfair. And one day she said he slapped her, but he didn't.'

'How do you know that?'

'I saw. They were arguing and then later I heard Ashleigh tell Mummy he'd hit her, but I know he didn't.'

'I see. Anything else?'

'Can't remember. I'm friends with Polly now and I won't push her again.'

'Good girl.'

Did Angie's comments add anything to what I already knew? Ashleigh had obviously felt unfairly treated and that her stepfather loved his birth children more than he did her. But that didn't mean she'd go to the lengths of claiming he'd raped her if it wasn't true. And Fatima had said there'd been other times he'd sexually abused her. Also, there was the medical evidence from the hospital where Ashleigh had sought help, although I remembered Selina had told me it was inconclusive and didn't link the assault directly to Tim.

With all this going round in my head, I took Angie and Polly to school and then had to stop off on the way home to do some food shopping. Once I'd unpacked I took my fostering folder from the locked drawer in the front room and began flicking through the pages. I wasn't sure what I was looking for, but what I found was Mel Robinson's business card. She was one of the two police officers from the Child Abuse Investigation Team who'd visited us and spoken to Polly and Angie shortly after they'd arrived. She'd left her card in case the girls remembered anything that might be significant, but this wasn't really significant, was it? They'd already told the officers about the arguments between Ashleigh and her stepfather. And yet …

I turned the card over and back again, and thought some more.

I'd already made a fool of myself once when I'd told Fatima that Angie had heard her parents on the night Ashleigh claimed her stepfather had raped her, feeling it was significant. I didn't want to do it again.

But on the other hand …

The minutes ticked by and then I grabbed my phone before I could change my mind again, and keyed in the numbers from the card. To my relief it went through to voicemail. I hesitated and then left a message. 'It's Cathy Glass, foster carer for Polly and Angie Fletcher. Could Mel Robinson or Kierston Smith give me a ring, please? It's nothing urgent. My number is … Thank you.'

I ended the call with my heart racing. They might not even return my call if they were very busy, I told myself, and tried to concentrate on something else, all the while running through what I would say if they did call me back.

Mel phoned an hour later and after swapping pleasantries of hello, how are you, there was an awkward silence as I struggled to begin.

'I'm assuming you have a lot of evidence against Mr Fletcher,' I began. 'I mean, apart from what Ashleigh is saying.'

Mel was silent for a moment and then said gently, 'I can't really discuss that.'

'No, of course not. I'm so sorry. It's just that I've got some concerns.'

'About what?'

'Some of the things the girls are telling me. Angie in particular. They're more relaxed with me now and less guarded in what they say about life at home. It's probably nothing, I don't know ...' I tailed off.

'Best if you tell me and I can decide if it's relevant,' Mel said patiently.

'Yes, of course. When you saw the girls they told you a bit about the arguments between Ashleigh and her step-father and that she wasn't happy at home.'

'I remember.'

'There were a lot of arguments and Selina usually took the side of her husband. But Angie tells me that on at least one occasion Ashleigh made up something that wasn't true – I think to gain her mother's sympathy. Angie said that, once, Ashleigh told her mother her step-father slapped her during an argument, but Angie was watching and knew it didn't happen.'

'That's interesting.'

'Also, Angie has told me that she heard her parents arguing on the night she and Polly came into care. That was the night Ashleigh said her stepfather raped her, but according to Angie he was at home. I don't know the timeline of that evening, but Angie said Ashleigh and her stepfather had argued at dinner, then Ashleigh left, slamming the front door as she went, so that would be early evening. She then heard her parents arguing about Ashleigh on and off during the evening and that night. The last time was at one-thirty in the morning. She has a clock in her bedroom and I know she can tell the time.' I paused.

'Do you think Angie would make it up to try to protect her father?' Mel asked.

'She hasn't the guile to do that, and when she told me it came out naturally. I thought you should know, as I understand Selina is saying that Tim was with her for the whole of the evening but she can't prove it. Now Angie is saying he was home too. I appreciate she's only six, but I am sure she's telling the truth. I wrote it in my log notes and also told their social worker, Fatima Hadden.'

'What did she say?'

'She didn't think it was significant as Ashleigh is claiming her stepfather sexually abused her at other times.'

'Hmm. It would have been good to be told, though.' So it seemed that Mel was taking my concerns seriously, which gave me the courage to continue.

'There are some other things that are niggling me too.'

'Yes?'

'I don't know Ashleigh at all. I've never met her and have only spoken to her briefly on the phone. But she wasn't at her foster carer's for long when it all fell apart. You know she's living with her father now?'

'Yes, we were advised of her new address. Why did she leave her carer? Do you know?'

'According to Ashleigh, Janet wasn't nice to her and didn't make her feel welcome. Janet had just returned to fostering after a long break so maybe she didn't handle some things right, I don't know. But Ashleigh had a list of complaints, including that Janet was vegetarian and refused to cook her meat. That she was only allowed a short shower each day rather than a bath, and she wasn't given her allowance on time. Janet says it's not true and that Ashleigh didn't want to be there and made life difficult for her. Janet was very upset about the things Ashleigh told her social worker and said they were lies. She also found some money had gone missing from her purse. Then a couple of weeks ago Ashleigh had an argument with her father and phoned Janet asking if she could return there to live.'

'So Ashleigh had little concept of the trouble she'd caused?'

'No.'

'Is she still living with her father?'

'As far as I know. I spoke to them both when this happened. Trevor Masters, Ashleigh's father, told me that the argument was about Ashleigh not going to school. She had been telling him she'd been going but hadn't. When he found out he was cross and told her off for lying to him, so she phoned Janet and asked to go there. They patched it up, but what I'm saying is that it seems Ashleigh can fabricate things and doesn't always tell the truth. I think she's very mixed up, is feeling hurt, and sometimes acts before she thinks. There was an incident while she was at Janet's where she claimed she was pregnant and then she wasn't.'

'I don't think we know about that.'

'Janet had decided she needed to be firmer with Ashleigh about coming-in times and who she was seeing, so she got ready to give her a good talking to. Since Ashleigh had arrived at Janet's she'd been coming and going as she pleased. But as Janet started Ashleigh burst into tears and said she was pregnant. Of course, Janet was shocked and didn't continue with her lecture. She immediately phoned Fatima, who visited that afternoon, by which time Ashleigh had decided she wasn't pregnant and it must have been a false alarm. Between phoning Fatima and her arriving, Ashleigh said she'd started a period. At the time it crossed my mind that it was very good timing, and I wondered then if Ashleigh had been telling the truth. I mean, Ashleigh wouldn't be the first troubled young person to make up something to gain sympathy and attention.'

'No, indeed,' Mel agreed.

'That's it, really. I was in two minds about telling you but decided you should know.'

'Yes. I am glad you did. I'm not sure where we are exactly with the investigation, so I'll check. If necessary, we'll see Ashleigh again, and Polly and Angie. In the meantime, let us know if anything else significant comes to light.'

'I will.'

As we ended the call I felt relieved and exonerated. My concerns had been building for some time and now I'd been able to share them. Whether what I'd said changed anything remained to be seen, but at least the police knew.

CHAPTER TWENTY-FIVE

MORE WORRY

September gave way to October and a blustery wind began to dislodge the leaves from the trees. I bought Angie and Polly new winter coats: navy for school as was required, and bright, colourful padded jackets for weekends. I hadn't seen Selina or Tim outside the school again since that first day. If they were there they were parked discreetly, and I guessed that didn't matter as long as the girls didn't see them.

So far none of the parents had approached me as Selina had feared they might. There wasn't really much opportunity when we were going into the playground a class at a time in a socially distanced queue and then leaving straight after. Some parents did form small groups outside the school and talked for a few minutes once they'd collected their children, but most went straight home. I had seen one small group looking at me quizzically as I passed, but no one had tried to talk to me. Angie told me that one of them was Belle's mother. I knew that Belle and Angie had been friends last term so I asked Angie if she would like me to try to organize a playdate with her in a park or similar, which was allowed.

'No, Mummy wouldn't like it,' she replied.

I assumed something must have been said about this during contact. Polly wasn't asking to see any of her friends, so I didn't pursue it. But at the end of the first week in October, when the schools had been back for over a month, the woman I knew to be Belle's mother broke away from the others she'd been talking to and stopped me as I was about to cross the road with the girls.

Lowering her mask to speak, she said, 'A few of us were wondering if Selina is all right. We haven't seen her here all term and she's not replying to our messages.' I felt Angie tense beside me.

'Yes, she's all right,' I confirmed.

'We've seen you bringing her children to school and collecting them but without Selina or Tim.'

'That's correct, I'm helping them out.'

'Is Selina ill?' she asked, clearly hoping for more details.

'No. In fact, I'll be seeing her shortly, so I'll pass on your best wishes.' And with a smile I took the girls' hands and we continued across the road.

As they got into the car I glanced over. Belle's mother had returned to the group and all three were looking at us. If they were good friends with Selina and Tim then they were probably genuinely concerned for them, but Selina had told me early on she wasn't replying to messages from friends, and I respected her decision. It was for her to tell them what she wanted them to know, if anything. It's a situation I've encountered before when taking a child I'm fostering to and from school. I would never share information about the family with anyone except the school, unless I was asked to by the child's parents.

As I drove to contact I asked Angie again if she wanted to meet up with Belle.

'No, she's not my friend any more,' she replied.

'OK, love. If either of you want to see any of your friends, tell me and I'll try to arrange something.' It's important for children to cultivate and maintain friendships, and sometimes it's more difficult for children in care.

I received a copy of Angie's and Polly's Personal Education Plans (PEPs) in the post. A PEP is a document that sets out the goals and attainments to help a child or young person in care reach their full academic and life potential. All children in care have a PEP and it forms part of their care plan. Normally, as the foster carer, I attended PEP meetings held at the child's school, but as meetings were being kept to a minimum the Deputy Head, who was also the designated teacher for looked-after children, had drawn up the PEPs and Fatima had approved and signed them. I read them both and then filed them in the folder. There were no surprises; the girls were a good average for their age.

Paula had settled back into work. Sometimes we watched television together in the evenings, although not as much as we had done while she'd been furloughed. She had other things to do now during her evenings and also wanted to relax in her room. I made a point of watching the evening news. It always gave the daily Covid toll – the numbers of those testing positive and those who had sadly died after contracting the virus. Worryingly, the numbers testing positive were rising again, especially in some regions. Rather than impose tighter measures or another complete lockdown, the government was implementing regional lockdowns. So far the area where I lived was unaffected, but that could change if the R number went up. We were reminded to be careful – hands, space, face.

On Tuesday afternoon of the second week in October, I'd just settled in front of my computer with a sandwich and a mug of tea when Janet phoned. I hadn't heard from her since Ashleigh had asked to return to live with her. I knew straight away that another drama was unfolding.

'You'll never guess what!' she began. 'I've just had the police here looking for Ashleigh. It seems she's gone missing.'

'Oh dear.'

'No warning. I just opened the front door and there they were! Two police officers with their car parked outside for all the neighbours to see. I nearly had a heart attack. I thought something had happened to one of my family. Then they told me they were looking for Ashleigh.'

'What a shock for you,' I sympathized.

'It was. They said her father had reported her missing this morning and they were checking all the places she might be. I said they could have phoned and saved themselves a trip, but they wanted to come in and have a look around.'

'That's usual,' I said. 'They'll go to her parents' home too and the homes of her friends – anywhere she could possibly have gone. Do you know what happened to make her run away?'

'No, they didn't say.'

Janet was more interested in telling me about the police visit than the reason Ashleigh might have run away. I appreciated how unsettling it was to have the police suddenly arrive on your doorstep. But if a young person goes missing, even if it's your child, the police will usually search the family home and any other homes where they might be.

Towards the end of the call Janet told me she was thinking of fostering again.

'That's good news,' I said encouragingly.

'A younger child,' she added.

'Good luck. Let me know how it goes.' I felt sure she had something to offer.

I wound up the call, finished my sandwich and now-cold tea, and returned to the computer screen. Ten minutes later my mobile rang again, and it was Ashleigh's father, Trevor.

'I hope I'm not interrupting anything, but have you heard from Ashleigh?' he began. 'She's missing and I'm very worried.'

'No, I haven't,' I said. 'Janet just called and told me she was missing. The police had been there looking for her. I'm sure they'll find her soon. In my experience young people are rarely missing for long.'

'That's what the police said but I can't just sit here and wait for news. I keep trying her mobile but it's off. I'm sure there's something the matter with Ashleigh. Something is bothering her, but I can't get to the bottom of it. She's not the girl I used to know.' He sounded very worried and stressed.

'She was badly abused,' I pointed out. 'It will take a long time for her to recover from that.'

'You think that's what it is?'

'Yes.'

'But why run away? This is her home. She's been offered counselling, but she doesn't want it.'

'What happened to make her leave?' I asked. 'School?'

'No, I don't think so. To be honest, I'm not sure. We had a police officer here yesterday. Mel Robinson, from the Child Abuse Investigation Team. But Ashleigh didn't seem worried by it. She'd already met the officer when she was at her foster carer's and she was very pleasant. She wasn't here for long and asked Ashleigh to confirm a few things in her statement. As I say Ashleigh didn't seem upset by her visit and couldn't really add any more than she'd already told them. I wondered if that had triggered something, but she seemed fine after they'd gone. She had an early night and then must have left during the night. When I went into her room to wake her for school I found her gone.'

'Perhaps it is to do with school,' I suggested.

'Maybe. I don't know.' He sighed. 'But why not talk to me about it, instead of running away and causing me all this worry? The police officer they sent this morning asked about Ashleigh's boyfriends, but as far as I know she isn't seeing anyone. Do you know if she is?'

'No. Sorry, I don't know.'

'Perhaps her mother or Janet has been able to tell them something,' he said. 'But this isn't going to help our application for Ashleigh to stay with me permanently. She hasn't thought about that. She's telling the social worker she wants to live with me and then clears off! What will they think? Anyway, I won't keep you. Please call me if you do hear from Ashleigh.'

'Yes, of course, I will.'

As the call ended I wondered if Mel's visit had anything to do with the conversation I'd had with her, but why it should result in Ashleigh running away I had no idea.

I tried Ashleigh's mobile number, but as her father had said her phone was switched off. I tried again before I left for school to collect Angie and Polly, but it was still off. I didn't tell the girls Ashleigh was missing. I didn't see any reason to. They were very young, hadn't seen Ashleigh for two months and didn't have a close bond with her. Whether their mother told them was up to her.

When we phoned Selina that afternoon she sounded utterly wretched, I assumed from the additional worry of Ashleigh now being missing, although she didn't mention it to the girls. As usual she didn't want to talk to me and today her conversation with the girls was very short. She asked them about school and if they were doing their homework and that was it, really.

'I think Mummy is unhappy,' Angie said.

'Yes,' I agreed. 'Hopefully she'll feel better tomorrow.'

I called Ashleigh's phone again that evening, but it was still off. Had she answered I would have tried to find out what was wrong and persuade her to contact someone to let them know where she was. It was possible she'd already been found. I wouldn't have been told as a matter of course, as I wasn't fostering her. Once Angie and Polly were in bed I texted Trevor: *Is there any news of Ashleigh?*

No, came his immediate reply.

I tried Ashleigh's phone again before I went to bed and it was still off. Although Ashleigh wasn't my responsibility,

I was concerned for her as I would be for any child or young person I knew who was missing.

When I woke the following morning I called her phone again and it was switched on, although she didn't answer. I left a voicemail message: 'It's Cathy, Angie and Polly's carer. Can you let me or your father know you're safe, please?' It was only 7 a.m.

I checked my phone every so often as I helped the girls get ready for school. Then before we left I texted her father: *Any news about Ashleigh? Her phone is switched on now. I left her a message.*

I took the girls to school and returned home, having not heard anything from Ashleigh or Trevor, then shortly after 10 a.m. he phoned. 'She's been found,' he said, immensely relieved.

'Thank goodness she's safe,' I said.

'She was at the home of her old boyfriend. I don't know the details yet. Ashleigh was too tired to talk last night and just wanted to go to bed. It was three o'clock before we were home, so I'm leaving her to sleep in.'

'The police found her?' I asked.

'No. The parents of the boyfriend insisted she phoned me to let me know she was safe.'

'That was sensible of them.'

'Yes. I went over and collected her straight away.'

'Have you told the police she's been found.'

'Yes. Thank you so much for your concern. You can't imagine how relieved I am she's been found safely. But I still need to talk to her about what's wrong and why she ran away.'

'Give her my love,' I said, and we said goodbye.

I was relieved too and hoped that Ashleigh would be

able to confide in her father and tell him what was wrong. Trevor Masters came across as reasonable, kind and caring, unlike the ex-husband Selina had portrayed. I guessed that was a result of an acrimonious divorce and not being able to work together over matters connected with Ashleigh.

We had contact that afternoon and it was still being held in the play area at the rear of the Family Centre, weather permitting, so I didn't see Selina at the start, only at the end. As usual she said the bare minimum to me, although I always said hello and asked her how she was, to which she usually shrugged or nodded. I assumed she'd been told Ashleigh had been found, although it was impossible to tell from her demeanour. She didn't look relieved or upset, just numb. It seemed to me she was shutting down in order to cope. I also noticed that her limp was worse. Perhaps she was in pain or taking stronger medication and that was the reason she seemed distant and robot-like. I didn't know, and she certainly wouldn't have appreciated me asking her. The days when we'd talked as we'd walked to the park were long gone. Usually the foster carer's relationship with the child's parents improves with time, but ours had deteriorated.

That evening Janet telephoned with the news that Ashleigh had been found.

'Yes, I know, thank goodness,' I said.

'How do you know?' she asked.

'Trevor Masters told me.'

'Do you know why she ran away?'

'No.'

'I think I might phone him and ask. I'm sure that girl is hiding something. I thought so while she was living with me.'

'I don't really think it's appropriate to phone him,' I said. 'She's home, that's all that matters. You're not her foster carer any longer so there's no reason for you to know.'

'Apart from curiosity,' Janet said.

'Exactly.'

Whether she did phone Trevor Masters or not I don't know.

The rest of the week ran smoothly, then on Friday something happened that was to eventually change everything, although I didn't know it at the time.

CHAPTER TWENTY-SIX

I'VE BEEN SO STUPID ...

Friday was another blustery autumn day. Contact was still being held outside to minimize the spread of coronavirus, and as usual a member of staff took Angie and Polly in through the side gate. I walked to the local shop to buy a few groceries, then I returned to the centre and sat in my car until it was five o'clock and time to collect the girls. I rang the security bell and waited for Selina, Angie and Polly to be let out. Normally they all appeared together, but today Angie and Polly came out first with the contact supervisor. Selina followed, phone pressed to her ear.

'She's just had to take an important call,' the supervisor told me. Which was slightly unusual, as phone calls were discouraged during contact. She stood aside to let Selina out and closed the gate behind her.

I took the girls' hands and we began towards my car as Selina followed, still on her phone but listening rather than talking. She said 'yes' a few times and then, 'I don't know.'

'We need to say goodbye to Mummy,' Angie said as I opened the car door for them to get in.

'You will, as soon as she's finished on the phone,' I said.

I helped them into their seats and fastened their belts, which Selina normally did.

'We haven't kissed Mummy goodbye,' Polly said.

'You will.'

I waited by the open car door for Selina to finish her phone call and say goodbye to the girls.

'We never knew his name,' I heard her say. 'No. I see.' She was silent and then said, 'I'll tell him now.'

Ending the call, she came to the car and seemed very flustered. 'I need to go,' she said to no one in particular. Then she stood for a few moments, looking around as if unsure what to do next. Clearly whatever the call had been about had deeply affected her. Good or bad news, it was difficult to tell, but the silent, withdrawn lethargy I'd seen in her in the past had gone, replaced by a heightened state of alert.

'I've got to go,' she said to the girls, suddenly leaning into the car. 'I'll speak to you tomorrow.' Quickly kissing them, she straightened and hurried to her car.

I closed the rear door and by the time I'd got into the driver's seat Selina had driven away.

'Mummy didn't wave,' Angie said.

'No, love, I think she's in a hurry. We'll phone her tomorrow. I thought we might go to the cinema in the morning,' I added to distract them as I drove off.

'Yes, I want to go,' Angie said.

'Me too,' Polly agreed.

'Excellent.'

Later, Angie asked why her mother had been in such a hurry and I said I didn't know, but that there was nothing for her to worry about. I could understand why it was playing on her mind given Selina's abrupt change in behaviour after taking the phone call.

The following morning I texted Ashleigh saying I hoped she and her father were well and reminding her to phone Angie and Polly when she had the chance. She didn't reply.

Paula came with us to the children's Saturday-morning cinema, which made it even more of an occasion for Angie and Polly. They loved it when she came on outings or played with them. In the afternoon Lucy, Darren and Emma dropped by for a couple of hours, which was great. After they'd gone I waited until 5 p.m. to phone Selina. Although it wasn't a school day, it made sense to keep to the same time so we all knew where we were.

I went out of the living room to make the call. As it rang I briefly wondered what sort of mood Selina would be in, and if she'd recovered from yesterday's shock, whatever it might have been. To my surprise she wanted to talk to me. 'Sorry I rushed off yesterday, but I needed to speak to my husband quickly.' She sounded upbeat and positive.

'That's all right,' I said.

'There's been a development,' she continued. 'The police were trying to contact Tim, but he wasn't answering his phone. We've finally got the evidence we need to prove Tim is innocent!' I could hear the excitement and relief in her voice.

'Really?'

'Yes. Ashleigh's boyfriend, Freddie, has told the police he was with Ashleigh on the night she claims Tim raped her. I've been telling the police all along Tim was with me, but they didn't believe me until now. Now they have the evidence they need.'

'Why didn't her boyfriend tell the police this before?' I asked.

'He thought he would be in trouble because they were having underage sex. But after Ashleigh ran away from her father and he fetched her back, Freddie told his mother and she took him to the police station where he made a statement.'

'I see. So have the police dropped all the charges against Tim?' I asked.

'Not yet, but they will. We're planning to have Polly and Angie home on Monday, as soon as we've spoken to our solicitor.'

'You haven't spoken to him yet then?'

'No, it was too late yesterday. Their office was closed.'

'Does Fatima know what's happened?'

'Not yet. She had gone home too. So we'll phone them first thing on Monday morning and we'll pick up the girls in the afternoon. Maybe straight from school. You aren't saying much. Aren't you pleased for us?'

'Yes, of course, but I wouldn't tell Angie and Polly yet.'

'Why ever not?'

'These things can take time. Has Ashleigh admitted she lied?'

'I've no idea. I haven't spoken to her. But we're not waiting any longer. The police have the evidence they need to show Tim is innocent, so the girls can come home.'

But I feared this wasn't going to be as quick and straightforward as Selina hoped. From what she said the police hadn't dropped the charges, and what about all the other times Ashleigh was claiming Tim had abused her? Was she with her boyfriend then too? Also, Polly and Angie were now the subject of care orders, unlike when they'd first come into care when it had been a voluntary agreement – a Section 20. Now a court order would be needed to return them home, which would mean their legal team putting together a case and presenting it to the judge. As of yet they weren't even aware of this new development. It also crossed my mind that Ashleigh's boyfriend had possibly made this up. Not likely, but the police would need to verify what he was saying. And last but not least, before the girls were returned home the social services would need to be satisfied they would be safe there, which wouldn't happen overnight. Imagine the outcry and lasting damage to the girls if they were returned and Tim abused them.

'I think it could take a while to sort out. So best not tell Angie and Polly,' I said again.

But that wasn't what Selina wanted to hear, and the first thing she said to the girls was, 'I've got some really, really good news for you. You know I had to rush off yesterday, well, it was because I had just heard that we have the evidence we need to prove your daddy didn't hurt Ashleigh. You and I knew that all the time, but we had to prove it and now we can!'

Angie and Polly didn't know what to say, and Selina continued to tell them what she'd just told me.

'Selina, I really think you need to talk about something else,' I said.

'Why? Don't you want them to come home?'

'Of course I do, but we don't know for certain when that will happen.'

'I do. They're coming home on Monday.'

I appreciated that all the weeks of stress had taken their toll on Selina and now there was a glimmer of hope she was grasping it. But this wasn't good for the girls. Standing, I took the phone off speaker and left the room.

Out of the girls' earshot, I said, 'Angie and Polly might not come home on Monday and if they don't after you've promised, they are likely to be very disappointed and upset. Better to play it safe for now and talk about something else.'

'I'll talk to them about whatever I want,' she replied.

'Selina, I have been asked to monitor phone contact. If it becomes upsetting for the girls then I will have to stop it.'

'Not for much longer,' she snapped. 'OK. Have it your way. Put them back on and I'll talk about something else.'

But of course the damage was done.

'Are we staying here or living with you?' Angie asked her mother, confused.

'You're staying there for the weekend,' Selina said, then she asked what they'd been doing today. But their minds were on other things and they kept returning to them going home and didn't have anything to say about the cinema or any of the other things they'd been doing that day, despite me prompting them.

As they said goodbye Angie asked, 'Are we coming home soon?'

'Yes,' Selina replied.

After they'd finished on the phone I tried to explain that when children in care returned home it often took many days, sometimes weeks, to arrange, and I'd tell them as soon as I had any details, but for now we'd carry on as normal. They were very unsettled for the rest of the evening, and I answered their questions and comments as best I could. I quietly explained to Paula what Selina had said. Having had plenty of experience of children leaving us – either to return home or move to permanency – she shared my scepticism about anything happening on Monday. That evening, when I wrote up my log notes, I included what Selina had told me and her daughters, as I was expected to.

On Sunday the girls wanted to make cards for their mummy and daddy, which I helped them with. Then Paula baked cakes with them. We went for a walk in the afternoon, but they were still unsettled and kept asking if it was time to phone their mother yet, as they had done when they'd first arrived.

When it was 5 p.m. I made the call away from them. I told Selina they were unsettled and asked her not to talk to them about going home on Monday.

'I won't,' she said curtly. 'But I don't know why they should be unsettled. This is their home.'

'They've been with me for over two and a half months,' I said. 'That's a long time in a young child's life.'

I heard her sigh. She clearly didn't agree with me, but when she spoke to them she kept off the subject of them going home and deflected their questions as best she could. At the end, when she said, 'See you tomorrow,' they assumed she meant at home. I had to explain it was more likely to be for an hour at the Family Centre.

* * *

That evening I emailed Fatima an update and asked for clarification about what was happening tomorrow so I could tell the girls. I assumed she'd read the email first thing on Monday morning.

The following morning I took the girls to school as normal, then said goodbye and that I'd see them at the end of the day. I didn't hear anything from Fatima and I was becoming increasingly concerned as the day passed. Sometimes information doesn't always reach the foster carer when it should. Having still not heard anything half an hour before I had to leave to collect the girls from school, I telephoned Fatima.

'Is contact going ahead this afternoon?' I asked.

'Yes, why shouldn't it?'

'Did you receive my email?'

'About?'

'What Ashleigh's boyfriend is saying.'

'Oh, yes, that. Goodness knows why Selina thought Angie and Polly would be going home today. It won't affect contact. I need to speak to her. It's on my to-do list. I'd better phone her now.'

I collected the girls from school.

'Are we seeing Mummy?' Angie asked me.

'Yes, love, at the Family Centre as usual.'

'We're not going home?'

'No, love.'

'I like seeing Mummy,' Polly said, happily.

I smiled. 'Good.'

When we arrived Selina's car wasn't in the car park as it usually was.

'She must be a bit late,' I said as we went up the path.

The member of staff who let us in the side gate said Selina had phoned to say she was on her way and asked me to wait with Angie and Polly until she arrived. It was the first time I'd ever known her to be late for contact. The contact supervisor was in the play area too, and Angie and Polly rode on the tricycles that had been put out. Selina arrived fifteen minutes late and it was clear she'd been crying. Subdued and downcast, she didn't acknowledge me and went straight to the girls and hugged them. I called goodbye and left. When I returned to collect them at the end Selina was no better. Ignoring me, she took the girls to my car and then concentrated on getting them in before saying goodbye.

'Are you all right?' I asked her, concerned, after she'd closed their car door.

'No,' she said, and went to her car.

But she did remember to wave as we both drove away.

'Mummy was sad,' Angie said in the car.

'Oh dear. I am sorry. I hope she is better soon.'

'It's because we can't go home,' Angie said.

I nodded and assumed it had been talked about at contact.

Once home, I bathed the girls and then we ate. After dinner I heard Angie read, and Paula read them both a story before I took them up to bed. They seemed to be over the upset of not going home, and back into our routine. They hadn't mentioned it all evening. I am continually amazed by children's resilience and their ability to pick up the pieces of their lives and carry on. I kissed them goodnight and gave them a hug, then, leaving the light on low, left them to go off to sleep.

Downstairs I made a mug of tea and took it into the

living room where I checked my phone. There was a missed call from Ashleigh, but she hadn't left a message. I assumed she was phoning to speak to her sisters, so I texted: *Angie and Polly are in bed now. Can they speak to you tomorrow a bit earlier?* I was pleased she'd finally called to talk to them and was sorry we'd missed her call.

A few minutes later my phone sounded with a text message. It was from Ashleigh: *It was you I wanted to speak to.*

Odd I thought, but one thing I'd learnt from being a parent and from years of fostering is that if a child or young person wants to talk to you then you make yourself available and listen, whether they are your child or not.

I'm free now. Shall I call you? I texted back.

No reply, then my phone rang and Ashleigh's number showed on the display. I silenced the television as I answered her call.

'Hello, love. How are you?'

'Not good,' she said, her voice low and flat.

'What's the matter? Are you at your father's?'

'Yes, but he doesn't know I'm phoning you. I'm in my room and he's downstairs watching television.'

'What's the problem?'

Silence, then, 'I'm in a lot of trouble and I don't know what to do.'

'Can you talk to your father about it?'

'No. He'll be so angry.'

'What is it? Can you tell me? Although he will need to know.'

More silence and then I heard her sobbing.

'I've been so stupid ...' and her voice trailed off.

CHAPTER TWENTY-SEVEN

A FAMILY TORN APART

The line was still open and I could hear Ashleigh crying quietly. I waited for her to recover enough to talk. I assumed she was going to tell me about her boyfriend going to the police, but I could have been wrong.

Eventually she sniffed and said, 'You know I ran away?'

'Yes, love.'

'I went to Freddie's house. He was my boyfriend.'

'OK.'

'But his mother phoned my dad and he came and got me.'

'Yes.'

'Then, after I'd gone, Freddie told his mother that I'd made up all the stuff about Tim raping me, and she took him to the police station and he told them.' So Selina had been right, on this count at least.

'And did you make it up?' I asked.

'Yes,' Ashleigh replied in a small voice. 'The police want to see me again, but Dad doesn't know. He is going to hate me when he finds out. I'll have no one. I don't know what to do.' Her voice caught as she stifled another sob.

I tried to remain calm and objective. Ashleigh needed help and advice, not condemnation.

'Your father won't hate you, but he needs to know,' I said. 'He's going to be upset and annoyed, but from what I know of him I'm sure he'll do the right thing and stand by you. He phoned me the night you went missing, and he was very worried. But you do need to be honest with him and the police.'

'I made it all up,' Ashleigh said in the same trembling voice. 'All the things I said about Tim sexually abusing me were lies. He never did any of those things. I don't like him and he doesn't like me. He was always going on at me, but he never touched me like that. I just wanted to leave home and live with Dad, but I can't tell the police that.' Her voice broke as she stifled a sob.

I took a deep breath. 'You have to tell them. Tim has been unfairly accused of a shocking crime, one of the worst. His life and your mother's are in ruins. If what you are saying is true then Angie and Polly are in care need-lessly.'

'It is true,' she blurted. 'Tim never touched me, I swear. I think that policewoman knew I was lying. She came here and asked me more questions. That's why I ran away. I never meant for Angie and Polly to go into care. I thought it would just be me that could leave home, which is what I wanted.'

I chose my next words very carefully.

'Ashleigh, you've made a big error of judgement, but now you can start to put it right. You have to tell your father and the police what you have told me.'

'Will I be in a lot of trouble?' she asked.

The short answer was yes.

'You have caused your family a lot of anguish and heartache, but you can begin to put it right by telling the truth and apologizing.' There was also the matter of perverting the course of justice and wasting police time, for which she could be prosecuted, but I didn't say that.

'It was Dad who gave me the idea,' Ashleigh then said. 'Not that I'm blaming him.'

'What do you mean, he gave you the idea?' I asked, a new fear gripping me.

'I'd been wanting to live with him for a long time and he wanted me to, but Mum and Tim wouldn't let me. Dad and I were talking about it one time and he said, "If you accused him of abuse they'd have you here quick enough." I know he didn't mean it, but it gave me the idea. So I said Tim raped me, and abused me at other times to make it convincing.'

I swallowed hard.

'So none of it was true?' I asked, wanting to be sure.

'No. It was all lies. It's true that Tim and I don't like each other, but he never touched me like that.'

I was quiet for a moment, trying to come to terms with the enormity of what Ashleigh was telling me. I could have cried out and been so angry for everything she'd put her poor family through – and indeed was still going through. I remembered Polly's and Angie's distress when they'd first arrived, Selina's raw anguish as someone who'd lost everything. I could hear her thinly masked heartbreak when she spoke to the girls on the phone and struggled to hold it together for their sakes. But it was no use being angry with Ashleigh and risk her closing down or running away again. She needed to do the right thing and admit what she'd done. Taking a breath, I kept my tone even.

'Ashleigh, the first step to putting all this right is to tell your father, then he will be able to support you when you see the police.'

'I can't!' she cried desperately. 'I know I've let him down. Can you tell him? Please.'

'It would be better coming from you.'

'I can't. Really, I can't.'

'All right. Calm down. I'll speak to him, but he's going to want to talk to you after.'

'Yes, I can do that, but I just can't bring myself to tell him. I've been hiding up in my room all evening.'

'Is there anything else he needs to be told when I speak to him?' I asked.

'No. Oh, yes. You'd better tell him I was never pregnant when I said I was at Janet's. I said it to stop her going on at me. And she looked after me OK. I just didn't want to be there.'

'So you made that up too?'

'Yes.'

'I'll tell Fatima. Janet was very upset at the way you left. Anything else you want to tell me while you have the chance?' I asked, wondering if there was no end to this girl's deceptions. She clearly had little idea of the misery she'd caused.

'No, honestly. That's all. Will you tell him now, please?'

'Yes.'

'I'm staying in my bedroom until you do.'

'All right. I'll phone him now.'

My stomach churned as I ended the call. I couldn't believe how stupid, irresponsible and selfish Ashleigh had been. It seemed the lies just tripped off her tongue when it suited her. How could she not have realized what she was doing by making all those false allegations? She'd ripped her family apart and crushed her mother.

Of course her father was going to be angry and very disappointed in her. I would have preferred to tell him in person, but it was late now and he lived an hour's drive away. I drank my now-cold tea and then pressed Trevor's number. He answered immediately.

'It's Cathy Glass.'

'Yes, hello, everything OK?' he asked, surprised to hear from me.

'Not really. Trevor, I need to talk to you. It's something very important. Have the police been in touch with you recently?'

'Not since they came here to see Ashleigh the night she ran away.'

'And you haven't heard from them since?'

'No.'

'So you're not aware that Freddie went to the police station?'

'No. I've had a couple of missed calls from a private number, but no one left a message. Why? What's the problem?' he asked, anxiety in his voice.

'After you collected Ashleigh from Freddie's home the night she ran away, he told his mother that what Ashleigh had said about Tim was a lie.'

'Why would he say that?' he asked naively.

'Because it *was* a lie. Tim didn't rape or sexually abuse Ashleigh. She made it up. She's just telephoned me from her bedroom and admitted it, and has asked me to tell you.'

I heard the silence and could picture his shock and incomprehension.

'Trevor, are you still there?'

'Yes.'

'Ashleigh asked me to tell you because she's worried you'll be angry with her.'

'With good reason!' he said, his voice rising. 'I can't believe what you're telling me. She made it up?'

'Yes, but it's not going to help, being angry. She knows she's done wrong. Now she needs to start trying to put it right.'

'I can't believe this,' he said again. 'Yet I knew there was something wrong with her when she first arrived. What a fucking mess! So none of it's true?' he asked incredulously.

'No. She says Tim never touched her sexually at all. They didn't get on, but he didn't sexually abuse her. She also said she was never pregnant as she claimed while she was at Janet's, and that all the bad things she said about her carer were made up.'

'Jesus! Why?'

'So she could live with you. She's just told me that one time you were talking about her living with you, and you said that if she claimed Tim had abused her they'd move her quickly.'

'My God! I might have said something like that, but I never meant for her to take it seriously and do it. I don't like the guy, but to say that when it wasn't true! I wouldn't wish that on my worst enemy. He's lost his own kids because of her. The poor sod.'

'Yes,' I said.

'Does anyone else know?'

'Selina is aware that Freddie went to the police station with his mother and told the police he was with Ashleigh on the night she claimed Tim raped her, but I don't know the details or what else he said. There's a chance one of the officers who came to see you may already have had some suspicion. Ashleigh thought so – that's why she ran away after their visit.'

'And Ashleigh has told you all this?'

'Yes, just now. She's waiting in her bedroom until I've finished.'

'What a fucking nightmare. I'm still struggling to believe she'd do something like this.' He paused and I heard his heartfelt sigh. 'I suppose I'd better phone my ex and tell her that Ashleigh has admitted to lying.'

'I'd be inclined to let the police deal with it,' I suggested. Feelings would be running high, and Tim and Trevor had already had one fight. 'I think talk to Ashleigh and then tell the police.'

'I really can't believe she would stoop so low,' he said. 'All those lies and the problems she's caused.'

'I know. I don't think she realized the repercussions. She told me she didn't think Angie and Polly would be taken into care.'

'That's the trouble with Ashleigh. She doesn't think! What's to stop her making up allegations against me if she doesn't get her own way? She's done it to Tim and that foster carer. I could be next.'

Which of course was a real fear.

'Right. I'd better calm down before I speak to her,' he said.

'Let me know if I can be of any help. But she does need to tell the police as soon as possible.'

'Yes, I know.'

We said goodbye and I stayed where I was, sitting on the sofa. I hoped I'd done the right thing in telling Trevor, but Ashleigh had asked me to, and he was her father and guardian so he needed to know. So often in fostering we have to make decisions that aren't in any training manual. He was clearly upset and annoyed, understandably, but would he be able to support Ashleigh through whatever lay ahead?

My thoughts then went to Selina and her unfailing support and loyalty for Tim. As far as I knew she had never doubted him. My eyes filled. That poor woman. She'd been through hell. Her husband had been accused of a heinous crime by her eldest daughter, resulting in her losing all her children into care. How quickly this could now be put right I didn't know, and it crossed my mind to phone Selina, but I decided against it. I'd leave it to Fatima and the police to deal with. What I needed to do was type up my log notes while it was all still fresh in my mind as it could be needed in evidence, especially if Ashleigh changed her story again.

I sat at my computer in the front room and typed, using Ashleigh's words as much as possible. I included not only what she'd told me about Tim, but about Janet too. There was a lot to include, and I was typing for nearly an hour. It was important I got it right and included the details. My notes would be read by Fatima and possibly the police and judge too. I read through them and, satisfied, emailed the update to Fatima so she'd have it first thing in the morning.

I went to bed that night with my head full of Ashleigh and deeply saddened by her behaviour. I understood that teenagers could be impulsive and she'd been unhappy living with her mother and stepfather, but there were other ways to address it. Discussing how she felt with them would have been a good start, and if that hadn't worked then she could have talked to another responsible adult she trusted. There was her maternal grandmother, who she'd been close to at one time, or a teacher – all schools offer pastoral care – or she could have confided in a doctor or church minister. If all that failed then as a last resort she could have gone to the social services and asked to be taken into care. There were so many other options apart from unjustly accusing Tim.

Of course I found it difficult to sleep that night, and the following morning I woke early still thinking about Ashleigh and the family she'd torn apart. I tried to concentrate on Angie and Polly and getting them ready for school, but what that poor family were going through was never far from my mind. I checked Paula was up and then made breakfast. I hadn't heard anything from Trevor or Ashleigh, so I didn't know if they'd contacted the police last night or were waiting until this morning. I took the girls to school and by 9.30 a.m., as I was driving home, I assumed Fatima had read my email.

The day slowly ticked by. I was on tenterhooks wondering what was going on. It was mid-afternoon before Fatima replied to my email. She simply acknowledged it and said she would be in touch. I guessed there was a lot going on, but until I heard anything different I would keep to our routine. I collected the girls from school, brought them home, gave them a drink and snack and then let them watch television. At 5 p.m. I phoned Selina as usual. She didn't want to talk to me and it seemed she didn't know of the latest development. I sat on the sofa with the girls, phone on speaker, as they spoke to their mother. The conversation lasted about fifteen minutes and Selina finished by saying she'd see them tomorrow.

Paula arrived home from work and we all ate together. Then she played with Polly while I helped Angie with her homework, some of which was online. I took the girls to bed and Paula kissed them goodnight. Once they were settled, I told Paula of Ashleigh's confession. She was as shocked and upset as I was.

'She needs help,' Paula said, meaning counselling or therapy.

'Yes, she does,' I agreed.

The following day, having heard nothing to the contrary, straight after school I took the girls to the Family Centre for contact. Selina's car was already in the car park as it usually was, but it wasn't until I got out that I realized she was still inside it. I assumed she must have arrived slightly later than usual and just ahead of us. Her car door opened and she rushed towards me. For a moment I thought she was going to hit or push me, but then she threw her arms around me and wept on my shoulder.

CHAPTER TWENTY-EIGHT

COURT HEARING

'Thank you, thank you so much,' Selina said as we hugged. Then she drew back. 'Sorry, I shouldn't have hugged you.' She meant because of the risk of transmitting Covid. 'We're going to court on Friday to have Angie and Polly returned,' she said, her eyes spilling tears.

'So Ashleigh has admitted what she's done to the police?'

'Yes. Thanks to you and Freddie.' Her manner was more relief rather than jubilation.

There was a tap on the car window and we both looked at Angie and Polly, who were still in my car as the child lock was on. They were staring worriedly through the window, wondering what was the matter. I opened the door to let them out.

'Don't worry, I'm not telling them yet,' Selina said quietly to me, before wrapping her arms tightly around the girls and hugging them for all she was worth.

She didn't have to tell them; they could see something was going on as their mother couldn't stem her tears.

'Are we going home?' Angie asked.

'Not just yet, love,' Selina said, wiping her eyes. 'But we are hoping it will be soon.' Which both girls accepted. Living with me had become the norm.

I went with them to the main door of the Family Centre, as it was my job to see the girls safely in. Once I'd pressed the security buzzer a member of staff opened the side gate and I said goodbye, adding that I'd see them in an hour. I returned to my car and switched on the radio, relieved and pleased that at last something positive was happening. Five minutes later Fatima phoned.

'Have you taken Polly and Angie to contact?' she asked. For a moment I thought I wasn't supposed to, but no one had told me otherwise.

'Yes, just now. I'm outside.'

'Fine. It's likely to be their last one. We're in court on Friday and we're anticipating that the judge will make an order for Angie and Polly to be returned home. We have no objection and it's unlikely the Guardian will raise any objection. Ashleigh will remain in care. I've talked to Mrs Fletcher and what we're thinking is that Polly and Angie will stay with you Friday night so you can say goodbye, and then you'll move them on Saturday. Video-call Mr and Mrs Fletcher on Friday. It's half-term holiday from school next week so they will have the whole week to resettle at home.'

'That sounds good,' I said. I couldn't stop myself from smiling. 'How is Ashleigh?' I then asked.

'Upset and full of remorse. Which reminds me, I need to speak to Janet's supervising social worker and set the record straight there. Any questions?' she asked, clearly in a hurry.

'I don't think so. I am pleased.'

'I'll phone you once we're out of court on Friday and confirm the move.'

We said goodbye and I rested my head back and closed

my eyes. I was delighted but wouldn't be completely reassured until the judge had made the court order to return Angie and Polly home. The case would be held in the family court responsible for children in care. The allegations against Tim would have been heard in a criminal court, but I assumed that any charges against him had now been dropped or soon would be.

I stayed in my car, the radio playing easy-listening music on low. Thank goodness Freddie had told his mother and then the police, I thought; without him, none of this would have come to light. I was also pleased that I'd raised my concerns with Mel. Her follow-up visit to Ashleigh seemed to have been the catalyst for her running away, which had prompted Freddie to confide in his mother, who'd taken him to the police station. So often in fostering all we have is a little bit of evidence – a chance word spoken by a child – and a gut feeling. I could have so easily ignored what Angie had said about overhearing her parents quarrelling on the night Ashleigh claimed Tim had raped her. Had Fatima placed more emphasis on that, questions about the validity of Ashleigh's claims might have been raised earlier. But she'd been dismissive of my concerns, feeling Angie's comments weren't relevant given her age and the other 'evidence', which turned out to be lies.

At 5 p.m. I got out of my car and went to the side gate of the centre to wait for Selina and the girls to come out. I expected Selina to be in the same positive mood as when she'd gone in, but she came out looking anxious.

'What's the matter?' I asked as we headed for my car.

'I've just had a phone call from the hospital. A bed has become available and the surgeon can operate on my leg on Monday, but I can't accept. I'll be in hospital a week, possibly longer, and there's no visiting due to Covid. I can't not see Angie and Polly when they've just returned home. I'll have to postpone it.'

I could see her problem, although I'd noticed that her limp had been getting worse, despite the stronger pain-killers she was taking.

'It's likely to be months if I miss this chance,' she added, clearly in a dilemma.

'Perhaps discuss it with Tim and Fatima?' I suggested. Fatima should be told.

'I will, but I really can't see a way around it. Tim is back at work. I could have asked my mother to help out, but she has a heart condition now, brought on by all the stress.'

'I am sorry.'

She nodded. 'Ashleigh has a lot to answer for,' she said quietly to me.

'Have you spoken to Ashleigh?'

'No, only to her father. We had a long talk. We should have done that ages ago. I think our animosity allowed Ashleigh to manipulate the situation. I will see her again, but not just yet. It's too raw. We need to get Angie and Polly home and our lives back.'

I opened the car door and Selina saw the girls in, kissed them goodbye and closed the car door. We looked at each other.

'Well, if all goes to plan on Friday, the next time we meet I'll be bringing the girls home,' I said. 'I'll phone tomorrow at the usual time for contact, but Fatima said to video-call you and Tim on Friday.'

'Yes, that's what we've agreed. Give us all a chance to readjust and for you to say goodbye.'

'Thank you.'

We gave each other an elbow bump this time rather than a hug, and Selina returned to her car as I got into mine.

'Mummy was happy today,' Polly said.

'Good.' I smiled.

'She's hoping we'll go home,' Angie said. 'But she's said that before.'

'We'll have to wait and see, but it's not so bad living with me, is it?'

'No,' Angie agreed. 'If we can't go home, can we stay with you?'

'That would be for your social worker to decide, but I'd like that.'

On Thursday I went shopping to buy the girls leaving presents and cards. I chose matching silver bracelets as a memento of their time with us. I also had plenty of photos and their Life Story Books for them to take with them. It's important that children in care or those who have been in care have a record of that period in their lives to supplement their own memories and share with their permanent family.

Once home, I began packing the clothes the girls didn't need and the toys they rarely played with, for there wouldn't be much time on Friday once we got the news. I put the holdalls out of sight in my bedroom as I didn't want their presence unsettling the girls. Had we not had Covid restrictions in place, I would have organized a little leaving party for them, but it would just be Paula, the girls and me on Friday evening so I'd cook their favourite meal and ice some cakes. I'd also arrange for

Adrian, Kirsty, Lucy, Darren and Emma to say goodbye via video call.

As I worked I realized that, possibly for the first time ever, my hopes and happiness for the children leaving outweighed my sense of loss. Of course we would miss the girls, they'd been part of my family, but they should never have been brought into care in the first place. It was right they were going home, and it should be as soon as possible.

When we phoned Selina after school she was anxious and wanted to speak to me first. 'Our solicitor says it's an open-and-shut case,' she said. 'But I won't believe it until I hear the judge tell us we can take Polly and Angie home.'

'I'll be thinking of you,' I said, and prayed nothing would go wrong.

Selina hid her worries as best she could from the girls and talked about other things, including their day at school. She also told them what their daddy was doing – the first time she'd mentioned Tim in a long while, although he didn't talk to Angie and Polly; perhaps he'd been advised not to for now. I thought there was going to be a massive readjustment in their household when the girls returned home.

Selina had said they were in court first thing on Friday morning, so as I was driving the girls to school I thought they would be on their way now. I could imagine how nervous they were feeling. It's daunting going to court, especially with so much at stake. Selina's solicitor believed it would be an 'open-and-shut case'; even so, from what I knew I thought it was likely to take up most of the day. I just hoped it wasn't adjourned or postponed, as I'd known happen in other child-care cases, usually because a document or report that should have been before the judge hadn't arrived.

I was surprised and concerned when at 12 noon Fatima phoned.

'We've just come out of court,' she said. 'There's a problem.'

'Oh no, what?' I gasped, and my stomach clenched.

'The judge has made the order, the girls will be going home, but not straight away. I need to run something past you.'

'Yes?' I asked, my heart pounding as I wondered what she was going to say.

'Mrs Fletcher has to have an urgent operation on her leg. She has been advised that if she postpones it any longer she is like to do irreversible long-term damage. Her mother can't look after Angie and Polly, and Mr Fletcher will be in work for most of the week. The girls are settled with you, so could you keep them until Selina is out of hospital?'

'Yes, of course,' I said, relieved that this was all. 'Selina wants me to?'

'Yes. It's the best option. The girls will go home for the weekend, so take them as planned on Saturday morning – you can arrange the time with Mr and Mrs Fletcher. Then collect them on Sunday evening. Mrs Fletcher wants to phone the girls from hospital each day, and Tim will phone too. He wants to see them on Wednesday and has taken the day off work, but he's asked for you to stay. You can arrange the time and place between yourselves.'

'All right.'

'I'll let Joy know what's happening, and can you tell Angie and Polly? I won't have time to get to see them today. I'll phone next week.'

'Yes, I'll tell them,' I said.

Cheered and reassured, I felt my pulse gradually settle, although I wondered why Tim wanted me to stay when he saw the girls on Wednesday. I put away their leaving presents and cards for now, but I would still cook their favourite dinner as I'd planned. It could be a celebratory meal, rather than their leaving do. On a high, I texted my family's WhatsApp group to let them know. I couldn't wait to tell Angie and Polly the good news.

I told them as soon as they came out of school.

'We're going to video-call your mummy and daddy today and then you are going home tomorrow for the weekend. I will come and collect you on Sunday evening and you will stay with me while Mummy has her operation, then, once she's well enough to go home, you will too.'

'Why can't we see Mummy?' Angie asked. It was a lot to take in, so I explained it all again, then answered their questions, of which there were many. Eventually they understood and were, of course, delighted.

Once home, I bathed the girls and changed their clothes, then at 5 p.m. I stepped out of the living room to video-call their parents on my tablet. Selina was there ready but looked deep in thought.

'I hope I've made the right decision,' she said. 'I could be in hospital for more than a week.'

'You have — you must have your operation,' I said. 'The girls will be fine here with me. I can keep them for as long as necessary, and you and Tim can phone as often as you like.'

'Thank you. The surgeon told me I should have had the operation years ago and if I left it much longer I'd end up on crutches or in a wheelchair. I don't know what I would have done if you hadn't been able to look after Angie and Polly.'

'Perhaps Tim could have taken more time off work?' I suggested.

'He won't,' she said, frowning. 'Did Fatima ask you to stay with him on Wednesday?'

'Yes. I said I would.'

'Good. He's worried sick that the same thing could happen again. That's why he wants you to stay.'

'You mean, he's worried about another allegation being made?'

'Yes. It will be ages before he feels confident around his children again, if ever. He used to be completely involved and helped me bath the girls and so on, but now he's saying he can't risk being left alone with them in case a chance remark is misinterpreted. This has ruined him. I can't see how he will ever be the same again.'

The poor man, I thought. How utterly dreadful to be made to feel that way through no fault of his own.

I said something reassuring along the lines that once the girls were home hopefully Tim would be able to relax into his role again.

'I hope so,' Selina said.

I took the tablet into the living room. There was no need for me to supervise telephone contact now, but I sat with them anyway, holding the tablet so both Angie and Polly could see.

'Daddy! Daddy!' they cried as Tim appeared and sat beside Selina.

'Hello,' he said, with a broad smile. But I was struck by how gaunt he looked.

I'd only seen Tim briefly before, online and in the photograph the girls had in their bedroom. He was slender then, but now he looked emaciated. His cheeks were sunken and there were dark hollows under his eyes – I assumed from all the worry and stress. Thankfully the girls didn't notice. This was their daddy and that was all that mattered.

To begin with he and the girls weren't sure what to say to each other and Selina had to keep propping up the conversation, but gradually they all relaxed and it became more natural. The girls told him what they'd been doing and about life with me. They were on the phone for nearly an hour and before they said goodbye I arranged with Selina and Tim that I should bring the girls at 10 a.m. tomorrow for their weekend visit. I said I'd also bring some of their belongings that they no longer needed.

As the call ended I heard Paula's key go in the front door. Two very excited girls ran down the hall to greet her, babbling about seeing their daddy and going home. I explained the arrangements to Paula and she was pleased for them. Angie and Polly wanted to go upstairs with her, then waited on the landing while she washed and changed out of her office clothes. Then they all came down for dinner. It was the girls' favourite meal – fish fingers, chips and beans, followed by jelly, ice cream and the cupcakes I'd iced. We also had lemonade in wine glasses to celebrate their good news.

After dinner they wanted to play games, so it was 'like a party', Angie said. Paula and I played with them until nearly 9 p.m., when we took them up to bed. They were tired out and fell asleep immediately. Paula and I kissed them goodnight and returned downstairs where we sat in the living room with mugs of tea and reminisced. The distressing circumstances in which Angie and Polly had arrived; how much they'd missed their parents before they'd gradually settled in; the nice outings we'd had; Polly starting school, then discovering they should never have been in care as the allegations against Tim were false. We talked about it all. Paula was aware that sometimes children in care make unfounded allegations against their carer and the devastation that can bring. Often carers stop fostering as a result, even when the allegation has been shown to be untrue. Foster carers have a 'safer caring policy', which aims to protect all family members, but if an allegation is made it's very difficult to disprove it, just as Janet and Tim had found.

We wondered if perhaps in some cases too much emphasis was placed on the young person's claims. I remembered Selina saying there was very little evidence against Tim, only what Ashleigh was saying, and that her statement gave few details. She'd said the medical report was inconclusive, that Ashleigh had had sex that night, but there was no trace of Tim's DNA. Neither was there any trace of his DNA or semen on her underwear or the bedsheets the police had taken away. Should the case against Tim have been thrown out sooner? We didn't know.

But on the other hand, what is the alternative if an allegation is made? That an abused child who has finally found the courage to speak out isn't believed? It's difficult, and clearly each case is different, but unfounded allegations ruin lives.

CHAPTER TWENTY-NINE

A BROKEN MAN

The following morning the girls were up early. Polly said she had a tummy ache, which I put down to nervous excitement. It went after she'd had some breakfast. I put the bags I was taking into the car and Paula waved us off at the door. The girls chatted excitedly as I drove but fell silent when I turned into their road and parked outside their house. The last time they'd been here was on that fraught night when they'd been taken from their home in tears.

'All right?' I asked them, turning in my seat.

They nodded but didn't say a word. Then the front door opened and their parents appeared.

'Mummy! Daddy!' they cried.

I quickly got out and opened the rear door and they ran down the path. 'Mummy! Daddy!' They couldn't believe their eyes.

Tim scooped them up and held them tightly. His eyes were tightly shut and his face creased with emotion as he was finally able to hold his children again. I thought there must have been many times in the past when he'd believed this moment would never come. As they hugged each other I quietly took the bags from the car and carried them up the path.

I was invited in for coffee and stayed for about an hour. To begin with the girls were cautious and not sure what to do. Then, with Selina's encouragement, they rediscovered their toys and bedroom and began to feel at home again. I noticed that Tim was taking his cue from Selina and spent a lot of time just looking at his daughters as if he couldn't believe they were actually there. When it was time for me to go I wished them a nice weekend and arranged with Selina to return on Sunday evening around six o'clock to collect Angie and Polly. She had to be up early on Monday morning to go to the hospital.

It was a strange weekend for Paula and me. The girls hadn't gone – indeed, we weren't sure for certain when they would be leaving – but they weren't here. The house was very quiet, and we suddenly found time to do those little jobs we'd been meaning to do for a long while. Looking after two young children is wonderful, but it is full-on. We visited Lucy, Darren and Emma on Saturday afternoon; Adrian and Kirsty were busy, so later we video-called them. Saturday evening Paula and I watched a film together, but by Sunday afternoon we were looking forward to seeing Angie and Polly again. I couldn't begin to imagine what their parents had felt like when they weren't seeing them.

Paula came with me and met Tim and Selina for the first time. As expected, the girls were reluctant to leave, wanting to stay at home, so we had to explain that that wasn't possible as Daddy would be at work and Mummy was going into hospital to have an operation.

'We'll phone each day,' I told them. 'And you're seeing Daddy on Wednesday.'

'Three sleeps,' Paula said, and Tim smiled.

'Tomorrow we're going to a farm to see lots of animals,' I added.

'That'll be fun,' Selina said encouragingly. 'You can tell me all about it when we speak on the phone.'

'And me,' Tim said. 'I'm home about six so any time after that.'

Parting was just as difficult for Tim and Selina as it was for the girls, but together we encouraged them into the car and they said goodbye, although they looked very sad.

'Good luck for tomorrow,' I told Selina. 'Phone when you feel up to it.'

'I will,' she replied, and shivered.

She was obviously anxious – it was a big operation – and Tim put his arm around her.

'Wave,' Paula told the girls as I drove away.

They did, and the last image we had was of Tim with his arm around his wife and them both waving until we were out of sight.

It was a pity Paula wasn't able to take time off work during the half-term break, but I had something planned each day for the girls. On Monday we went to the farm, which was about a thirty-minute drive away. I had my phone with me the whole time, but only Joy called. I assumed Selina was being operated on or drowsy from the anaesthetic. The girls enjoyed themselves. It was a full day out, although they were looking forward to speaking to their parents. I video-called Tim at six o'clock and he said that Selina had only just come out of surgery, but the operation had gone to plan. He spoke to the girls and reassured them that their mother was all right but still very sleepy, so she'd phone them as soon as she could.

On Tuesday I took them to an activity centre, although some of it was still closed due to Covid restrictions. As we ate the picnic lunch I'd brought with us Selina video-called my phone. She was propped up on a mound of pillows in a hospital bed and looked pale, but she was happy to see the girls. They were worried, having never seen anyone in hospital before.

'My teacher had an operation last year,' Angie told her mother seriously.

'I remember,' Selina said. 'Your class made her a "get well soon" card. So where are you now?'

'At an activity centre,' Angie replied.

'Are you having a good time?'

'When are you going home?' Angie asked.

'I'm not sure yet, love. Probably in a week,' Selina replied. 'They are going to get me up tomorrow.'

'Can't you get up?' Polly asked, even more worried.

'Not by myself, I need some help,' Selina said.

'Do you have to stay in bed all day?' Polly asked, as if it was a punishment.

'For now, to rest my leg, but it will soon get better and then I will be able to do all the things I used to, maybe more.'

'Have you seen Daddy?' Angie wanted to know.

'I video-called him. I'll speak to him again later. Enjoy the rest of your day and I'll call you again when you're home.'

They blew kisses to each other and waved goodbye. But seeing their mother in hospital was both reassuring and worrying for Angie and Polly.

'Why can't she get up?' Angie asked.

'Because she has to rest after the operation.'

'I hope she can get up soon,' Polly said.

'Yes, she will.'

'What have they done to her leg?' Angie asked.

I explained as best I could from what I knew.

Once home, I texted Selina to say we were back and to call when she was ready. I didn't want to phone her in case she was sleeping. A few minutes later she video-called and looked much brighter. Her cheeks had some colour in them, she'd combed her hair and was sitting more upright in bed. She and the girls talked for about twenty minutes; Angie and Polly had lots of question about the operation and what it was like being in hospital.

I waited until after dinner to phone Tim to make sure he was home from work. He hadn't been in long. He and the girls talked mainly about their mother being in hospital. Tim told them that once she was home she would need a lot of help to begin with and wouldn't be able to drive for some months. He asked them what they would like to do tomorrow when he saw them for the day, and after some thought they decided they just wanted to be at home.

'Sure?' he asked.

'Yes,' Angie said, and Polly nodded.

'Is eleven o'clock all right to bring them?' he asked me. 'That will give me a chance to speak to Selina after the consultant has done his rounds.'

'Yes, that's fine. And you still want me to stay?'

'Yes, please.'

* * *

I took another couple of bags containing the girls' belongings with us on Wednesday. Angie and Polly were very excited to be seeing their father again and spending time at home. Although they knew their mother was in hospital, when we arrived Polly was surprised to find she wasn't there. Tim and I explained that she was in hospital recovering from having her leg mended. The girls decided to go to their bedroom to play. Tim made me a coffee and as we sat in the living room we could hear the girls running around upstairs, jumping off the bed and generally having fun.

'I'm not keeping you from anything, am I?' Tim asked.

'Only the housework,' I said.

He smiled. 'There's not much of that here without the children.' Then his face grew serious. 'Selina explained why I wanted you to stay?'

'Yes. I understand your concerns, but it won't happen again. You don't have to worry.'

He shook his head despondently. 'I can't believe how much Ashleigh must have hated me to say those dreadful things. If I'd had any idea how she felt, I would have done things differently.' He ran his hand over his forehead in anguish. 'Ashleigh was my first experience of being a father and I seemed to do all right when she was young. But as she got older she resented me more and more. I used to do most of the disciplining – you know, tell her off if she was late home or didn't do her schoolwork or was rude to her mother. Maybe that was wrong, but Trevor never told her off, and Ashleigh seemed to be getting out of control.'

'I know it can be difficult bringing up stepchildren, and the teenage years can be challenging anyway. But it's very unusual for a young person to go to the lengths Ashleigh did.'

'I suppose I should find that reassuring,' he said dejectedly.

'It's bound to take time to rebuild your lives,' I said.

'Trevor told Ashleigh to apologize to me, but I don't want anything to do with her. I understand Selina will want to see her, but I'm afraid she'll have to do it without me. I would rather Angie and Polly had nothing to do with her, heartless though that may sound. I know they're half-sisters, but there were times after it happened when I actually thought about suicide. The only thing that stopped me was that I'd be leaving Selina to cope with all this mess alone, and it would have made me appear guilty.' His eyes filled and his mouth drew down as he fought back tears.

'I am sorry,' I said, and waited while he composed himself.

'I thought the arguments Ashleigh and I had were part of normal teenage life – you know, bucking the rules,' he said. 'But she must have hated me so much. She would shout that I wasn't her father and tell me to piss off and worse. I would tell her off and Selina would take my side. We had some dreadful arguments.'

'I know. Angie and Polly overheard an awful lot.'

'I'm sorry they did. I'll have to make it up to them. Goodness knows how, though.'

There was little I could add beyond that I thought time was a great healer. I'm not sure my words were of much comfort. Tim had been to hell and was still finding his way back. While we'd been talking, all the noise upstairs had stopped and it had become mischievously quiet.

'I think maybe check on Angie and Polly,' I suggested. 'It's gone very quiet up there.'

'Yes. Good idea.' He stood. 'Will you come?'

'Sure.'

I went with Tim, but the girls weren't up to mischief. They were lying on their beds and Angie was reading to Polly.

'Good girls,' I said.

'We're downstairs if you want us,' Tim said, and we returned to the living room where he carried on talking. I think he needed to unburden himself.

He talked about the night Ashleigh had accused him, when he'd been taken to the police station, and he'd had to take off his clothes and give samples to be checked by forensics. He said he was in shock and felt like a criminal, although he knew he was innocent. When word got out of what he'd been arrested for some of his neighbours had shunned him and one had called him a pervert.

'It will be the same at school,' he said. 'I'm dreading it. Selina won't be up to taking the girls for some time, so I will have to. My boss has said I can go in late and leave early and then make up the time online at home so I can do the school run.'

I nodded.

'I used to be actively involved in the school. It was a big part of my life, but now I don't even know which classes the girls are in.'

'Angie is in Raven class and Polly is in Robin class,' I said. 'I can write down the start and finish times, although it's all on the school's website. You have to wear a mask when you take and collect them.'

He nodded. 'I just know other parents will be talking about me, pathetic though that sounds.'

'Have you told the Head, Elizabeth Hambridge, you are not being prosecuted as Ashleigh has admitted to making it all up?'

'No, I thought the police would do that.'

'I would tell her just to make sure.'

He gave a small nod. 'I know I've got to start getting my life back and doing the things I used to do, but it's difficult. The thought of going into that playground for the first time when other parents will know what's happened makes me want to run.' He paused thoughtfully and looked at me. 'I don't suppose you'd come with me when I take and collect them on the first day?'

'I can do, if you wish.'

'It would help.'

'OK. I'll be there.'

'Thank you. Whatever must you think of me?'

I thought he was a broken man who needed a lot of support.

We talked some more about other things, and then Tim stood and said he would make us lunch.

'Would you like some help?' I offered, also standing.

'No, I can do this, at least,' he said with a rueful smile. 'Perhaps you could check on Angie and Polly? Tell them lunch will be ready in about twenty minutes.'

'Will do.'

I went up to the girls' bedroom. They were now rummaging in the storage boxes under their beds, which were full of toys and games. I passed on their father's message and then stayed with them as they wanted to show me their toys. When Tim called us for lunch we went down together and into their kitchen-diner where the table was laid with china, cutlery and napkins. I'd been expecting a sandwich lunch, but Tim was setting out a quiche, which looked homemade, boiled new potatoes, peas and a mixed salad.

'That looks delicious,' I said, taking a seat at the table.

'Daddy is a good cook,' Angie said.

'Did you make the quiche?' I asked as Tim joined us.

'Yes, first thing this morning. I just had to heat it up. Cooking is something I can get right. Help yourself.'

The quiche tasted as delicious as it looked, and I told Tim how nice it was more than once. If ever a man needed his confidence rebuilding it was him. We talked about cooking as we ate, and I learnt that he also baked bread and cakes, and did most of the cooking when he was home at the weekends.

'I like Daddy's cooking,' Angie said.

'Me too,' Polly agreed.

'I am sure you do. So do I,' I said.

Tim smiled, pleased.

He'd made individual strawberry mousses topped with fresh strawberries for dessert. Once we'd finished we all helped clear the table and load the dishwasher and then Tim asked me what time I had to leave. I said around four o'clock and suggested we play some board games at the table. I'd seen plenty in the girls' bedroom. I usually involve families in activities like this when I am introducing children to their adoptive parents. It's fun and helps them bond. Tim and his children were re-bonding. The girls were keen and brought down some games, which we played for an hour or so. When Polly said she wanted to go to the toilet Tim asked Angie to go with her. She still needed some help, and Paula or I usually took her at home, but clearly Tim didn't feel comfortable doing that yet.

We played some more games and when it was time to go Tim presented me with a cake tin. 'Thanks for everything,' he said.

I lifted the lid and peered inside. It was a home-made triple-chocolate gateau with piped cream!

'You made it?'

'Yes.'

'Thank you so much,' I said.

'No, thank *you* for everything. I hope you enjoy it.'

'I am sure we will.'

Tim helped get the girls into my car and then waved as I drove away. Once he was out of sight Angie asked me, 'Do you like my daddy?'

'Yes, love.'

'Is he a good daddy?'

'I think so, don't you?' I glanced at her in the rear-view mirror.

She nodded and then smiled. 'I'm glad you like him.'

It was as though she needed my confirmation after all the bad things she'd heard about him.

CHAPTER THIRTY

END OF AN ERA

The girls and I had a day at home on Thursday after
three full days out. I organized indoor activities and
we also went out for a short walk. On Friday Tim phoned
to say Selina was being discharged on Saturday. It was
earlier than expected due to a sudden rise in Covid
patients. The number of those needing to be hospitalized
had risen and now anyone who could be discharged was
being sent home to free up beds. Tim was going to collect
Selina on Saturday, but he didn't know what time yet so
he asked if I could bring the girls home on Sunday morning, which was fine with me. It would also give him a
chance to get organized. Selina would be continuing her
recovery at home, and she was coming with a lot of equipment: crutches, a walking frame, a commode (as they
didn't have a downstairs toilet and she needed help climbing stairs) and a wheelchair, which she would need if they
went out. He said a nurse would be coming in to begin
with. 'I've arranged to take a few days off work, but
you're still OK to meet me at their school on Monday?'

'Yes, of course.'

I emailed Fatima and Joy with the arrangements,
packed the rest of Angie's and Polly's belongings, then on

Saturday evening served their favourite meal again – this time it was their leaving do. Paula and I gave them their presents, which they loved and wanted to wear immediately. We video-called Adrian and Kirsty, and Lucy, Darren and Emma, so they could say goodbye. The girls were excited to be going home but asked a number of times if we would still see them. I said I was sure we would, but I'd need to check with their mummy and daddy. Ultimately, whether we stayed in touch would be their parents' decision. Some want to, but others just want to put the past behind them and move on with their lives.

Of course Paula and I felt sad as we loaded the girls' bags into the car on Sunday morning, but we stayed positive. It was right that the girls were going home, and not before time. They would have been there sooner had it not been for Selina's operation. Sammy was restless, sensing something was wrong as the bags disappeared out of the front door. Angie and Polly spent a long time petting him and saying their goodbyes.

Paula came with me to return the girls home. She'd played such a big part in their lives and, like me, she was hoping to see them again. I would be seeing them the following morning when I took them to school with Tim, but for Paula this might be goodbye.

'You can come in,' Angie told us as I parked outside their house.

'Yes, we will, but we won't stay long.'

Paula opened their car door to let them out. Angie was carrying the empty cake tin I was returning to Tim.

I pressed the doorbell and after a moment Tim answered. Angie and Paula rushed past him and into the living room, eager to see their mother.

'How is Selina?' I asked.

'Pleased to be home, although she had a bit of a rough night. The nurse is coming later.'

Tim helped Paula and me unload the car and bring the bags into the hall. He wasn't wearing a mask, but we put ours on before going into the living room to see Selina as she'd just come out of hospital. She was on the sofa, the leg that had been operated on heavily bandaged and in plaster, elevated and resting on a cushion. The girls were now standing beside her looking at it warily and asking questions.

She smiled at us. 'Make yourselves at home.'

Tim offered us a drink, but we refused, saying we wouldn't stay long. We talked to Selina for a while but from a short distance. Presently, she yawned, apologized and said she felt tired and thought it could be the pain-killers. I felt it was time to go. Angie and Polly had lost their wariness at seeing their mother incapacitated and Angie was holding her hand while Polly was playing with her hair, something she liked to do with Paula and me.

We said a fond goodbye to Selina, Angie and Polly in the living room. Selina thanked us for all we'd done, so did Tim as he saw us to the door.

'See you tomorrow at 8.50,' he said to me.

'Yes, I won't forget,' I reassured him, for clearly taking the girls to school for the first time was still a big deal for him. 'And thanks again for the cake.'

'You're welcome.'

As Paula and I returned to our car the front door closed. The family that had been torn apart was together again. Well, almost. Ashleigh was no longer there and as far as I could foresee never would be. She'd ended that option when she'd made those allegations. I hadn't heard anything to the contrary, so I assumed she was still living with her father.

Once home I hoovered and cleaned what had been Angie and Polly's bedroom in case it was needed again for an emergency. I usually like to have a short break between one child leaving and the next arriving to recharge my batteries, but that wasn't always possible. I knew the number of children being taken into care was still rising. Later, Paula and I spent a relaxing evening watching a film and eating a Chinese takeaway.

On Monday morning Paula left for work as I left to go to Angie and Polly's school. I arrived five minutes early and parked in my usual spot. It was strange doing a school run without children in the car, as if I had forgotten them. A few minutes later I saw Tim drive past and park a little further up. I got out, put on my mask and walked towards his car. He stepped out of the driver's seat and looked around. When he saw me he smiled with relief.

'Great, you're here,' he said, joining me on the pavement. 'Thank you so much.' He put on his mask. 'I emailed the Head as you suggested, but she hasn't replied.'

'She may not have read it yet,' I suggested, for he seemed to be taking her lack of reply as a bad sign.

'Cathy!' Polly cried, pleased to see me.

'We're not going home with you,' Angie said a little moodily.

'Cathy knows that – don't be cheeky,' Tim told her, but I smiled.

'No, you're going home with your daddy,' I said. 'How is your mummy?'

'She had a better night,' Tim replied.

Both girls wanted to hold their father's hand to cross the road, so I was bit superfluous to requirements. I followed them along the short path and into the playground. A few other parents were ahead of us and some, having dropped off their children, were leaving. I hadn't really got to know any of them, mainly due to social distancing and the masks, but I noticed one mother who had a child in Angie's class look pointedly at Tim. He was concentrating on the girls so didn't see. I showed him where the girls had to go. As usual a TA stood just inside each classroom entrance, welcoming the children. I'd already explained to Tim that although start and finish times were staggered, if parents had more than one child at the school they could bring them in together.

Angie and Polly were still hugging and kissing their father goodbye when the Head, Elizabeth Hambridge, appeared from another door. Mask on, she came across the playground towards us. Tim saw her and straightened. I saw worry and concern in his eyes.

'Good morning,' she said brightly to us all, then, turning to Tim, 'Good to see you again. I got your email, thank you. We have a staff meeting this evening so with your permission I'd like to share its contents with my staff, then they can nip any gossip they might hear in the bud.'

'Yes, of course, thank you,' he said, relieved. 'That would be good. Thank you so much.'

'I assume Angie and Polly are home for good now?' the Head asked, glancing at me questioningly.

'Yes,' Tim said.

'I've just come today to show Tim where the girls go in,' I added.

'Great. And how is Selina after her operation?' she asked Tim.

'At home recovering.'

'Give her my best wishes. Nice to see you here. We're looking forward to having you on the PTA again. We've missed your input.'

'Thank you,' Tim said, but his voice caught. Her words meant so much to him.

The Head said goodbye and returned into the building. I waited while Tim finished saying goodbye to the girls. With a final kiss and a hug, they let him go and we watched them disappear into their classrooms. Suddenly I teared up as it hit me this would be the last time I saw the girls go into school. I couldn't talk for a moment; I was so emotional. I'd been with Polly on her first day – a milestone – and I loved them both dearly.

I was unusually quiet as we left the playground.

'Thanks again for everything,' Tim said once we were outside.

'You're welcome.'

We went to our respective cars and for a moment I sat gazing out of my side window at the school. It was the end of an era for me, but the start of a new one for Tim. I hoped that in time he would be able to regain his confidence and relax into enjoying his family again. But I knew it would be a long time, if ever, before he could truly put the past behind him.

EPILOGUE

Selina made a full recovery from her operation, although it was three months before she could drive or walk without an aid. Paula and I were invited to the girls' birthday parties in February and March of the following year. Tim seemed a lot more relaxed around the girls and had regained some of the weight he had lost. He'd made the party food, including the girls' birthday cakes, which were amazing.

At the time of writing Selina has phoned Ashleigh but hasn't seen her. Ashleigh didn't stay with her father but went to live with another foster carer. I don't know the reason. Tim, Selina, Angie and Polly attend family therapy to try to help them come to terms with the past and rebuild their lives. I understand Ashleigh is attending therapy too.

Although Angie and Polly were reunited with their parents, I am still haunted by the thought of what might have been if the truth hadn't come out. Parents, foster carers, nannies, teachers and others in positions of trust who work closely with children are vulnerable to false allegations. Investigations take time and might not always uncover the truth. After much thought

Janet decided not to foster again, and who could blame her?

Thank you for reading their story. For the latest on these children and others in my fostering memoirs, please visit https://cathyglass.co.uk/updates.

SUGGESTED TOPICS FOR
READING-GROUP DISCUSSION

────────────

If Angie and Polly had to leave home, why couldn't they stay with their maternal grandmother? Do you think that was the correct decision?

Selina was adamant that Tim was with her all evening on the night Ashleigh claims Tim abused her. Why wasn't her word sufficient?

This family was previously unknown to the social services and the children were being well cared for, so was taking them into care justified? If so, why?

How might the rift between Trevor and Selina and Tim have contributed towards the allegations Ashleigh made against her stepfather?

In protecting children, mistakes sometimes occur. Were mistakes made in this case? If so, what were they?

How might Fatima have allowed her own experience of an abusive childhood to influence her judgement?

Should a child's claims of abuse always be believed?

Ashleigh is shown to make things up; for example, what she said about Janet. At what point was it reasonable to doubt her testimony?

Ashleigh is clearly a very troubled young person. Why do you think that might be?

It was known from early on that Ashleigh and her stepfather argued. Should that have cast doubt on the validity of her allegations?

Trevor is worried that Ashleigh could make up an allegation against him. Are his concerns justified?

CHRONOLOGY

If you would like to read, or re-read, my books in chronological order, here is the list to date:

Cut	Damaged
The Silent Cry	Hidden
Daddy's Little Princess	Mummy Told Me Not to Tell
Nobody's Son	Another Forgotten Child
Cruel to be Kind	The Child Bride
The Night the Angels Came	Can I Let You Go?
A Long Way from Home	Finding Stevie
A Baby's Cry	Innocent
The Saddest Girl in the World	Too Scared to Tell
Please Don't Take My Baby	A Terrible Secret
Will You Love Me?	A Life Lost
I Miss Mummy	An Innocent Baby
Saving Danny	Neglected
Girl Alone	A Family Torn Apart
Where Has Mummy Gone?	

The titles below can be slotted in anywhere, as can my Lisa Stone thrillers: http://lisastonebooks.co.uk/:

The Girl in the Mirror	Happy Adults
My Dad's a Policeman	Happy Mealtimes for Kids
Run, Mummy, Run	About Writing and How
Happy Kids	to Publish

This list is also on the Books page of my website: https://cathyglass.co.uk/true-stories-cathy-glass/

Cathy Glass

One remarkable woman, more
than **150** foster children cared for.

Cathy Glass has been a foster carer
for 30 years, during which time she has
looked after more than 150 children, as well
as raising three children of her own. She was
awarded a degree in education and psychology
as a mature student, and writes under a
pseudonym. To find out more about Cathy
and her story visit **www.cathyglass.co.uk**.

Neglected

The police remove Jamey from home as an emergency and take him to foster carer Cathy

But as Jamey starts to settle in and make progress a new threat emerges, which changes everything.

An Innocent Baby

Abandoned at birth, Darcy-May is brought to Cathy with a police escort

Her teenage mother wants nothing to do with her, but why? She is an adorable baby.

A Life Lost

Jackson is aggressive, confrontational and often volatile

Then, in a dramatic turn of events, the true reason for Jackson's behaviour comes to light ...

A Terrible Secret

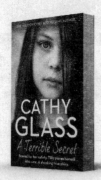

Tilly is so frightened of her stepfather, Dave, that she asks to go into foster care

The more Cathy learns about Dave's behaviour, the more worried she becomes ...

Too Scared to Tell

Oskar has been arriving at school hungry, unkempt and bruised. His mother has gone abroad and left him in the care of 'friends'

As the weeks pass, Cathy's concerns deepen. Oskar is clearly frightened of someone – but who? And why?

Innocent

Siblings Molly and Kit arrive at Cathy's frightened, injured and ill

The parents say they are not to blame. Could the social services have got it wrong?

Finding Stevie

Fourteen-year-old Stevie is exploring his gender identity

Like many young people, he spends time online, but Cathy is shocked when she learns his terrible secret.

Where Has Mummy Gone?

When Melody is taken into care, she fears her mother won't cope alone

It is only when Melody's mother vanishes that what has really been going on at home comes to light.

A Long Way from Home

Abandoned in an orphanage, Anna's future looks bleak until she is adopted

Anna's new parents love her, so why does she end up in foster care?

Cruel to be Kind

Max is shockingly overweight and struggles to make friends

Cathy faces a challenge to help this unhappy boy.

Nobody's Son

Born in prison and brought up in care, Alex has only ever known rejection

He is longing for a family of his own, but again the system fails him.

Can I Let You Go?

Faye is 24, pregnant and has
learning difficulties as a result of
her mother's alcoholism

Can Cathy help Faye learn
enough to parent her child?

The Silent Cry

A mother battling depression.
A family in denial

Cathy is desperate to help before
something terrible happens.

Girl Alone

An angry, traumatized young girl
on a path to self-destruction

Can Cathy discover the truth
behind Joss's dangerous behaviour
before it's too late?

Saving Danny

Danny's parents can no longer cope
with his challenging behaviour

Calling on all her expertise, Cathy
discovers a frightened little boy who
just wants to be loved.

The Child Bride

A girl blamed and abused for dishonouring her community

Cathy discovers the devastating truth.

Daddy's Little Princess

A sweet-natured girl with a complicated past

Cathy picks up the pieces after events take a dramatic turn.

Will You Love Me?

A broken child desperate for a loving home

The true story of Cathy's adopted daughter Lucy.

Please Don't Take My Baby

Seventeen-year-old Jade is pregnant, homeless and alone

Cathy has room in her heart for two.

Another Forgotten Child

Eight-year-old Aimee was on the child-protection register at birth

Cathy is determined to give her the happy home she deserves.

A Baby's Cry

A newborn, only hours old, taken into care

Cathy protects tiny Harrison from the potentially fatal secrets that surround his existence.

The Night the Angels Came

A little boy on the brink of bereavement

Cathy and her family make sure Michael is never alone.

Mummy Told Me Not to Tell

A troubled boy sworn to secrecy

After his dark past has been revealed, Cathy helps Reece to rebuild his life.

I Miss Mummy

Four-year-old Alice doesn't understand why she's in care

Cathy fights for her to have the happy home she deserves.

The Saddest Girl in the World

A haunted child who refuses to speak

Do Donna's scars run too deep for Cathy to help?

Cut

Dawn is desperate to be loved

Abused and abandoned, this vulnerable child pushes Cathy and her family to their limits.

Hidden

The boy with no past

Can Cathy help Tayo to feel like he belongs again?

Damaged

A forgotten child

Cathy is Jodie's last hope. For the first time, this abused young girl has found someone she can trust.

Run, Mummy, Run

The gripping story of a woman caught in a horrific cycle of abuse, and the desperate measures she must take to escape.

My Dad's a Policeman

The dramatic short story about a young boy's desperate bid to keep his family together.

The Girl in the Mirror

Trying to piece together her past, Mandy uncovers a dreadful family secret that has been blanked from her memory for years.

About Writing
and How to Publish

A clear, concise practical guide on writing and the best ways to get published.

Happy Mealtimes
for Kids

A guide to healthy eating with simple recipes that children love.

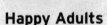

Happy Adults

A practical guide to achieving lasting happiness, contentment and success. The essential manual for getting the best out of life.

Happy Kids

A clear and concise guide to raising confident, well-behaved and happy children.

CATHY GLASS WRITING AS
LISA STONE

The new crime thrillers that will chill you to the bone . . .

THE COTTAGE

Is someone out there?

TAKEN

Have you seen Leila?

THE DOCTOR

How much do you know about
the couple next door?

STALKER

Security cameras are there to
keep us safe. Aren't they?

THE DARKNESS
WITHIN

You know your son better than
anyone. Don't you?

Be amazed
Be moved
Be inspired

Follow Cathy:

 /cathy.glass.180

 @CathyGlassUK

www.cathyglass.co.uk

Cathy loves to hear from readers and reads
and replies to posts, but she asks that no plot
spoilers are posted, please. We're sure
you appreciate why.

MOVING
Memoirs

Stories of hope, courage and
the power of love . . .

Sign up to the Moving Memoirs email and you'll
be the first to hear about new books, discounts,
and get sneak previews from your
favourite authors!

Sign up at

www.moving-memoirs.com